THE MOST BEAUTIFUL PLACE ON EARTH

THE MOST BEAUTIFUL PLACE ON EARTH

Wallace Stegner in California

Matthew D. Stewart

The University of Utah Press
Salt Lake City

The Defiance House Man colophon is a registered trademark of The University of Utah Press. It is based on a four-foot-tall Ancient Puebloan pictograph (late PIII) near Glen Canyon, Utah.

Library of Congress Cataloging-in-Publication Data

Names: Stewart, Matthew D, 1982- author.
Title: The most beautiful place on Earth : Wallace Stegner in California / Matthew D. Stewart.
Description: Salt Lake City : University of Utah Press, [2022] | Includes bibliographical references and index.
Identifiers: LCCN 2021042925 (print) | LCCN 2021042926 (ebook) | ISBN 9781647690557 (cloth) | ISBN 9781647690564 (paperback) | ISBN 9781647690571 (ebook)
Subjects: LCSH: Stegner, Wallace, 1909-1993—Criticism and interpretation. | California—In literature. | West (U.S.)—In literature.
Classification: LCC PS3537.T316 Z926 2022 (print) | LCC PS3537.T316 (ebook) | DDC 813/.52 [B]—dc23
LC record available at https://lccn.loc.gov/2021042925
LC ebook record available at https://lccn.loc.gov/2021042926

Errata and further information on this and other titles available online at UofUpress.com

Printed and bound in the United States of America.

Cover photo: Wallace Stegner writing in his Los Altos Hills study. Courtesy Special Collections, J. Willard Marriott Library, The University of Utah.

TO KATIE

CONTENTS

ACKNOWLEDGMENTS

After barely surviving a blizzard during the winter of 1906–1907, Wallace Stegner's greenhorn cowboy, Rusty Cullen, decided he "did not think that he would ever want to do anything alone again, not in this country." While I did not risk frostbite in the completion of this book, I am most grateful to the people who were willing to trek along with me. Without them I would be stuck in a drift somewhere, but the errors that remain are certainly my own.

The Syracuse University History Department and the Maxwell School challenged me and offered great support, both intellectual and financial. Thanks especially to Susan Branson, Martin Shanguhyia, Osamah Khalil, Michael Ebner, Mikkel Dack, Norman Kutcher, Sarah Hamersma, Patti Bohrer, Faye Morse, and the late Ralph Ketcham. Christina Leigh Docteur was a tremendous encouragement, as were Dan Olson-Bang and Glenn Wright from the Graduate School. I'm especially grateful to the readers who read the first draft in full and offered valuable comments: Grant Reeher, Jeffrey Gonda, Bob Wilson, and Mark Schmeller.

Thanks also to my fellow graduate students at Syracuse for challenging discussions and for the good word in the grad bay, especially: Charlie Goldberg, Giovanna Urist, Shauna Soljour, Scarlett Rebman, Jesse Hysell, Davor Mondom, Phil Erenrich, Elissa Isenberg, John Barruzza, Bob Searing, Jonathan Wilson, Nick Mason, Torie Fritz, Sarah Stegeman, Eunyoung Gay, Francis Akouwah, Humphrey Mensah, and Jerry Robinson.

The seeds of this book were first watered in a writing group that was one of the highlights of my time at Syracuse. Thanks to Paul Arras and Elisabeth Lasch-Quinn for organizing, to Michael Ebner for support, and to Tom Guiler, Namhee Lee, Andrea Catroppa, Sravani Biswas, Dave Wolken, Yoshina Hurgobin, and Alex Elias for such rich conversations at Phoebe's.

The Friends of the Marriott Library at the University of Utah generously supported two trips to Utah. In Special Collections, thanks to Greg

Thompson and Judy Jarrow for helpful assistance and for sharing their Stegner lore.

In one of the most serendipitous moments of the creation of this book, the Idaho Humanities Council chose "Wallace Stegner and the Consciousness of Place" as the theme for their 2017 Summer Teacher Institute. Special thanks to Rick Ardinger for hiring me as a facilitator, and to Tara Penry, Dick Etulain, Jenny Emery Davidson, Judy Austin, Mike Branch, and Cindy Wang, in addition to all the teachers who participated, for making it a fun and stimulating week.

I'm grateful to be publishing this book with the University of Utah Press. I'm especially grateful to Tom Krause for his support for the book, and to Dick Etulain, William Handley, Hannah New, Jessica A. Booth, Pat Hadley, and Ginny Hoffman for valuable help during the editing and production process.

To my colleagues and students at The Ambrose School: thank you. There are too many of you to list, and I'm so glad to work with all of you.

Thomas Gowen, John Stegeman, Jeff Bilbro, Paul Arras, Nick Smith, Amanda Patchin, Joe Gerber, Chris Maiocca, Heather Jennings, Jason Peters, Tara Penry, and John Murdock came along at various stages of the book to read drafts and pull me out of ruts. Eric Miller, Robert Corban, and Elisabeth Lasch-Quinn were the conversation partners that steered me towards Stegner in the first place, and this book will always remind me of them and of my gratitude for their friendship. Betsy's careful pencil notes guided me from outline to finished draft.

My in-laws, siblings and siblings-in-law, and their kids made our trips to Maryland, Idaho, and Virginia fantastic adventures. Thanks to Kelly and Marline, Becca and Scott, Taylor and Melanie, Brent and Lindsay, Tim and Ali, Sam and Amber, Cynthia, Dylan, Bradley, Annie, Grayson, Ellie, Jack, Hattie, Evelyn, Caroline, Mae, Maren, Henry, Grace, and Griffin.

I did not need to study someone with as tumultuous a childhood as Wallace Stegner to know how wonderful my parents are. Thank you, Mom, and thank you, Dad.

To Donovan, Lucy, and Robert: my heart is full, and I hope you will enjoy reading this someday. I am happily indebted to Katie for more than I can repay in the life we share together. She makes it easy to believe the words we etched on our wedding rings almost a decade ago: "to love and live beloved is the soul's paradise, both here and in heaven."

THE MOST BEAUTIFUL PLACE ON EARTH

Figure 1. Wallace Stegner wrote in this study nearly every morning from the time the family moved into their home in Los Altos Hills in 1949 until his death on April 13, 1993. He lit a wood stove and a cigar, then commenced typing in a two-fingered hunt-and-peck style. The Stegner house was torn down after it was sold in 2011, but his study was preserved on the property and remains as of 2021. Courtesy Special Collections, J. Willard Marriott Library, University of Utah.

Wallace Stegner in the Most Beautiful Place on Earth

This is the most beautiful place on earth. There are many such places. Every man, every woman, carries in heart and mind the image of the ideal place, the right place, the one true home, known or unknown, actual or visionary. A houseboat in Kashmir, a view down Atlantic Avenue in Brooklyn, a gray gothic farmhouse two stories high at the end of a red dog road in the Allegheny Mountains, a cabin on the shore of a blue lake in spruce and fir country, a greasy alley near the Hoboken waterfront, or even, possibly, for those of a less demanding sensibility, the world to be seen from a comfortable apartment high in the tender, velvety smog of Manhattan, Chicago, Paris, Tokyo, Rio, or Rome—there's no limit to the human capacity for the homing sentiment.

—Edward Abbey[1]

After all, what are any of us after but the conviction of belonging?

—Wallace Stegner[2]

Home is a notion that only the nations of the homeless fully appreciate and only the uprooted comprehend.

—Wallace Stegner[3]

Wallace Stegner (1909–1993) spent the formative years of his childhood on a desolate prairie in Saskatchewan without any modern conveniences. He lived most of his adult life in what is now one of the most luxurious places in the world: Los Altos Hills, California, right in the heart of what would become Silicon Valley, formerly the Valley of Heart's Delight.[4] He traversed western spaces on foot and on horseback, and by bicycle, raft, car, train, and plane. In his childhood, he entered western towns and cities as a prairie runt of the working class, as a backward Canadian worthy of scorn for his unfashionable T. Eaton catalogue sweater and elk-hide moccasins, and as an unwitting member of the criminal underworld.

As an adult, he was welcomed to western cities as the distinguished guest of universities, conservationist groups, political organizations, literary societies, and book clubs. He acted as a representative of Stanford University, the Sierra Club, and the federal government of the United States. He was the promising future of the New West for one generation of westerners and wise man of the Old West for another. He was simultaneously the epitome of the Establishment for counterculture icons like Ken Kesey and reviewed dismissively twice within a year in the pages of the *New York Times Book Review*.[5] He died on March 28, 1993, due to injuries sustained during a car accident on a western highway in Santa Fe, New Mexico, having lived and written his way through some of the most momentous changes in world history. He had experienced about as much of the American West in all its variety as was possible to experience on the scale of one human lifetime.[6]

It is a tragic irony that Stegner's death was caused by an accident on an American highway.[7] He had written that, "like many Americans, especially the poorer kinds," he was "born on wheels."[8] George, his father, was an inveterate gambler on resource booms throughout the West, whether wheat in Saskatchewan to feed the soldiers of Europe during the Great War or whiskey in Salt Lake City during Prohibition; none of his schemes paid off as quickly as he hoped before the family was off to the next western space to try again. His mother, Hilda, was not educated past her teen years and had married young to his then dashing and adventurous father to escape Iowa farm life with her rigidly pious Lutheran family. The romance wore off, and she found that she longed instead for "the beauties and strengths and human associations of place."[9] After moving to Redmond, Washington, she refused to go to Saskatchewan with George when Wallace was four years old. The family was divided, and Hilda was forced to leave Wallace and his brother in an orphanage in order to work. She eventually took her sons out of the orphanage and returned to her family in Iowa before deciding that they would move to Saskatchewan and stick with George even as he continued to uproot the family from place to place throughout the Mountain West.[10] George had less capacity for sticking, and Hilda died of breast cancer in Salt Lake City, attended only by Wallace and a kind nurse.

Though as driven—albeit in much different directions—as his father, Stegner sought place like his mother and could only with great effort and decades of writing think about his father without feeling some level of anger, especially after George had abandoned Hilda on her deathbed in 1933.[11] George met a violent end in 1939. As the *Salt Lake Tribune* reported it on June 16 of that year: "Former Mining Man Shoots Woman, Self to Death in Salt Lake Hotel." Stegner's brother, Cecil, had preceded his mother in death from pneumonia in 1931. With his father's death in 1939, Stegner found himself without any significant connections to his personal past. The *Salt Lake Tribune* article that reported his father's murder-suicide summed up his situation: "Only known survivor of Stegner's is a son, Wallace, formerly of Salt Lake City and now teaching at the University of Wisconsin."[12]

At the age of thirty, then, Wallace Stegner had no immediate family. What was left of his past was located primarily in his own mind. Because of his father's restless roving across the West, he had no "artifacts of memory," no long-time family friends, no close relatives, no hometown, and no home.[13] He was orphaned in the present with no place to which he could return and no felt sense of "a personal and possessed past."[14] He turned to writing at least in part as a means of self-therapy, writing being "cheaper than other methods."[15]

He was not completely alone, however, or reduced to the exploitative relationships of necessity that are the fate of many who find themselves in desperate circumstances. By the time his father died, he was happily married to Mary Page Stegner, to whom he would remain married until his death, and had developed rewarding and sustained friendships. He had also experienced some professional success. But this did not remove the emotional desire to comprehend intellectually the cultural, moral, political, and geographical dimensions of his family tragedy and his sense of being cut off from any story spanning more than one human generation.

This book offers a sympathetic account of Stegner's attempt to remedy this estrangement. He was particularly well equipped to do so. To borrow Edward Abbey's evocative phrase, Stegner was blessed (or cursed) with an acutely refined "homing sentiment." After following in the footsteps of his parents by moving from place to place for the next six years of his life—ironically, as Stegner wanted very much to avoid the path his father took at his family's expense—Stegner and his family finally settled in Los

Figure 2. Wallace and Mary in Alaska with the National Park Service, 1965. Wallace and Mary married in 1934 and remained married until Wallace's death in 1993. This photograph of the Stegners was taken in Alaska in 1965 while Wallace was serving on the National Parks Advisory Board, to which he was appointed by Secretary of the Interior Stuart L. Udall. Courtesy Wisconsin Historical Society, WHS 74157.

Altos Hills and fitfully but determinedly made a home there until he died in 1993. This effort was worked out in countless ways that are lost to history; the novels that reveal this process, however, are not.

The heart of this book is my close reading of the three novels he wrote while coming to terms with the home that he and his family made in Los Altos Hills, California. In my reading of these novels, I place Stegner's characters in conversation with Stegner himself, the historical record, and his many readers. Stegner's homemaking was no easy task, and ultimately, I come to the conclusion that Stegner more or less gave up on the idea that he could make a home in California with a durable sense of place. My account of this attempt is thus a tragedy valuable more for the catharsis and wisdom it offers than for any political project it might suggest. What Stegner wanted out of his place was not possible for him to create on his own; it was as if he were trying to rebuild a torn spider's web with his fingers.[16]

The Amputated Present

A consistent theme in Stegner's California novels is the cultural damage imposed by a society incapable of seeing more than what he called the "amputated present."[17] Consider the life circumstances of the four of his protagonists who most resembled him (though Stegner always protested readings of his work that traced lines too directly from his life to his fiction). Bruce Mason, the protagonist from *The Big Rock Candy Mountain* (1943) and then *Recapitulation* (1979) several decades later, is a lifelong bachelor who becomes a diplomat. Brief sections of *Recapitulation* suggest that he is well liked by his colleagues and respected in his profession, but over the course of the novel we find that he has insulated himself from emotional connections of almost any kind. He has sealed himself off from his past (for understandable reasons that are explored sympathetically in the novel). Though kind and polite to his acquaintances, he is seemingly unattached to any of them. When he dies, the Mason family will be remembered by no one, Stegner implies.

Joe Allston, the protagonist of two short stories and a novella written in the 1950s, and, later, the novels *All the Little Live Things* (1967) and *The Spectator Bird* (1976), is a literary agent who, "at the bottom of the

Depression," chooses to be a "talent broker" instead of a "broke talent."[18] Though his marriage is one built on mutual love and respect, Joe never knew his father and became more distant from his mother throughout his life. In his recollections, Joe's past is another lifetime and social class ago; he worked his way out of his humble origins and then, without realizing it, found himself estranged from his past and with no capacity to reconnect to it. Joe's relationship to his son Curtis is fraught, and in *Live Things* it is revealed that Curtis died of a probable suicide. Joe's story is largely an attempt to work out a future without the son he imagined in it.

Lyman Ward of *Angle of Repose* (1971), the book that won Stegner a Pulitzer Prize and remains his most widely known, is a Bancroft-winning historian who does have a substantive personal past but is, like the others, peering into a future that seems cut off from the "amputated present." Lyman informs his readers that he is retreating into research of the past for the purpose of escape: "I'd like to live in their clothes for a while, if only so I don't have to live in my own."[19] He has a son, but his son is alien to him; further, he is recently divorced and restricted to a wheelchair by a disease that has required the amputation of his leg.

Finally, Larry Morgan of *Crossing to Safety* (1987) is also without a substantive personal past. Unlike the rest of the protagonists, Larry's future is more promising, even if also vague. In fact, Stegner's last novel is one of the few in his whole oeuvre that presents a modestly hopeful future for a protagonist. Notably, it is also one of his few novels that is set outside of the American West. In sum, both Bruce and Joe are essentially pastless and futureless. Lyman is futureless and Larry is pastless. All of them are living in a present that feels decidedly cut off from a living past and future.

These are men who are living in a society that obscures their past but are too old to be compensated for this loss with a new and exciting future. All they have is a contextless, boring present—even the relative privilege of their situation seems only to highlight their loneliness. Joe Allston summarizes the situation well, when he asks himself how, "without dramatic events or high resolves, without tragedy, without even pathos, a reasonably endowed, reasonably well-intentioned man can walk through the world's great kitchen from end to end and arrive at the back door hungry."[20] Ultimately only Larry seems capable of participating in a living, multigenerational community. And all of them seem to believe it should be otherwise.

What exactly did Stegner seem to want for his protagonists? What did he want them to "see a little better"?[21] Or what did he think they saw and might help readers see a little better? What was missing? As white men from the upper middle class, the protagonists of Stegner's novels do not suffer personally from an unjust social hierarchy. They may or may not suffer from the empty universe or the weight of a false identity being forced on them by an uncaring commercial order, and they are not overburdened by the angst that so captured many middle-class and elite Americans during this era.[22] They are not attempting to run away or escape; they are not stifled. Instead, they are weightless and spinning like an astronaut cut off from the shuttle.

They suffer primarily from their disconnections from the past and the future in any one particular place. They have only a present but wish for more; they are alienated in a certain sense but would not use that term. They are lonely and they are seeking clarity not about the "nothingness" they inhabit as modern suburban bourgeois, but about conditions more immediate to them: meaningful attachment to actual people and actual places.[23] Though the narrators of his 1960s and 1970s books were especially critical of hippies, these characters have typically dropped out in some way themselves and are trying to justify their lives as exiles in the suburbs. But Stegner never allows them peace in their exile, and he typically suggests that they have learned that dropping out is impossible and dehumanizing.

In what is the most concise summary of this element of his work in personal terms, Stegner wrote:

> I had grown up a migrant, without history, tradition, or extended family, in remote backwaters of the West. . . . And so, though I was susceptible to the dialectic of those who declared their independence of custom and tradition and the dead hand of the past, I had no tradition to declare myself independent of, and had never felt the dead hand of the past in my life. If the truth were told, and it now is, I was always hungry to feel that hand on my head, to belong to some socially or intellectually or historically or literarily cohesive group, some tribe, some culture, some recognizable and persistent offshoot of Western civilization. If I revolted, and I had all the appropriate temptations, I had to revolt

away from what I was, and that meant toward something—tradition, cultural memory, shared experience, order. Even my prose felt the pull of agreed-upon grammar and syntax. Eventually, inevitably, I was drawn to what I most needed.[24]

This "toward something" that Stegner describes is another key focus of this book. A unifying theme of Stegner's California novels is the hope that living in a present with a "possessed past" versus an "amputated present" might prompt the development of "sticker virtues" that might create new possibilities for community.

Using two phrases from Stegner's corpus of writing, I study his complex endeavor to achieve the "conviction of belonging" in the "formless non-community" of the California Midpeninsula.[25] Stegner wrote books that imagined attempts to think back to attachment and maturity—to, in his words, "tradition, cultural memory, shared experience, order"—rather than west to freedom, movement, and fluidity.[26] Though the historical record suggests this experience was not unique in lived experience or in popular art, it is at least rarer as a theme in American writing with aspirations to lasting literary value, especially in the twentieth century.[27]

Boomers and Stickers

Being the son of his restless, boom-chasing father but also of his place-loving mother, Stegner eventually developed two terms that summarized the dynamic that brought such turmoil to his young life: "boomers" and "stickers." In this paradigm, the boomers are those who approach western resources as "grave robbers might approach the tomb of a pharaoh" in an "extractive frenzy"; the stickers are those who "settle, and love the life they have made and the place they have made it in."[28] These two categories can be used reductively, but, following Jeffrey Bilbro, I see the categories instead as "prophetic pry bars" whose stark distinctions are meant to jar sensibilities with recognition and potential for reform.

Stegner hoped that the stickers might create the possibility for multi-generational western places that had the capacity to bind people together, to build communities that would survive individual members. Stegner defined "place" most precisely in a late essay, "The Sense of Place."

Stegner wrote: "At least to human perception, a place is not a place until people have been born in it, have grown up in it, lived in it, known it, died in it—have both experienced it and shaped it, as individuals, families, neighborhoods, and communities, over more than one generation.... [Space becomes] place only by slow accrual, like a coral reef."[29] As this definition suggests, there are no shortcuts to place; time is the necessary foundation.

The experience of coming to terms with one's home place, of reckoning with the homing sentiment and its demands, is, of course, hardly unique. Stegner's effort to do so rewards careful study, however, because he made great art out of his attempt, left a detailed historical record of it, and just so happened to try to make a home in what would become one of the most influential places in the world over the course of the latter half of the American Century. It is also the case that he played a significant role in shaping the direction of American fiction during his lifetime.

It is difficult to overstate Stegner's fervent belief in the value and power of fiction. His reverence for the form did not fade, even as the form itself changed significantly over the course of his lifetime. Despite his prodigious efforts on behalf of institutions and in other forms of writing, fiction was always where he placed his greatest hope. This may come as a surprise to those who know him primarily as the author of his famous "Wilderness Letter" and as the articulate citizen-spokesman of and for the landscapes and places of the American West.

By the early 1980s, he admitted to historian Richard Etulain that "I would like now and again to be asked to review a novel instead of another book on western geography, geology, or water problems. But they don't take you as a literary man, you see. When they want a novel reviewed, they go somewhere else."[30] It was a poignant admission. His reflection on the "Wilderness Letter" twenty years after it was published also evinces a slight bitterness regarding the way his work as a citizen seemed to overshadow his work as a novelist: "This letter, the labor of an afternoon, has gone farther around the world than other writings on which I have spent years."[31]

The two major biographies that have been written about Stegner's life and work reflect these two sides of Wallace Stegner, sometimes focusing on one side at the expense of the other. Jackson Benson's, which was built on thorough readings of Stegner's whole corpus of work, a series of interviews Benson did with Stegner in the years before he died, and extensive research, is set primarily in terms of Stegner's life story and the development of his literary craftsmanship. Benson focuses chiefly on the maturation of Stegner's literary voice. It was limited in that Benson had developed a close friendship with the Stegners over the course of his interviews and then, in the wake of Stegner's death, struggled with the tension between his more critical arguments and Mary Stegner's increased sensitivity about her husband's legacy.[32]

Philip Fradkin's biography of Stegner tells his life story as well but sets it primarily in terms of his affinity for the West and his role as a prominent defender of western places. He is also concerned with articulating the reasons for Stegner's eventual despair over the state of the West later in his life. He argues that Stegner's "major flaw" was that "ultimately he could not adapt to the region that had formed him and that he had defined and represented so eloquently."[33] Both books are comprehensive and neither fails to make connections between these two major ways that Stegner influenced the American public during his lifetime.[34]

In this book, however, I focus more carefully on Stegner's devotion to fiction as a mode of thought meant to serve, build, and protect western places as places. I think his work in fiction is less easily separated from his work as a citizen. Instead of using Stegner's sense of himself as novelist and citizen, as reinforced by later interpreters, I start instead with another of Stegner's ideas, the "anguished question," and use it to guide my inquiry into his thought regardless of the genre or form that it took. This allows me to elaborate on the connections between his various works in richer ways.

In an essay written for his last essay collection, Stegner wrote: "The guts of any significant fiction—or autobiography—is an anguished question. The true art of fiction, in which I include autobiography, involves putting that question within a plausible context of order."[35] Using this category in the way that I use it means I am pushing it past Stegner's way of posing it. Without claiming that everything Stegner wrote came from somewhere deep in his soul, I argue that the anguished questions he acknowledged as inspiration for his fiction are relevant to his formal scholarly efforts as well as his work as a citizen. In a diary entry from 1976, Stegner reflected on the tangled goals of his fiction more candidly than he might have in a published essay:

Fact is, a novel's setting and general outline and essential action are often only a framework for something else—rumination about life, as often as not. And rumination may be truly personal, a writer using a character as a mouthpiece for his own ruminations; or it may be speculative, a writer using a character such as Allston or Ward as a sort of experimental vehicle, letting him ruminate, as it were, to see what he thinks. It is a good deal like the anthropological ideal of getting outside the culture, stepping back to gain perspective. It is also curiously like a scientific experiment—an attempt to experience life within circumstances and in characters that are created for the experiment and should not be intruded upon by authorial prejudices or even preoccupations. Undoubtedly there are writers who know what they think, and write their books to air what they think. I, on the contrary, seem generally to be asking questions, maundering around and being amazed by the complexity (beauty, anguish) of the most ordinary people and events. Like Dreiser, I suppose I am going to leave this world knowing less than when I came.[36]

Stegner created artistic worlds that had integrity to them and explored a wide range of questions in those worlds, in the attempt to make sense out of the world he actually inhabited. They were moral laboratories of a sort. There is intellectual content to Stegner's fiction that goes beyond strictly "aesthetic" or "political" categories. While few scholars would defend such divisions in theory, the legacy of the moralistic tales of the Victorians writing in the Genteel Tradition on the one hand, or the agit-prop associated with the Popular Front of the 1930s on the other, left American writers with very prominent negative examples of a "prescriptive aesthetics," or propaganda posing as fiction.[37] At its worst, such work was aesthetically worthless and perhaps not even entertaining, or, for the more politically oriented, simply a useless diversion from more valuable political action.[38] It was a tendency to be avoided at all costs. Further, regardless of theoretical conviction, many readers are simply repulsed by fiction that is overtly ideological and didactic. Nonetheless, Stegner practiced a form of fiction that yields more insight if his novels are considered in the "novel of ideas" category, in which the "intellectual" and "aesthetic" content of a novel are not easily disentangled.

This is not because an occasional character in a Stegner novel engages in a witty conversation against hasty and destructive suburban development or some other conservation issue. Such remarks are a feature of Stegner's fiction, but a tendency he studiously avoided as much as possible. Rather it is to emphasize that, for Stegner, the American West would only become a "geography of hope," in his terms, if its communities managed to enlist the loyalty of generations of stickers, who would build and maintain—and love—cultures that were adapted to the place.

In the American postwar context, he considered fiction and, to a lesser extent, history and other forms of nonfiction, essential resources for that effort. In Stegner's vision, fiction was a means of enlightening people to their existing or missing connections with places and other people. In the words of William Bevis, he "imagined" and "wrenched" the "conception of 'western' from forms of escape to forms of belonging."[39] This attempt was not separate from an aesthetic experience but was in fact part of the way that Stegner believed fiction worked when at its most powerful. It was at least the fiction he found most compelling.[40]

In sum, Stegner's fiction should not be reduced to either soft political argument on the one hand or hard ideological fiction on the other; I see his books instead as artifacts that demand an aesthetic and intellectual response, that encourage a form of holistic thinking that is obscured by more one-dimensional modes of thought. Incorporating fiction into intellectual history allows for a mode of inquiry that is not as easily separated into formal and informal categories. Close reading of fiction can point towards ways that ideas are entangled with moral reasoning, sensibility, and emotion, seemingly intangible matters that fiction is uniquely poised to illuminate.[41]

Stegner's Significance

Stegner wrote prodigiously, and as founder of the Creative Writing Program at Stanford University, he both materially enabled and inspired—sometimes as a figure to write against—the fiction of a whole generation of American writers.[42] Over the course of his lifetime, he published thirteen novels, dozens of short stories, and nine nonfiction books, in addition to hundreds of articles for newspapers, magazines, journals, and even calendars.[43] In the 1970s, he won two major American awards for achievement in literature, as *Angle of Repose* won the 1972 Pulitzer Prize and *The Spectator Bird* won the 1977 National Book Award.

By 2009, on the one-hundredth anniversary of his birth and sixteen years after he died, he was hailed by journalist Timothy Egan as the "uber-citizen" of the West.[44] He was raised to almost mythical status—journalist David Gessner used the term "Saint Wallace the Good" to describe the extent of his apotheosis for a generation of westerners—toward the end of his life and especially after his death.[45] Through his work, he provided histories, concepts, words, and metaphors to westerners to express what they had felt and thought about their lives and histories but could not quite articulate for themselves. Dorothy Bradley, an eight-term member of the Montana House of Representatives, wrote that for her and other westerners, Stegner was their "translator of the land ethic" for the West—the writer of "little scraps of paper in [our] pockets," serving as both "compass" and "inspiration."[46] In a 2016 lecture, environmental historian Mark Fiege recounted his own experiences reading *The Big Rock Candy Mountain* (1943) many years after it was published. The novel affected him so deeply that at one point he threw it against a wall.[47] As Fiege's example suggests, Stegner's words have resonated for several generations of readers.

Other than for western literary scholars, writers, historians, and environmentalists active from the 1940s to 2020s, however, Stegner has never been quite prominent enough to be studied without a justification of his historical significance.[48] Further, his apotheosis as the great citizen of the West has in some cases led to an undermining of his actual work, and was also accompanied by a slow-burning scandal that called into question how much recognition he deserved for *Angle of Repose*, his most well-known book (this scandal is discussed in chapter 4). His work has never been read as widely outside of the American West as he would have liked, and his popular reception has been limited in that none of his books has been made into a major film. Others also question whether his attempt to come to terms with his place in the West was too accommodating of what was ultimately white settler–colonialism (this issue is discussed in chapters 2 and 4).

Starting with the most concrete measure of his significance as a writer, then, a large proportion of his books have been reprinted numerous times and remain in print, with *Angle of Repose* and *Crossing to Safety* attracting the most modern readers.[49] Stegner's name also graces various institutions throughout the West. In most cases, it is used to evoke a sensibility that is still publicly meaningful. Ironically enough, the Stanford Creative Writing Program, which still issues Stegner Fellowships, is probably the institution that does the least to maintain his name within its living institutional memory.[50] Other places do more to maintain their connections to Stegner's legacy: the Wallace Stegner Award is granted by the Center of the American West at the University of Colorado–Boulder for "a sustained contribution to the cultural identity of the West through literature, art, history, lore, or an understanding of the West," and Montana State University hosts the Wallace Stegner Chair in Western American Studies and sponsored a conference on Stegner's work as recently as May 2019.[51]

Aside from these more tangible manifestations of his influence, ideas that he developed, translated, and refined remain relevant in literature and history and the genres of memoir, nature writing, and environmental writing. Even if never a household name (by novelist standards) nationally, his work has inspired steady criticism that has usually led to some exploration of his life as well, since his work often drew on personal experience.

His life and work have been the subject of two full-length biographies and several shorter works, and his work has been the subject of substantive criticism in hundreds of articles, theses, and dissertations.[52] He has appeared as one of the principal figures in many books of literary criticism and literary history, with one scholar even naming the existence of a "Stegnerian Spatial Field" in her analysis of the western literature of the era.[53] He continues to resonate in more popular works as well, with David Gessner's *All the Wild that Remains: Edward Abbey, Wallace Stegner, and the American West* (2015) being the most prominent recent book.[54]

Organization of the Book

The ideas that influenced Stegner and that he then channeled for his own use only to be redirected for other uses are not easily confined to distinct chronological periods.[55] Nonetheless, there are two chronological frameworks that shape this study, however porously. The first starts with Stegner's move to California in 1945 and ends with his death in 1993. Given the significance of place in his thought and the thematic focus of this study, Los Altos Hills, California, is particularly significant as it was the place where Stegner lived for most of his life. Stegner's published writings about California, and especially his fiction set in California, sharpen the focus even more, so the primary chronological emphasis is ultimately the 1950s through the 1970s.

Chapter 1 begins with Stegner's family's move to California. In the context of his developing regional vision as expressed in early articles and books, the chapter traces Stegner's attempts to build a range of institutions in California as well as his first writings that either adopted the state as its subject or used it as a setting for fictional work. Chapter 2 explores a research project that Stegner undertook with funding from the Wenner-Gren Foundation and as a member of the Stanford Center for Advanced Studies in Behavioral Sciences (CASBS) in the mid-1950s. This project and the book that came out of it, *Wolf Willow* (1962), illuminate Stegner's understanding of western history and his own past in more comprehensive terms and also highlight his growing commitment to fiction as a resource for addressing the questions he thought most important to explore in his historical moment.

The subsequent three chapters include close readings of three novels: *All the Little Live Things* (1967), *Angle of Repose* (1971), and *The Spectator Bird* (1976). The novels are united by location, themes, and a first-person narrator who opens the book with ruminations and something of a thesis. Two of these three books won major awards, so they also mark the summit of Stegner's national recognition as a writer of American fiction. Each of the readings reveals ways that Stegner and his readers addressed the cultural changes of the 1960s, adding nuance to the historiography of an era that has more often been marked by polarization. The conclusion is focused on Greensboro, Vermont, the place where Stegner chose to have his ashes spread after his death. Greensboro served as a realistic but still at times utopian foil for Stegner's exploration of the western "formless non-communities" that are the focus of the previous chapters. Together, these chapters illuminate the different ways that Stegner attempted to understand the limits of community and the practice of place in the American West while deepening our own understanding of the era in American history more broadly.

Chapter 1

To Los Altos Hills

Americans cleave to the things of this world as if assured that they will never die, and yet are in such a rush to snatch any that come within their reach, as if expecting to stop living before they have relished them. They clutch everything but hold nothing fast, and so lose grip as they hurry after some new delight.

An American will build a house in which to pass his old age and sell it before the roof is on.

—Alexis de Tocqueville, 1835[1]

The moderns, carrying little baggage of the kind that Shelly called "merely cultural," not even living in traditional air, but breathing into their space helmets a scientific mixture of synthetic gases (and polluted at that) are the true pioneers. Their circuitry seems to include no atavistic domestic sentiment, they have suffered empathectomy, their computers hum no ghostly feedback of Home, Sweet Home. How marvelously free they are! How unutterably deprived!

—Wallace Stegner, *Angle of Repose*[2]

As for many Americans, the impending conclusion of World War II filled Wallace Stegner with exhilaration and survivor's guilt. He was in the process of completing his contribution to the American postwar order, a series of articles commissioned by *Look* magazine that revealed the fault lines of racial and religious discrimination in the United States and called for a more just postwar peace. Since the series was focused on the nation as a whole, the final observations required Stegner and his family to make their way west. The series would later be published as one of Stegner's first nonfiction books, *One Nation* (1945), and the sections about the West would serve as his opening chapters.

The Stegners had been living in Massachusetts while Stegner taught at Harvard. Despite Stegner's ambition and his desire to join the midcentury republic of letters, the West beckoned. The *Look* assignment opened an opportunity. The publication of *The Big Rock Candy Mountain* in 1943 had secured his reputation as a novelist, and he had developed friendships at Harvard and at the Bread Loaf Writer's Conference (where he met Robert Frost and Bernard DeVoto, among others) that presumably seemed secure enough to survive by mail. Whether it was confidence lifted by the success of *The Big Rock Candy Mountain* or just a decision to move west regardless of the consequences, the Stegners had decided that their trip west would be one way and that they would not return to Harvard after his leave was over.

In a letter to his good friend Phil Gray on April 23, 1944, Stegner noted his draft status as 2-A with relief and announced: "And I guess we've decided to move west for good, no matter what comes up after this Look job. I wouldn't advertise that yet, since I'm still technically on leave, but I don't expect we'll come back to finish up our three years here. Instead we shall probably make the 2,000,003'rd immigrant into California since the outbreak of war, and rent us an abalone diver's shack at Santa Rosa or somewhere."[3]

He was not wrong about joining the masses of people migrating to California. As 17 percent of the total American defense output during World War II was spent in California, the war years had brought around 8 million new residents to California, in addition to another 3 million who were military-in-training or in transit. By 1950, the population of the state as a whole was listed as 10,586,223 and it would climb to nearly 35 million by the end of the twentieth century.[4]

The Stegners eventually made it to the beach but were hardly living in a diver's shack. Soon after the letter to Gray, Stegner and his family were living in the "gardener's cottage" on the Gardiner Hammond Estate in Montecito, California.[5] In a letter to Richard Scowcroft, he described their situation: "Rumors leak back to me . . . that we are living in a mansion with six baths. Tain't so. Is only three, one of which is tired and won't work any more. House is a little tired all over, really. But we still like the palms and the eucalyptuses and the pines and the beach and the private golf course."[6]

By June of 1945, the Stegners' idyll in Santa Barbara was at an end and they were on their way to Palo Alto, Stegner having been offered a job in the English department at Stanford. With this move, he joined another significant migration, as the nine-county region surrounding the San Francisco Bay Area "became home to 676,000 more people, 330,000 more jobs, and $2.5 billion more in annual income" just between 1940 and 1947, with "per capita wealth of the region reach[ing] the highest level in the nation," as reported by Margaret O'Mara.[7]

In another letter to Phil Gray, written shortly after arriving in Palo Alto in July of 1945, Stegner offered the following assessment of Palo Alto and Stanford, the institution in which he would teach for the next twenty-six years, and the metropolitan area he and his family would make their home until he died.

> California, that is Palo Alto, is not wilderness, coming at three thousand an acre and selling altogether too fast at that price. It is very pleasant country, for all that: golden wild-oat hills dotted with marvelous old liveoaks and bay trees, with a dark pine-covered ridge of the coast range behind, and in front the hills dropping down over orchards and town to the bay, and beyond the bay the barren gold ridge of the San Jose Mountains with Mount Diablo coming up in the midst of it. There are views to knock your eye out all over these hills.... [We] have just enlisted ourselves in a cooperative building group which is about to buy 250 acres of the most marvelous hill land back of the campus about three miles.[8]

To Stegner, the attraction of his new environs was the proximity to nature, and particularly western nature, even if not quite "wilderness." His evaluation of Stanford was much less enthusiastic: "The university seems a pleasant place. So far we have seen no great signs of distinction.... It seems to be mainly army and women, to the naked eye, and the ivy moulders on the Stanford Bowl for lack of organized sports [*sic*]."[9] Though mildly dismissive of the university (and of military students and women) and betraying concerns, which proved to be accurate, about the impending growth and development of Palo Alto, the overall tone of Stegner's letters from the period was delight at finally being out west again after his sojourn in Madison and Cambridge.

He exulted in his return to the landscapes of the semi-arid West. Being without home in the interpersonal sense, he at least knew he was at home in the flora and fauna of the West. The university might be uninspired, but there is also a hint of confidence that it is merely temporary; after all, they had only just offered the job to Stegner. Stegner was not necessarily wrong in his dismissal of Stanford. Stegner had moved there at a critical phase in the history of the university, when it was laying the groundwork for its transition from, as George Packer called it, a "country club of the California elite" to a world-leading university.[10] His confidence in its trajectory also proved to be accurate, as Stegner was able to convince a funder to help him start the creative writing program not long after he arrived, which went from promising to elite within a few years.[11]

Eager and buoyed by a sense of promise and hope, then, Stegner became a Californian. The Stegners were renting a home near campus and excited about their options for future housing. The cooperative Stegner mentioned in the letter to Phil Gray was the Peninsula Housing Association (PHA), and the members had organized to build a planned community in what became Ladera, California. Stegner had written a series of four generally positive articles on cooperatives for *The Delphian Quarterly* from 1942 to 1943, so he was already a convert to the cooperative idea.[12] The cooperative was also opposed to restrictive covenants and included several black families as early members. It was a chance to put the principles he had espoused in *One Nation* into practice.[13]

Stegner was so enthusiastic about the project that he wrote a short article about it, one that is nearly utopian in its description of their plans. Stegner was excited about the project for many reasons. First, it offered "middle-income families" a chance to build their own home at a reasonable price rather than having to settle for "an overpriced cheesebox" that allowed for no discussion of design from the owner. Further, because it was new and being planned cooperatively, "beauty, convenience, [and] the pleasures of country living open ordinarily only to the very wealthy" would be built into Ladera "from the very beginning." The people were occupationally diverse as well, with Stanford professors, engineers, airline pilots, many teachers from public schools, accountants, insurance agents, auditors, federal, state, and city employees, a professional baseball player, a longshoreman, a dentist, writers, photographers and publishers, mechanics, nurses, composers, architects, industrial designers, bakers, carpenters, geologists, chemists, and retired army colonels listed in Stegner's account.

These members of the community had the opportunity to plan "not merely their own homes but their whole neighborhood, their whole town." But that was not all, as the cooperative was also a signal that the members were "measuring the ability of the American public to throw off a system that has proved utterly incompetent and even antisocial" by cooperating in a "spirit that used to animate barn raisings when democracy was younger and simpler." In summary: "When [the PHA] completes the project . . . [i]t will have created not merely 400 modern homes of sound and beautiful design, but an entire new community. This community is new from the grassroots up."[14]

The new community could not escape the legacy of redlining based on race, however, and the members were not approved for Federal Housing Authority (FHA) loans because the PHA included the three black families as members. Some members, against the Stegners' objections, proposed a compromise that would allow minority members into the development, but only in a number equal or lower than the percentage of minority residents in California as a whole. In January 1948—in the same month and year that the U.S. Supreme Court was hearing the *Shelley v. Kraemer* case that would prohibit racially restrictive covenants—the compromise passed 78–75.[15] Even with the compromise, the cooperative still failed to acquire FHA loans. When faced with the possibility of expelling the existing minority members in order to obtain the loans, the Stegners resigned and the co-op was disbanded. Eventually the tract was resold to a developer who built a subdivision that included houses tied to restrictive covenants that qualified for FHA loans. Three years of cooperative dreaming had failed.[16]

In the wake of that disappointment, the Stegners instead commissioned a house to be built in the relatively remote (at the time) Los Altos Hills in 1948 and moved into it in 1949. It was a beautiful California Modern home, situated at the top of a hill with a view of the valley and other hills of the region, and stylish enough to be featured in both the August and December editions of *House and Garden* in 1952. The articles praised the house for its open floor plan and use of landscaping to both protect privacy and allow for porousness between indoor and outdoor spaces around the home.[17] Even if not living in the cooperative community they had hoped to help build, it is not too far-fetched to suggest that Stegner and his family had reached the "big rock candy mountain" that had always eluded his parents. Further, he was an accomplished author and a promising young professor at what was becoming one of the nation's premier universities.

It was a hopeful and exhilarating time, and over the next few decades Stegner was among the Californians intent on building a California that might embody the "geography of hope." The Wallace Stegner who put this phrase into the consciousness of his fellow environmentalists and embodied a certain western, liberal, humane sensibility is crucial to understand and will be the primary focus of this chapter. For a westerner who had experienced the deprivations of culture in several western form-less non-communities, and who had also experienced the exhilaration of the wilderness experience, the suburbs seemed a place that one might be able to build a real western place, one more suited to human flourishing than other spaces.

Bourgeois Utopias

With this move, Stegner became a resident of a western suburb. More accurately, a suburb of a western suburb, since Palo Alto was a suburb of San Francisco. Though Stegner had experienced variations of the rural West in several locations and the urban West in Salt Lake City, this was the first time he lived in what would soon become the dominant frame-work for the organization of western space in the postwar decades. The suburbs of California, and particularly the suburban spaces of what became Silicon Valley, have been the subject of historical inquiry from a wide range of angles.[18] The growth of the suburbs is one of the most consequential changes in a whole host of consequential changes in the postwar half of the American Century. Here I am primarily concerned with elaborating on Stegner's sense of the suburbs as a retreat from the broader world, and the effects of this suburban ideal on the possibility of community in these places.

Suburbs resist easy definition. In Robert Fishman's long history of the suburb, *Bourgeois Utopias: The Rise and Fall of Suburbia*, suburbs are marked by single family homes on large plots leading to a low-density

environment, economic dependence on a large city, the exclusion of all
industry and most commerce, and class homogeneity. These concrete
characteristics promote what Fishman defines as the true mark of the
suburb, an aesthetic ideal grounded on the marriage of city and country.[19] These suburbs served as a "refuge for a privileged minority."[20] Fishman's "true suburbs" have been killed by their own success, as places
like Los Angeles have increasingly become more like low-density cities than places that blend city and country. Rooted in the first wave of
industrialists' attempts to build their own approximations of the English
aristocratic estate without giving up the possibility of continuing to work
in London, Fishman's true suburbs are pre-automobile and as such distinguished from more modern versions of the suburb, such as those in
postwar California.[21]

For Stegner, the Bay Area suburbs where he settled had the promise
to unite the two ways of life he most sought to experience. They offered a
chance for him to achieve one version of the American Dream, to experience the "conviction of belonging" in both wilderness and civilization.
As he wrote in "The Wilderness Letter": "For an American, insofar as he
is new and different at all, is a civilized man who has renewed himself
in the wild."[22] In one of his more lyrical descriptions of his childhood in
Saskatchewan, Stegner wrote of a nighttime experience in 1915, after traveling in a wagon across fifty miles of prairie to start a homestead with
his father and brother, when he felt this sense of belonging and renewal
in nature:

> Then in the night I awoke, not knowing where I was. Strangeness
> flowed around me; there was a current of cool air, a whisper-
> ing, a loom of darkness overhead. In panic I reared up on my
> elbow and found that I was sleeping beside my brother under a
> wagon, and that the night wind was breathing across me through
> the spikes of the wheel. It came from unimaginably far places,
> across a vast emptiness, below millions of polished stars. And
> yet its touch was soft, intimate, and reassuring, and my panic
> went away at once. That wind knew me. I knew it. Every once in
> a while, sixty-six years after that baptism in space and night and
> silence, wind across grassland can smell like that to me, as secret,
> perfumed, and soft, and tell me who I am. It is an opportunity I

Figure 3. Wallace, Mary, and Page Stegner in Yosemite National Park in an undated photo from the 1950s. Courtesy Special Collections, J. Willard Marriott Library, University of Utah.

wish every American could have. Having been *born lucky, I wish I could expand the opportunities I benefited from, instead of extinguishing them* [emphasis added].[23]

While this experience was not an exception and Stegner wrote many lyrical passages about his experiences of the natural world and the sense of belonging he felt in it, he also at times wrote about the deprivations of life lived in relatively open spaces; he did not believe in the romantic primitivism of Thoreau, or in John Muir's "galling harness of civilization."[24] He wanted to belong in both geological time and human time. In another essay, reflecting on his experience lecturing in Greece, Stegner tried to reckon with the difference between his unknown past and the burdens of an overbearing glorious past:

> History clangs like bronze in [George] Seferis' poems; *the felt knowledge of a continuous past and present* informs every line. . . . Those Greek writers must have been a little astonished to hear a man who had grown up without history come carrying culture back to Athens. Some of them said frankly that they envied me, for a glorious past can be a burden to a writer living in a diminished present. But *I envied them more than they envied me for what they had was what I had spent my life hopelessly trying to acquire* [emphasis added].[25]

Characteristically, Stegner argued against himself on this issue. Was he, by virtue of his childhood experiences in Eastend, born lucky (as in the first passage) or born deprived (as in the second)? Regardless of which assessment was pulling more strongly on him at any given moment, these passages suggest why Stegner was attracted to the Bay Area suburbs as they existed in the late 1940s. Like many others, he wanted to live where it was possible to have both the "soft, intimate, reassuring" wind of the wild spaces and, at the same time, access to the arts and institutions that create and sustain human civilization. Stegner was clearly going to California to stay and to build. His first decades in California were filled with an impressive amount of institution building, not to mention writing.[26]

Stegner's Regional Vision

Given these commitments, Stegner moved to California as a fellow traveler in the American regional movement as elaborated most clearly by historian Robert Dorman. Dorman frames this movement, which is more coherent in his book than it was as a distinct historical movement, as "an alternative route to modernization" that attempted to resist through regional development both nostalgia and the "acids of modernity" described by Walter Lippmann.[27] What united the movement, according to Dorman, was the belief that commitment to region could be a "means toward a richer, freer, and more humane way of life."[28] In such a vision,

> Region was more concretely, indeed, programmatically envisioned to be the utopian means for reconstructing the nationalizing, homogenizing urban-industrial complex, re-directing it toward an accommodation with local folkways and local environments. The region, it was hoped, would provide the physical framework for the creation of new kinds of cities, small-scale, planned, delimited, and existing in balance with wilderness and a restored and rejuvenated rural economy.[29]

Dorman's regionalists—Lewis Mumford, B. A. Botkin, Mary Austin, Howard Odum, and others—were also united by the attempt to push beyond merely a "style of personal confrontation with local culture, tradition, or landscape" and to attempt to instead "fashion regionalism into a democratic civil religion, a utopian ideology, and a radical politics."[30] While Stegner's political engagement was uneven, he did at least share one of the guiding maxims of the movement: "Rejecting the 'mine and move' philosophy that had laid waste to America's landscape as well as its democracy, they would proselytize a new guiding maxim: 'stay and cultivate.'"[31]

Stegner's first article for a national publication offered a defense of regionalism in Iowa, the heart of the 1930s regionalist movement. "The Trail of the Hawkeye: Literature Where the Tall Corn Grows" appeared in the July 30, 1938, edition of *The Saturday Review of Literature*. He followed that article with three other articles on the topic of regionalism before 1940, with two in the *Delphian Quarterly* and one in *Publisher's Weekly*.[32]

The first of these articles was a short and hopeful description of the previous generation of Iowa writers and the reversal of the tendency to "revolt from the village" by revolting instead from "regimented industrial cities." Instead of being merely the state where "the greatest boast is the production of taller corn and huger hogs than any other region in the world," Iowa had, with the presence of Paul Engle and Grant Wood, among others, "become as fit a subject for books, and as reputable a state for a writer to live in, as any other." Stegner blessed the movement as a healthy one: "Cultural regionalism is the philosophy of many Iowa writers today, but the movement is liberalizing rather than the reverse. In a society moving toward complete industrial regimentation there is a profound need for the preservation of healthy provincialisms, as Josiah Royce pointed out as far back as 1902." Even better, the cultural regionalism in Iowa was not much marked by "the aggressive sectionalism that has colored the literature of the South."[33]

A few lines indicated Stegner's evolving appreciation of the power of place. The first was a short description of what exactly made someone an Iowa writer. Noting first the difficulty of a precise definition, Stegner settled on a definition that reveals his sense of what a regional identity comprised at the time. Iowa writers are those who grew up there or "who spent so considerable a part of their early lives in the state that they were indelibly marked by their environment." In the case of an Iowan, this marking came from a "society probably more rural in its philosophy than that of any state in the union."

Though he stopped short of praising rural society outright, it is not hard to guess where his sympathies lay. Stegner concluded with two short descriptions of essential ingredients of regional art, both of which aligned him with other regionalists of the Depression era. First, he suggested the necessity of a coherent culture—"the homogeneity of the state, the stability and conservatism of its society, the unbroken tradition of people living in much the same way for four generations, gives a solid cultural earth for the artists to dig in"—a "profoundly essential element in lasting art." Next, he emphasized the necessity of a university, where there is "a congenial intellectual environment for the artist" which "ought to be sufficient reason for a good deal of hopefulness about the future of Iowa literature."[34]

Stegner continued looking at regional infrastructure in his next article, "A Decade of Regional Publishing," in *Publisher's Weekly*, which appeared on March 11, 1939. The article described the history of Caxton Press in Caldwell, Idaho. The article began with a description of the great sloughing off of the accoutrements of culture forced by the migration of white Americans across the continent. Several generations later, the "culturally expatriated sections of America are now trying to climb back towards civilization" at times with "laughable results" but in other ways that are "hopeful and even portentous." The presence of the press demonstrated an attempt toward regional "intellectual autonomy" against long odds, most notably a regional market of less than a million people, by Stegner's estimate.

William Gipson, the editor of Caxton Press, received high praise. Though Gipson was "a local patriot" and a "devout regionalist" and "Idaho booster" who embraced "one of the principal jobs of any regional press," the "effort to make their region known to Idahoans and the world at large," Gipson was "also a lover of books" with a broad range of books that are not simply western. He was not one to settle for mere regional distinction, but a publisher who believed that "'fine books are the most worthwhile things made by twentieth century men ... [who] hope some day to produce the finest trade editions being made in the world today.'" Stegner acknowledged that such a statement might make "a student of printing smile" but also suggested that the endeavor was more hopeful than it might appear.[35]

Two articles on regionalism for *The Delphian Quarterly* reveal more plainly that Stegner was invested in regionalism as a philosophy. In his articles for *Saturday Review* and *Publisher's Weekly*, Stegner emphasized that the regionalism of Iowa and Idaho via Caxton Press was not antagonistic to cosmopolitan and urbane values. However, his articles in *The Delphian Quarterly*, a much smaller publication than the other two, suggest that Stegner saw regional presses as uniquely liberalizing. Stegner argued that the "regional presses are of a different and much more vital breed" than previous small boutique presses. Recent regional presses have pushed beyond these "pleasant and fairly harmless" versions and have "been absorbed into a larger movement: the movement for literature interpreting the regions of America in their own terms, with a deep reliance on the patterns of emotional and social behavior that link a writer to his audience and make him not a man apart but a Voice from within."

Stegner again presents a very hopeful picture for Caxton Press in Idaho, but his highest praise goes to the University of Oklahoma Press, which "has elected to do, honestly and thoroughly, the job that a private or subsidized press is best adapted for: the interpretation of its immediate region." He also praises Prairie Press of Iowa as a publishing venture that "has been representative of the best in the regional movement: enthusiasm for the region itself, and loyalty to its cultural patterns, combined with distinguished good taste in the actual bookmaking." The Countryman Press of Weston, Vermont, has "proclaimed the virtues of the country against those of the city, the hinterlands against the metropolis" while attempting to "bring books to a segment of the population which has never used them before. Vermont farmers have to be coaxed into such a thing by degrees; he sells them twenty-five cent pamphlets."

Stegner concluded his essay on six regional presses with an argument for the value of decentralized publishing. After noting that publishing can reduce costs through economies of scale, he wrote, "But there are those who would be glad to give up some of the efficiency for a more democratic, undominated, and dispersed organization." Failure to cultivate smaller presses makes it more likely for "minority opinion . . . simply to be manufactured out of existence." Efficiency breeds uniformity, and "uniformity is not so far removed from regimentation, and regimentation is not democracy."[36]

"Regionalism in Art" included Stegner's description and defense of regionalism as an artistic philosophy. Regionalism is not "motivated by chauvinism or patriotic local pride"; rather, it "merely means that the artist must express, if he is to express anything at all, the things he knows best, the knowledge that is both of the brain and the blood." The artist needs to be "emotionally as well as intellectually linked with his materials"; the artist needs to "deal with the patterns of the culture out of which his own life has grown." It is only this "intense interest in the particulars" of life that allows for "universal expression of human character and living." Crucially, however, this is not something the artist can do alone. Regional art is only possible where several conditions obtain, including: "a fairly uniform way of life"; a "continuous tradition of settled existence within fairly limited patterns"; and, unsettlingly, "if not a homogenous race, at least a race whose stamp has been accepted by the bulk of the populace." In short, there must be a "generic 'culture'" or, in the words of Thomas Hart Benton, "'a way of living rather than a precious juggling of excerpts from half-read books.'"[37]

Stegner demonstrated sincere faith in the power of the local to express the universal: "Art speaks most clearly to the immediate society from which it came" and can also speak to the nation, but "at its best, if it rises above the level of merely competent art, it speaks to all humanity." This kind of art transcends; it is too valuable to be reduced to regional chauvinism or naked politics:

Regionalism, cultural regionalism, is not an antiquarian fad like the cult of the hillbilly. It is contemporary, and it deals by preference with the usual rather than with the unusual, with the essentially normal rather than the picturesque, with cultures which are continuous and vital rather than with the isolated and the moribund. It is not concerned with "causes" and class struggles and political faiths, except as those touch the lives of the people and the patterns of the local life. The moment an artist loses his primary interest in human beings as people, and feels the impulse to throw his weight on one side or another of a cause, he loses his status as an artist, no matter how important his job as tractarian or propagandist may be. His job is no longer to enrich the understanding, but to coerce it, and that is not art. Regionalism is not a fighting doctrine, or a doctrine that needs even to be conscious in the artist's mind. It is simply the recognition of the simplest truth about art: that the artist wastes his time and talent by trying to speak of anything but his own life and his own people and his own culture.

As these articles demonstrate, Stegner was attempting to sort out several related questions. First, he was looking at regionalism as a question of identity. What did it mean to be from a region and to be marked by it? Could one's region of origin be escaped? Was it healthy to escape? Or was it healthier to stay? Second, he was looking at regionalism in relation to infrastructural circumstances, such as publishing houses and critical journals. Could someone write from a region that is not New York, or not equipped with material means of supporting writers? Third, he was looking at regionalism as a cultural movement. In what ways could regionalism promote or retard the production of art? Fourth, Stegner was a regionalist in the sense that he was committed to the conservation of landscapes and nature. Stegner came to his regionalism honestly, as he lived in Iowa in the 1930s, as much a notable home of regionalism as any other place due to the presence of Grant Wood and others. It is intriguing to wonder whether he would have conceived of himself as a westerner in the same way had he not spent his most intellectually formative years in Iowa in the 1930s.

One Nation

This regional vision informed one of Stegner's first nonfiction books, *One Nation* (1945), a book originally commissioned as a series of articles to be published in *Look* magazine. Despite the drift of the title, the book itself included strong arguments for regionalism as a means of promoting a stronger and healthier nation.

One Nation was a real career risk for Stegner, however. Beyond the fact that Stegner left his job at Harvard to take on the project, *Look* was fairly tame; it made *Life*, its closest competitor, look like a vehicle for hard-hitting investigative journalism. For example, the June 27, 1944, issue included an article titled, "A Guy Named Joe." The subject? Just Joseph Stalin, expert in Arctic meteorology and a fan of James Fenimore Cooper.

This is admittedly a humorous example, but it is consistent with the overall tone. *Look* had a way of making everything look tame, even dictators. Articles on tense topics such as spouses returning from active duty tended towards banality and sentimental assurance. According to the index, Stegner's articles on race were the only articles that included the word "Negro" from January 1944 to December 1945.[38] In contrast, *Life* ran an editorial that was harsh on the South just after Gunnar Myrdal's *An American Dilemma* was published, and in 1943 included an article on black soldiers and a lengthy photo essay castigating the role of whites in the Detroit riots. So why write for *Look* just after securing one's reputation as a "serious" novelist?

Stegner took the job for several reasons. Most immediately, he wanted to be on the road, and he wanted to be on the road in the America West. He missed the West and felt like he was simply marking time at Harvard. Though he was critical of his father's restless roving, old habits died hard and wartime gas rationing was cramping him, as was the new role Harvard had adopted to meet the demands of the army. This included an increased teaching load and curriculum shaped too directly to meet national security needs.[39] Salaries at Harvard were low, so being paid well to take trains across the country was very appealing. Further, he did not think he was above journalism, even for *Look*. He was more focused on the notion that he might reach a wider audience, especially given the topic, which he thought might do some good for the nation. "Wartime patriotism took strange forms," as he told Richard Etulain later.[40]

So it was that by March 1944 he began research for the new project. He was influenced most strongly by Myrdal's *An American Dilemma*, which had just been published in January 1944.[41] Another important influence was Carey McWilliams's *Brothers Under the Skin*, published in 1943.[42] Lillian Smith's *Strange Fruit*, as well as the research of Roi Ottley, Charles S. Johnson, and John Lawlah were also cited briefly.[43] He began his investigative research in Boston, where he was attempting to understand the complexities of a recent outbreak of Irish Catholic anti-Semitism that had resulted in the assault of several Jews.

This initial research resulted in an article published in the July 1944 issue of the *Atlantic Monthly* titled, "Who Persecutes Boston?" Though the article itself was sensitive to the fact that the Irish and Catholics in general were not immune from persecution themselves, and argued that "the Roman Catholic Church is not in the least responsible for the anti-Semitic outbreaks in Boston," the sentence that followed was more incendiary: "But it could do more than any other agency or institution to stop them, if it would."[44] The *Atlantic* editor who decided to print the article did not realize that the magazine was owned by Irish Catholics. The owners hated the article, and the editor's Catholic secretary resigned in protest.[45]

In the September 1944 issue of the *Atlantic*, the editors opened their correspondence section by noting that the *Atlantic* had been "severely criticized by the Catholic press" for publishing the article before ultimately defending Stegner and the decision to publish the article. They included two critical letters and six supportive letters in the correspondence. Samples from two of these letters are enough to give a general picture. The most negative letter came from Brookline, Massachusetts, and opens with the sentence, "In my whole life I have never read an article that has incensed me so much as 'Who Persecutes Boston?' by Wallace Stegner." One of the supportive letters came from a soldier who linked the battle against intolerance to American efforts in World War II: "The Germans and Japs are fighting us because we are bearers of the Judaeo-Christian cultural and religious spirit. . . . We believe in freedom, in democracy, in truth, and in justice for all. (Good God, we do, don't we?)"[46]

Stegner continued in his research but *Look* took note. By May of 1945, *Look* had decided that they would not be publishing the pieces as serial articles as originally planned and would instead condense the articles into one short article. Stegner would still have the opportunity to publish his original work as a book, and it was published by the fall of 1945. The article that ended up in *Look* magazine was not what Stegner had envisioned. In a letter to a friend, he said *Look* "got scared" because they were afraid "the public that reads *Look* ... just wouldn't take it."[47]

This decision could not have been taken lightly, as *Look* had paid Stegner and several photographers to do the work over the course of a whole year. They traded twelve or fourteen (depending whether the introduction and conclusion stood alone) serial articles, plus hundreds of photographs, for one five-page article that included seven photographs. Instead of race being a central focus of a major national publication for over ten issues, it managed to surface in only one issue. It is hard to gauge the impact of journalism, but this was certainly a lost opportunity for Stegner and, perhaps, Americans as a whole.

The differences between the article and the book reveal the boundaries of public discussion of "moralistic, state-activist racial liberalism" in the United States in the midcentury.[48] The most obvious difference between the two pieces is the regional emphasis.[49] *Look*'s article opened with a half-page photograph of a burning cross with five hooded KKK members giving the raised-arm Nazi salute. "Prejudice: Our Postwar Battle" is the headline. Regardless of what happens next, the reader has already been signaled to understand that this is a discussion of the South. The next page included another half-page photograph of two white men, one with a U.S. Army sweatshirt, supporting a black man in a suit clutching a hat in his hand, his face bloodied beyond recognition and his knees buckled. Without the caption or a glance at the bloodied rag in one of the white man's hands, which is overwhelmed by a wide grin on the face of the other white man, it looks like the white men are dragging a "trophy" beating in for the camera.

Again, *Look* seemed to point the reader towards the Jim Crow South. The caption informs the reader, however, that the two white men were actually rescuing the black man from other whites during the 1943 Detroit riots.[50] Nonetheless, the dominant features of the article were consistent with the American tendency to label racism as a regional problem confined to the South to minimize damage to the nation and its institutions as a whole.[51] Letting the photographs tell the story, as they tend to do in

Look, this is even more evident, as the story concluded with two half-page photos depicting racially diverse educational settings. In the first, a black woman is teaching a room full of white children in New York; the second depicted a classroom full of happy, boisterous children of "24 nationalities" singing "God Bless America" in a school in Los Angeles.

Stegner's book, on the other hand, opened with an introduction that included four short vignettes describing discriminatory acts against an interracial conference in St. Louis, Jews in Boston, Japanese Americans in Santa Barbara, and Mexican Americans in Los Angeles. The first photo in the book pointed to everyday discrimination with a photo of a club on a beach in Boston that says, "Private Beach—Gentiles." Though the introduction did move to description of the Jim Crow South within a few pages, the emphasis on racial discrimination as only a southern problem was challenged further by the first chapter, which opened with a map of California to illustrate the annual trek Filipino agricultural workers made following harvests of produce. This chapter then highlights the plight of male Filipino farm workers stuck in a rootless lifestyle, with little hope for marriage due to labor conditions, miscegenation laws that prevent marriage to non-Filipinos, and immigration laws that prevent more Filipino women from migrating to the United States.

Following the chapter on Filipino men, Stegner investigated Japanese Americans in internment camps, Chinese Americans along the West Coast, Mexican *braceros*, the *pachucos* of Los Angeles, the Hispanos of New Mexico, American Indians, blacks in the South, blacks who moved out of the South during the Great Migration, the black middle class, and, finally, Catholics and Jews. Assuming the order was chosen very deliberately, it suggested southern racism was the center of a national problem that varied only in degree. He made it abundantly clear that racism was a national issue. The conclusion contained this warning: "The caste system of the South is a weed which will grow as well in northern climates as in southern."[52]

Another crucial difference was that the book included short articles that attempted to interpret each culture from the inside, to the extent possible in a *Look*-sized article. While extreme poverty is obvious in some photos and other photos depict victims of brutal violence, the book as a whole tended to cover a wider range of life than the standard Farm Security Administration (FSA) shots. *One Nation* includes photos of parties, clean apartments and schools, shaves, dances—in general, the photos seem to be photos the subjects themselves might have actually placed on their own walls. The concern for "authenticity" manifested by most of the FSA photographers was missing, so there are parts of the book that look more like a photo album composed by the subjects for themselves than a documentary book composed by the photographer for an audience.[53] There are at least two possible interpretations for this decision.

First, it could have been that Stegner thought it necessary to dispel myths about race being linked to intelligence or any other desirable quality. Though scientific arguments about racial inferiority had been dispelled in many quarters by the 1940s, Stegner spent several paragraphs arguing against this claim in his book, suggesting that *Look*'s demographic still needed convincing. Photographs of "successful" minorities may have been included in order to provide visual evidence to support the textual arguments. The correspondence that followed the article in *Look* suggested that this was indeed a case that needed to be made. Readers wrote vehement denunciations of even the watered-down article: "You can entertain the thought that the Negro is your equal if you wish— but he isn't mine" and "Southerners have been brought up to consider themselves above the Negroes which, in the eyes of God, they are. When God created men, He never meant for them to be equal and they never will be. Race war is better than racial equality."[54]

At a more philosophical level and consistent with his regionalism, Stegner had great hope for the survival of the cultures he described, if they were respected enough to be included in the American system. It is telling that his version of the "American creed" came out as "diversity without disunity" rather than the more hopeful and more common "unity in diversity."[55] If Stegner's version with the double negative seemed less hopeful, it was also legitimately suspicious of the mission of assimilation that seems the inevitable outcome of the more popular version.

In most of his profiles, Stegner looked at how each group managed to maintain its identity and build community despite social, political, and economic disadvantages. Consistent with regionalist trends, he primarily argued that preservation of the cultural heritages of the groups rather than assimilation would promote a stronger national culture. For example, he praised the new federal policies for American Indians that reversed the more assimilationist policies of the past, even if in language that marked Indians as outside of the national "we":

> The new policy is removing that sense of shame, letting the Indian move in the world as an equal, though different, citizen. On that basis he probably will not only give more to America but take more from it. As a matter of fact, the prospect that the Indian cultures might survive along with the Indian people should hardly cause alarm. We are already tremendously in debt to those cultures.[56]

More indirectly, the photos could have just represented the optimistic tone of the book as a whole, published as it was in 1945, with Allied victory nearly assured and the American economy drastically improved since the Great Depression.[57] Especially in comparison to other books in the documentary genre from the late 1930s and early 1940s, Stegner's book was marked by undeniable confidence for the postwar world, even if Stegner also issued strenuous warnings about the potential dangers connected to demobilization in a racially charged atmosphere.[58] Throughout the book Stegner praised the Fair Employment Practices Commission of 1941, experiments in diversity such as an intentionally mixed-race school in Springfield, Massachusetts, and the fundamentally decent character of everyday Americans (such as the readers of *Look* magazine).

Stegner also believed that bottom-up movements among minorities were a source of hope: "In many ways, a time of racial tension is a time of hope, for it means that instead of being submissively held down, colored Americans are exerting an irresistible pressure upward."[59] He echoed this sentiment again in the conclusion: "We can measure the amount of progress they have been making in the past five years by the increasing racial tension that those years have brought. Prejudice gives way only with loud and groaning noises, but it gives when the pressure from below becomes great enough."[60]

Beyond the Hundredth Meridian

By 1954, Stegner's regionalism had begun to focus more on geography. In that year, he published *Beyond the Hundredth Meridian*, in which he studied John Wesley Powell's attempt to organize the American West by hydrographic basins to account for western aridity. *Beyond the Hundredth Meridian* was contemporaneous with high modernist masterpieces of midcentury liberal planning projects in California, notably the California Water Plan of 1957, the California Freeway System of 1958, and Clark Kerr's "A Master Plan for Higher Education" of 1960.[61] Here I am less concerned with an analysis of the book as a whole than I am with using it to highlight Stegner's regional thought.

Beyond the Hundredth Meridian is still considered a classic study of the American West, even if Stegner's scholarship and methods have been disputed and the book superseded—at least at the scholarly level—by Donald Worster's more thoroughly and carefully researched biography, *A River Running West*.[62] At the time, it was significant for lifting John Wesley Powell into the pantheon of proto-environmentalists at an important moment for the conservation movement, right in the heart of the Echo Park Dam controversy of the 1950s. Stegner wrote with relatively uninhibited admiration for Powell; in her review of Worster's book, Patricia Limerick said *Beyond the Hundredth Meridian* "might prove to be the last successful installation of a western American hero.[63]

Stegner thought Powell was a neglected hero and he wrote to recover Powell's ideal of disinterested public service and realistic vision for the American West, both of which he felt had been neglected by less worthy variations of the western hero. He saw in Powell the origins of a "usable past."[64] Stegner's Powell, the self-educated scientist who lost his arm in the Battle of Shiloh but still managed to raft the Colorado River and lead the second U.S. Geological Survey, in addition to becoming the first director of the Bureau of Ethnology at the Smithsonian Institution, is called upon for service against several "dragons of error, backwardness, and unchecked exploitation."[65] The "unchastened illusions" of boosters who, like William Gilpin, believed that the "rain followed the plow" were the most important enemies, but Stegner also posed Powell's disinterested commitment to science against Clarence King's chasing of the "rainbow with dollar signs on it" and his optimistic practical vigor against "tired and soured observers" like Henry Adams.[66]

Several principles of Powell's influenced Stegner's view of the West as a region. First, Powell insisted that the American West was a region that could not be settled and governed in the same ways that other

American regions had been. Against preconceived aesthetic paradigms that rendered newcomers incapable of truly seeing the region, inaccurate reports, and simple boosterism that benefited from misleading information, Powell insisted on the "inflexible fact of aridity" that "lay like a fence along the 100th meridian."[67] From his study of Powell, Stegner would also insist that it was impossible to study the West or develop coherent communities in the West without some understanding of the centrality of aridity.

First Attempts at California Fiction

As Stegner was finishing *Beyond the Hundredth Meridian* and becoming a major voice among midcentury California environmentalists and conservationists, he was also exploring the social and cultural tensions of his new home through his fiction.[68] It is in these stories that we see Stegner stepping into the role of the regional artist that he had praised when he was thinking through the regionalist movement in Iowa and elsewhere. Stegner started laying down a foundation of stories that might bind the California newcomers into a community, and shape the Midpeninsula into a distinct place.

He was no booster in these stories, however. If his nonfiction praised the John Wesley Powells of the West, his fiction tended more towards the dislocated musings of Henry Adams. Stegner started writing about California suburbs that approximated Los Altos Hills specifically by 1953.[69] The world that he created with his first novella set in his part of the Midpeninsula, with Joe and Ruth Allston and their home in Los Altos Hills at the center, proved fertile enough to support a novella, "Field Guide to Western Birds" ("Field Guide" hereafter), and two short stories, "All the Little Live Things" ("Live Things" hereafter), published in *Mademoiselle* in May 1959, and "Indoor-Outdoor Living," published in *Pacifica* in September 1959.[70] Two novels then followed, *All the Little Live Things* (*Live Things* hereafter), published in 1967, and *The Spectator Bird*, published in 1976. Stegner originally envisioned including all three shorter pieces in *Live Things*. The final product did include most of both "Live Things" and "Indoor-Outdoor Living" with only minimal changes, but *Live Things* only reveals faint traces of the outline of "Field Guide."

This was typical of Stegner's imaginative literature, as many of his short stories were later built into his novels. He was more concerned with the integrity of each piece on its own than with the integrity of the fictional universe that he was creating with all of the relevant pieces put together, so it is often the case that character names and circumstances change to fit the demands of each piece of fiction depending on the circumstances of its publication.[71] Viewed as a whole, however, this fictional world is intricately developed and significant for its commentary on a specific historical place and time. It is consistent with Stegner's vision for fiction as expressed in "Fiction: A Lens on Life," where he wrote, "It is often necessary for a writer to distort the particulars of experience in order to see them better."[72]

The Artist and the American Philistine

"Field Guide," Stegner's first piece of suburb fiction, fittingly begins, "I must say, I've never felt better." Even though already legendary for many years, the golden landscapes of California were luxurious and retained the capacity to surprise new migrants with their good fortune to be alive in such a beautiful place. It was almost uncomfortably beautiful, particularly for a generation that grew up during the deprivations and terrors of the Great War, the Great Depression, and World War II, as Stegner had. It was the tensions of the soft-liberal nouveau riche that Stegner explored in this first suburb story. Sometimes sympathetically, sometimes humorously, sometimes seriously, he explores how the new upper-middle class reckoned with their increasingly comfortable lives in the suburbs. At their best they embrace neighborly community. At their worst they are shallow, bored, and hypocritical.

Joe Allston, Stegner's narrator, is a sixty-six-year-old man, just retired from a career as a literary agent. Stegner imagined him into being when he was himself forty-four years old. Joe is sitting in his study, watching birds, astounded by the beauty of his surroundings, but nonetheless, with some uneasiness insisting to himself that he is satisfied. It is clear that after six months he has yet to adapt to the rhythms of retirement. He is weary of work and the trappings of his career, but incapable of rest or taking much interest in the work he has undertaken as his leisure. After a lifetime of chaos, home and leisure is too slow.

The birds distract and interest him much more than the memoirs that are purportedly the retirement project that lead him down each day to his study, a small detached studio a hundred feet from his house. One, an unidentified species of towhee, "a champion for pugnacity," strikes Allston as particularly vexing:

> Maybe he is living up to some dim notion of how to be a proper husband and father, maybe he just hates himself, for about ten times a day I see him alight on the terrace and challenge his reflection in the plate glass. He springs at himself like a fighting cock, beats his wings, pecks, flies up, falls down, until he wears himself out and squats on the bricks, panting and glaring at his hated image.[73]

Being a new resident of the suburbs, Joe is still identifying the flora and fauna and sifting through the differences between his past habitat and his current one. He and his wife, Ruth, are beginning life in the Peninsula suburbs after having moved from New York City because "even Yorktown Heights might be too close to Madison Avenue for comfort."[74]

Joe sees his new life in California as an escape to an unimpeachably beautiful western landscape. To take just one description of the place he is learning to love: "I watch the light change across the ridges to the west, and the ridges are the fresh gold of wild oats just turned, the oaks are round and green with oval shadows, the hollows have a tinge of blue." Within the same paragraph he reinforces his feeling of sanctuary by describing the chaos he has avoided, notably to the east, whether consciously alluding to Thoreau's "Walking" or not:

> Off to the east I can hear the roar, hardly more than a hum from here, as San Francisco pours its commuter trains down the valley, jams El Camino from Potrero to San Jose with the honk and stink of cars, rushes its daytime prisoners in murderous columns down the Bayshore. Not for me, not any more. Hardly any of that afternoon row penetrates up here. This is for the retired, for the no-longer-commuting, for contemplative ex-literary agents, for the birds.[75]

Figure 4. Stegner patio in Los Altos Hills, c. 1950s. Courtesy Special Collections, J. Willard Marriott Library, University of Utah.

These suburbs are closer to the Roman villa or the first London suburbs of the eighteenth century, a chance to experience something more like wilderness and leisure, than the energetic hum of upwardly mobile prosperity that defined suburbs like those of Orange County.[76] It is an escape to a wilderness sanctuary; the natural world is more widely present, the homes are more distinct, and the separation from the less-fortunate others is more dramatic. He is retiring from midcentury life, rather than climbing his way into it in the manner of his fellow Californians to the south.[77]

Stegner stages the central conflict of the story at that great artifact of midcentury California life, the poolside cabaña barbecue patio party. This party brings an opportunity for reflection on other western "birds," their fellow suburbanites. Stegner describes the scene as a "mulligan world, though it is made of prime sirloin."[78] Fittingly, in the context of the suburbs, it is leisure in a private place that brings the group together. Notably, leisure is the only thing that binds the formless non-community in almost all of these Midpeninsula stories. Guests include a music critic, a builder, wealthy philanthropists, a Pan-Am pilot, a piano teacher.

Everyone is seemingly new to the area, to each other, to the mores of the luxurious world they now inhabit. Postwar California prosperity has made the event possible. There is an air of exuberant wealth and almost effortless affluence: "Half the people here do not work for a living, for one reason or other, but they cannot be called idlers. They all do something, sometimes even good."[79] Most members of the group are wealthy enough that there is little distinction between their work and their leisure.

Stegner evokes the party as a lavish display on the verge of decadence. The Casement house, or "Casement Club," is built in the California Modern architectural style that would come to characterize the California suburban paradises popping up postwar at a rapid pace.[80] The architecture is sleek, the materials are of the highest quality, the pool is lighted, the patio is warmed by radiant heating—each feature is still novel enough at midcentury to evoke wonder from the nouveau riche gathered in Los Gatos.[81] There is still an aura of surprise and thrill to this scene—it has yet to decay into the cliché of stifling, entitled wealth—plastics!—that is evoked in the opening scenes of *The Graduate*, for example.[82]

In Allston's judgment, "The taste has been purchased, but it is taste." It "just misses being extravagantly beautiful; all it needs is something broken or incomplete, the way a Persian rug weaver will leave a flaw in his pattern to show that Allah alone is perfect."[83] The guests are treated to a "landslide, an avalanche" of delights: "a state fair exhibit of salads ... endive, romaine, tomatoes like flowers ... slabs of breast from barbecued turkeys, gobs of oyster dressing, candied yams dripping like honeycomb ... Shishkebab [*sic*] ... a smorgasbord of smoked salmon, smoked eel, smoked herring, cheeses ... ice cream confections shaped like apples, pears, pineapples, all fuming in dry ice."[84]

The benevolent if somewhat uneasy prosperity is in tension with the occasion for the party, the California debut of a young pianist and Jewish refugee from Poland, Arnold Kaminski. The barbecue is hosted by the Casements, Bill and Sue. Bill is a former lumber mill owner (of redwoods—interestingly, given his commitment to conservation, Stegner portrays him almost completely in a sympathetic light) and Sue is enamored—Joe implies no actual romance but thinks to himself that Bill should be suspicious—with Kaminski, who resides in a cottage on the Casements' property. She has invited Joe in hopes that he will be as enamored with his talent as she is and then proceed to open up opportunities for the young artist, given his connections in New York City. They are the two most honored guests.

Unfortunately for Sue, Joe and Kaminski regard each other with immediate and mutual suspicion. Though Joe has sold literature successfully over the course of his career, his associations with artists have not fostered respect but instead a jaded weariness with artists. The introduction does not go well. Joe is embarrassed by Sue's naked admiration of Kaminski and suspicious of Kaminski's disdainful appreciation of her idolatry. Kaminski returns Joe's suspicion almost immediately.

In Joe's words, Sue "stands outside the closed circuit of our hostility like a careless person gossiping over an electric fence" and proceeds to gush about both Joe's connections as an agent and Kaminski's musical genius. She is convinced that they need to know each other, and that they will immediately recognize their mutual responsibilities to each other. Joe and Kaminski know otherwise; they view each other across a great gulf. Joe sarcastically interprets what he imagines Kaminski's judgment of him must be: "I am not a Glandular Genius. I am not even an Artist, and hence I am not Sensitive." Joe is particularly annoyed by Kaminski's arrogance towards his host and her life, as he "stands there aloofly, not contaminating his art by brushing too close to Conspicuous Consumption." As Sue tugs Kaminski along to be introduced to other guests, Kaminski proclaims in a loud whisper, "For God's sake, how long is this going to go on? ... I am supposed to play for pigs who swill drinks and drinks and drinks. ... These are not the people to listen to music. ... They are the wrong people."[85]

At the same time as Joe is infuriated by Kaminski's display of ascetic and aesthetic superiority, particularly because it is so pointedly humiliating to his well-meaning but naïve host, Stegner makes it clear that at least part of the reason Joe is so agitated is that he is himself nagged by the opulence. Throughout the party, Joe maintains an internal dialogue in his mind between a former client of his, Murthi, an interpreter of Indian philosophy for westerners, and himself over the cosmic justice of such luxury: "In India, [Murthi] tells me, the only well-fed people are money-changers and landlords, grinders of the faces of the poor."[86]

Joe counters to himself: "But these people, I try to tell him, grind no poor. They are the rich, or semi-rich, of a rich country, not the rich of a poor one. Their duty to society is not by any means ignored. ... They give to causes they respect, and many of them give a great deal. And they don't put on a feast like this because they want to show off, or even because they are gluttonous. They do it because they think their guests will enjoy it; they do it to introduce a struggling young artist." In his mind again, Murthi replies: "You pay nothing for it. . . . It is nothing but self-indulgence. It smothers the spiritual life. In the midst of plenty, that is the time to fast." Joe's body forces an end to the internal dialogue: "I am too full to argue with him."[87]

Meanwhile, Sue grovels before Kaminski long enough to persuade him to play, even if among the debased bourgeoisie. Joe's ear is not quite perceptive enough to tell, but he thinks that Kaminski burlesques Sue's request for Chopin's Nocturnes, delighting her and simultaneously wink-ing to fellow sophisticates who know better. Sue swoons. Joe is almost converted by Kaminski's rendition of Bach, however. In an evocative image, Stegner describes Joe's reaction:

> As when, in the San Francisco Cow Palace, loudspeakers announce the draft horse competition, and sixteen great Per-cherons trot with high action and ponderous foot into the arena, brass-harnessed, plume-bridled, swelling with power, drawing the rumbling brewery wagon lightly, Regal Pale; ton-heavy but light-footed they come ... and above them the driver spider-braced, intent, transmits through the fan of lines his slightest command ... sixteen prides guided by one will, sixteen great strengths respondent and united; so the great chords of Bach roll forth from under the hands of Arnold Kaminski.[88]

Despite such a promising beginning, Kaminski stumbles and recov-ers, and then stumbles slightly again. Joe thinks he has taken on too much and that he knows it. Joe decides that he is a talented imposter, admirable if not so conceited, but nonetheless unworthy of a concert career. This is confirmed to Joe by the final selection, the Piano Pieces of Arnold Schoenberg, Opus Nineteen. Joe says that Schoenberg has been explained to him, but:

> no amount of argument can convince me that this music does not hurt the ears ... though I am prepared to admit that by long

listening a man might accustom himself to it, I do not think this proves anything.... The survival of the race depends upon its infinite adaptability. We can get used to anything in time, and even perhaps develop a perverted taste for it. But *why*? The day has not come when I choose to try adapting to Schoenberg [italics original, here and below].[89]

As he grits his teeth and waits for it to end, Joe realizes,

Kaminski *means* this Schoenberg. He gives it the full treatment; he visibly wrestles with the Ineffable.... He is putting himself into it devotionally, he *is* Schoenberg. I recall a picture of the composer on some record envelope—intense staring eyes, bald crown, temples with a cameo of raised veins, cheeks bitten in mouth grim and bitter, unbearable pain. Arnold Schoenberg, Destroyer and Preserver. Mouthful of fire and can neither swallow nor spit.[90]

The concert ends, and the western birds assemble to discuss. Sue demands Joe's assessment. He tries to be judicious, and remarks at one point that, perhaps, given the miniscule chances of success (on Kaminski's terms), Kaminski is better off contenting himself with teaching and performing occasionally with the local symphony. Sue is offended for Kaminski: "Can you imagine Arnold teaching grubby little unwilling kids to play little Mozart sonatas for PTA meetings?" This sets Joe off. He thinks to himself, "It is true that I can't imagine Kaminski doing any such thing as teaching the young, but that is a commentary on Kaminski, not on the young."

He tips his hand further: "Besides, I am the defender, self-appointed, of the good American middle-class small-town and suburban way of life, and I get almighty sick of Americans who enjoy all its benefits but can't find a good word to say for it." Joe is now in the mood to argue. When he makes a sarcastic remark, another guest calls him an "old cynical philistine."[91] The conversation turns to artists and agents, with the room against Joe. Stegner draws out the final inevitable confrontation between Joe and Kaminski. It starts with a provocation from Kaminski, who implies that agents are merely leeches. The guests banter about artistic genius and commercial perversion of art, with Joe playing the provocateur while Kaminski lurks, silent.

The other guests prepare to leave, and Joe sees Kaminski coupling off with the music teacher, who is at first flattered by the attention until she realizes that Kaminski is not interested in conversation about music. She leaves, distraught. Sue Casement notices and begins to wonder what happened, which proves to be Kaminski's undoing. He confesses that he insulted her because she invited insult with her priggishness. By this point drunk, he proceeds to unmask himself even further. It turns out that Joe is more correct about his artistic façade than he wished himself to be. Kaminski reveals that he is not a refugee from Poland but from South Boston, with a fake name, story, and accent. He reveals that he could tell Joe knew he was a fake and, in a drunken, self-pitying melodrama, tells everyone that he wants to fail, that he knows they all hate him, that there is nothing honest about him at all. Bill tries to usher him back to the cottage before anything worse comes out, and in the commotion, the melodrama turns to slapstick and Kaminski turns, stumbles, and lands in the pool.

Joe and Ruth stay until the situation is under control, then leave. Joe's cynical unmasking eye has proven to be too much, and his contempt turns to pity and sadness. He begins to see Kaminski with some level of sympathy. He and Ruth drive home quietly. Joe tastes the "stale bourbon in [his] mouth and knows [himself] for a frivolous old man." His thoughts return to the towhee and his glass door, assuming that it will return to his patio tomorrow. He will watch "the fool thing for as long as I can stand it, and ruminate on the insanities of men and birds." But then, when he "cannot put up with the sight of this towhee any longer," he will retire to his study and "sit looking out of the window into the quiet shade of the oak, where nuthatches are brownly and pertly content with the bugs in their home bark. But even down there I may sometimes hear the banging and thrashing of this dismal towhee trying to fight his way past himself and into the living-room of the main house."[92]

To Ruth, Allston says that he is "'just irritated that they don't give you enough time in a single life to figure anything out.'" The story ends with that sentence.[93] Through most of the story, Stegner writes Joe as a cynical observer who does not miss anything. Until the end, it is reminiscent of a Tom Wolfe exposé of artistic pretension.[94] Most of his cynicism is directed at Kaminski, but he also unmasks, even if more sympathetically, the other western birds as simpletons and self-conscious strivers putting on their own airs. The final unmasking of Kaminski is so complete and pitiful, however, that it proves unsatisfying. Joe himself is unmasked as well; he reveals to himself his own cynicism. The whole scene seems empty, the California suburb confirmation of the nearly contemporary theories of Erving Goffman's *Presentation of Self in Everyday Life* (1956), in which all public life is performance. Though Joe's anger at Kaminski's artistic snobbery builds through the whole evening, by the time Kaminski is pulled pitifully from the pool, Joe realizes that Kaminski is actually the climber attempting to make it to the inside.

Stegner also seems to suggest in this study that sentimentality can cut in multiple directions. Using James Joyce's short definition of sentimentality as "unearned emotion," Stegner's story turns the tables. Just as nostalgia can be sentimental, so can angst. He seems to dismiss the whole canon of works based on variations of J.D. Salinger's *Catcher in the Rye* (1951) as unearned angst.[95] Which was more sentimental, false, and destructive during this moment, the unearned angst of the disaffected or the unearned nostalgia of the bourgeois? (Or were either of these emotions truly unearned?)[96] Or is this really a matter of looking at a justification of perpetual immaturity versus a call for maturity? Who is worse off, the retired "American Philistine" whose opinions about art are dismissed out of hand by the truly enlightened, or the artist without an audience or a home and, at least in Stegner's view, a self-destructive streak that prevents him from belonging anywhere?

While Stegner justifies Joe's suspicion that the art world's standards are social judgments posing as artistic ones, exhibiting behavior closer to adolescent cliques than to an ideal republic of letters, he also looks sympathetically at those who play the game with motives that are always mixed. Ultimately, his judgment about Kaminski is that he uses art to distinguish himself from the masses rather than to communicate with other human beings, and that this vision of art was more likely to confirm him in his misery in a self-perpetuating cycle.[97]

The Brainless Power of the Twentieth Century

In the next two stories that would eventually become *Live Things*, Stegner introduced other tensions into the suburban world his characters inhabit. In his second Peninsula story, "All the Little Live Things," a short story featured in the May 1959 edition of *Mademoiselle*, Stegner went right to the heart of the matter with a reflection on death. Juxtaposed rather grotesquely among the *Mademoiselle* advertisements—six for girdles ("be a living doll"), one for a swimsuit, one for stationery, one for lipstick, one for eyelash crème, one for the "Madam X" wedge shoe, and, finally, one for the "Grip-Tuth Hairtainer"—it was a short story about Joe and Ruth's encounter with their neighbor Marian Catlin, who has recently died from cancer. This story served as the basis for the novel of the same name, which is explored in more detail in the next chapter.

Stegner's disgust with blind, destructive growth—what his former student Edward Abbey called the "ideology of the cancer cell"—is the theme that most shaped "Indoor-Outdoor Living," his third Peninsula story.[98] It was published in the September 1959 demonstration issue of *Pacifica*, a publication intended to be a monthly magazine published in San Francisco that never made it past the demonstration issue.[99] The only reason this exploration of blind growth is a tension is that Stegner dramatized the destruction of blind growth through a comic neighborhood drama about a friendly but simple-minded builder named Tom Weld. It is not always merely greed and the blind rush for profit that lead to development, but admirable qualities like the desire to build, work hard, and create opportunities combined with less admirable qualities, such as a lack of aesthetic awareness or sustained thought about long-term ecological consequences. It is perhaps Stegner chastising himself for being among the first to open the Los Altos Hills to development.

The Allstons had purchased their land from Weld, and though he is a bulldozer operator in the paving and contracting business who leaves his yard strewn with construction equipment, they anticipate a neighborly relationship with him. Their first clue that this might not be the case is that they observe Weld's dog stealing hens from their other neighbor, Dan Shields. Joe Allston meets Shields and asks him about it. With an eye to the humor of the situation, Shields tells him about the chickens and about Weld's incapacity to take responsibility for the dog's actions, which has led to Shields giving up on keeping chickens. Shields is too good-natured to force the issue. Weld completely misses the cues Shields sends; he simply admires the dog's cunning and amiably refuses to take responsibility for the dog, which eventually also impregnates the Shields' dog just for good measure.

Joe finds that Weld has the same attitude about his horses, which have begun to wreak havoc on the Allstons' new yard, a yard designed by a landscape architect. Joe heads over to speak to Weld about it, and Weld suggests Joe put up a fence to keep the horses out. Realizing that his problem with the horses will not be solved by acquiescence in the same way that Shields solved his problem with the dog, Joe notes that in California it is the responsibility of the owner to fence animals in, unlike in open-range states such as Texas, where Weld is from.[100] Weld says he'll have to see about it but does nothing.

Problems continue, with the horses stomping through the Allstons' recently poured cement, waking them up by pasturing on their backyard terrace, and breaking down the barrier fence that the Allstons installed as a temporary measure. Finally, Weld installs his own fence, but it is haphazard and shoddy, complete with a "backwoods cattle guard," accomplished merely by pulling alternating planks from the wooden access road bridge. The neighbors come to an uneasy peace and life goes on. Neighborhood crisis elevates the truce to a more genuine harmony when Joe sees fire on Weld's property when the Welds are away. He helps beat the fire back, saving the house. They are finally on good terms again and, consistent with the comic tone of the story, Weld then repays Joe's generosity with an unintentional insult.

The fire had burnt over a hilltop clearing that the Allstons admired as part of the view from their house. Weld, seeing that it was cleared out by a fire, decides to flatten it out as a field for his horses. Joe watches from his backyard as Weld, an "imbecile armed with the brainless power of the twentieth century," thoughtlessly bulldozes "the lovely curve of the hill" into a broad platform with the debris piled on all sides, with the result that it looks, in the classic western mode, "like a gravel pit, or the tailings of a mine." Watching with disgust, Joe imagines that the hill will likely be left that way, sparsely vegetated by invasive weeds, for many years. Weld is blissfully ignorant: "It did not occur to him that it was ugly, and so long as it didn't bother him why should anyone else be bothered?"[101]

If "Field Guide" was a half-defense of the American Philistine, the introduction of Tom Weld to the neighborhood reveals why Stegner only offered a half-defense. Stegner's Weld is a good-natured fool with too much power and too little respect for margins in a fragile environment. This philistine is incapable of being persuaded of values that go beyond his immediate purposes and there is nothing to be done but watch with regret.

Conclusion

Stegner moved to California with a firm set of regional commitments and almost immediately threw himself into putting them into practice. Stegner's first decade in California was marked by indefatigable institution building: aside from his work with the Stanford Creative Writing Program and the PHA, Stegner helped found two short-lived journals, *Pacifica* and *The Pacific Spectator*; served as the center of an attempt to establish partnerships with writers from several Asian countries following his tour in Asia on a Rockefeller Grant in 1951; and was active with the Sierra Club and other conservationist groups. He had also started a project with the Wenner-Gren Foundation, and then a few years later held a fellowship with the Stanford Center for Advanced Study in the Behavioral Sciences (CASBS). In his fiction, however, he had started to explore these regional efforts in ways that illuminated their more tragic dimensions and some of the perhaps irresolvable tensions that marked the place that he was trying to make a home. Though the social science venues provided him with funding and some valuable resources, he still found fiction to be the mode of thought that best allowed him to explore the questions and tensions he found most pressing.

Chapter 2

Village Democracy

*And everyone knows the magic perspective of memory—it keeps what we
loved and alters the relative size and value of many things that we did not
love enough—that we hated and resisted and made mountains of at the time.
It turns the dust of our valleys of humiliation, now that the sun of our working hours has set, into a sad and dreamy splendor which will fade into depths
beyond depths of unknown worlds of stars.*

—Mary Hallock Foote[1]

*Memory is a kind of homesickness, and like homesickness, it falls short of the
actualities on almost every count.*

—Ivan Doig[2]

*I imagine a past in which some truth lies. This past is a place that yields a
dense, almost impenetrable, imaginative growth. Historians can only hope to
tap this fertility and trim and discipline what grows so luxuriantly. Beyond
history's garden grates, the thick jungle of the past remains, and memory's trails
lead off into it.*

—Richard White[3]

Second Growth (1947) took its name from a term drawn from forestry.
A second-growth forest is one that has regrown to the extent that a prior
timber harvest is no longer evident. Stegner's first novel after *The Big
Rock Candy Mountain* (1943), the book explores the course of a single
summer and is more a series of vivid impressions than the saga of a
family in the West, as was *Big Rock*. *Second Growth* follows an ensemble
of characters as they reckon with generational change and the "carrying

capacity" of the fictional town of Westwick, New Hampshire. The forest is more important than any one of the trees in this book.

In his note on the fictional character of the book, Stegner told his readers that he was interested in the "cultural dynamism" of the town, "the conflict on the frontier between two ways of life, which is its central situation," a situation "that has been reproduced in an endlessly changing pattern all over the United States." The people and their village took form in Stegner's mind "not as portraits but as symbols."[4] This frank admission that he was looking at symbols would be heresy to the creative writing mantra of "show don't tell," but it also suggests that Stegner may have been more worried about offending the town than committing an offense against the literary standards of that moment. Regardless, his attempt to understand some of these processes in a specific place using the techniques of fiction mark this book as the beginning of a research trajectory that would culminate with *Wolf Willow* (1962) and, I argue, set a framework for his reflection on the experience of belonging and the lack thereof in the formless non-communities he later explored in his California novels.

Westwick was a thinly veiled version of Greensboro, Vermont, a place the Stegners had started visiting at the invitation of the Gray family, whom they met in Wisconsin in the late 1930s. By the time Stegner wrote *Second Growth*, they had spent several summers in Greensboro, and purchased property and spent a whole year there (uncommon for summer residents) while he was finishing *Big Rock* from May 1942 until early 1943.[5] Stegner's story of Westwick stages the old-town values against the summer newcomers in order to work through the survivals and losses.

As in actual second-growth forests, the community is in transition and older "species" are fighting newer species for space and prominence, and even survival, within the community. Human time and geological time have collided, and it is not clear which will win. The principal conflict is between the year-round residents of the town and the summer visitors. The summer visitors are mostly academics from Ivy League schools who build rustic Waldens with simple "think houses" for morning writing and lakefronts for afternoon swims. On special occasions, the town heads out on rowboats to listen to concerts broadcast over the lake.

Abe Kaplan is a relative newcomer who has lived in the village for five years as the only Jew in the town. He very quickly befriends a real new-comer, Ruth Liebowitz, who is visiting the town to experience the joys of it as described by a homesick friend who looks back on it with nostalgia even though she escaped it to live in New York. Abe is worried, correctly, that Ruth will be the victim of anti-Semitism in the town and quickly makes her acquaintance. Both are distant from their pasts and bond quickly over their shared love for the town's natural beauty, even as they are repulsed by the anti-Semitism that they experience from some of the town members. Abe stoically accepts this situation, and lives for his debates with the summer people from the universities. Abe and Ruth are married hastily that summer and, in addition to bouts of fear arising from their rash decision, Ruth struggles because even though they are respected in the town and part of the community economically, they are also subjected to social slights that signal they do not belong as full members of it.

Two young people from the town are also changed by the end of the summer. Andy Mount is a talented teenager whose father is "as worthless a good-for-nothing as the town had produced for two generations."[6] Stephen Dow, a summer visitor who is also the headmaster of a prestigious prep school, offers Andy a free education at his school, but at the cost of leaving the town and his mentor, John Mills, "a twelfth-century guild worker lost in the twentieth century."[7] Helen Barlow attended the University of New Hampshire and wishes to leave the town, but is bound by familial responsibilities and fear, and has been designated the successor to her teacher in her old elementary school. She has "been successfully educated away from her own life but not into the other."[8] The job does not satisfy her, and she is invigorated by her friendship and then a flash of a romance with Flo Barnes, an athletic summer visitor who tries to enliven her to new possibilities. Their summer fling is too much for Helen, however, and, "lost between two worlds," she commits suicide during one of the summer's evening concerts over the lake at the end of the summer.[9]

Her death is the seed of acceptance for the Kaplans, however, as hearing the splash in the water, Abe dives in after Helen. He fails to find her in the evening-dark water and nearly freezes to death in the process. As Abe recovers, Ruth is welcomed to the community in a new way when the women of the town bring her a basket of baked goods, a small gesture of respect. Andy chooses to leave the town at the end of the book to take Stephen Dow's offer to attend his school. By this point, John Mills has had a stroke and encourages Andy to leave. The reminder of his mortality offers a contrast with Helen's situation; while Mills' mortality is connected to Andy's renewal, Helen's parents' smothering is the indirect cause of her death. In one case the older species fosters the renewal of the younger; in the other, the older species starves out the younger. The town itself survives and ambles into its quiet future.

Second Growth proved to be a little too close to home for the residents. It was the second time Stegner had written fiction that caused conflict with the people that inspired the characters, and it would not be the last.[10] The Grays did not object to the novel as a whole, but still pushed back against Stegner's portrayal of the town. Responding to Phil Gray's criticism, Stegner wrote:

> You almost make me cry when you speak as if I had drawn G[reensboro] as a sinister place. Doomed, maybe; lost between two cultural configurations, maybe; losing its traditional values and uneasy with the new substitutions, maybe; narrow, with a tradition which in some ways is a cultural dry rot, maybe. But Sinister, yee! The dryrot is only partly dryrot.... it can come up with the old sick basket and the instant neighborliness in time of trouble as surely as it can come up with narrow piety and snobbishness. I certainly never thought I was making it sinister. I was only trying to make it complex, which it is, and if you want my own attitude you can find it in the idea attributed to Stephen Dow on page 208, the line beginning, "If he had not been able to believe ..."[11]

The passage to which Stegner referred, with some of the preceding sentences for context, follows:

> That was the trouble, he [Stephen Dow] thought ruefully, about trying to take refuge in simplicity. The lovers of the simple were too inevitably complex. The place had changed; something fine had gone out of it, or was going. Something that had been peculiarly and wonderfully native lay now like old John Mills with

half his face pulled into a stiff grimace and one side gone dead. Looking out into the square full of the invaders and contemplating how the whole life of the village had altered so that now it existed mainly to supply the campers, and lived only during the summer months, Mr. Dow felt a twinge of guilt. He had been the very first, and his responsibility was that much greater. If he had not been able to believe that out of the confusion of two ways of life there would come not only destruction but some survival, and not only survival but perhaps eventual enrichment, he would have gone away from John Mills's door feeling that his last visit had been less a farewell than an act of expiation.[12]

Here is one of Stegner's earliest reflections on the seemingly intractable tragedy associated with the attempt to escape from "history." History always follows, and with unpredictable results that cannot be anticipated. Stegner was concerned enough about the response to the book in Greensboro that he did not return for a year, though Phil Gray told Stegner that the character who most resembled Abe Kaplan, Louis Kesselman, was "almost over-exuberant" in his enthusiasm for the novel.[13] He was eventually welcomed back into the Greensboro community by those besides the Kesselmans. The ideas he broached in *Second Growth* stuck with him, however, and the town became more significant to him with time. It was especially intriguing to him in its relation to the town of his childhood: Eastend, Saskatchewan.

Stegner was generally suspicious of Stanford's transition to quantitative social science frameworks of research when they undercut the humanistic traditions that he believed essential to the university.[14] The criticism was not delivered out of ignorance, as from 1956–1957 Stegner held a fellowship with the Stanford Center for Advanced Study in the Behavioral Sciences (CASBS) that allowed him to experience such research methods firsthand.

Stegner's experience with the Stanford CASBS is notable for two reasons. First, the work brought out of him several theories about place and community in the West and gave him a set of ideas to work through. In succeeding chapters I highlight the ways these ideas worked themselves into his fiction. Second, the process brought out debates over the nature of Stegner's fiction and what he hoped to achieve with it. The most concrete result of the research program that he adopted was *Wolf Willow*. In his interview with Richard Etulain, Stegner called *Wolf Willow* a "librarian's nightmare."[15] The problem is indicated by the subtitle of the book (which Stegner did not like and which was a compromise with the publisher— though any suggested alternative subtitles have not survived): "A History, A Story, and a Memory of the Last Plains Frontier."[16]

Wolf Willow was not Stegner's most popular book but it is the book that included his most comprehensive attempt to understand place and community in the West, as well as the modes of thought that he thought most valuable for approaching those themes.[17] Though in his interviews with Etulain about thirty years after the research had been completed he referred to his "half-assed notion" of a project, Stegner did sketch out an ambitious agenda for himself and spent several years working on it in various forms.[18] If *Crossing to Safety* (1987) and *The Spectator Bird* (1976), along with *Wolf Willow*, are interpreted as outgrowths of this project, it was this research agenda that most shaped his scholarly work after the 1950s.

A self-consciously scholarly turn of this kind was not an implausible move for Stegner. He earned a doctorate in American literature at the University of Iowa with a self-described "very bad dissertation" on the nature writing of geologist Clarence E. Dutton during the depths of the Great Depression in 1935.[19] Though the research he conducted for the dissertation would point him to John Wesley Powell and crucial frameworks for interpretation of the American West that shaped his thought, it seems clear that he treated the dissertation itself as an exercise and moved on from it as quickly as possible.[20] He was more interested in writing fiction and the doctorate seemed primarily inspired by the circumstances of the Depression and the possibility that it would allow him to find a position that would support his writing. At the same time, as is suggested by his hostility to artistic pretension in "Field Guide," he did believe in study over inspiration and clearly respected scholarship.[21]

Within the covers of *Wolf Willow* are samples of each of the genres that Stegner used throughout his career to think about the West, as well as discussion of most of his "anguished questions." It is the paradigm for the ways that I will be reading Stegner's intellectual work in this book. What makes the book so fascinating is that it had a long gestation period and was the end result of Stegner's most formal scholarly efforts. It is therefore an artifact that demonstrates in a very compelling way how Stegner thought, what genre meant to him, and why he was so dedicated to fiction.[22] I believe that Stegner turned to fiction in *Wolf Willow* not because he thought it was simply a more effective means of promoting his social theories, but because he thought the genre communicated ideas that he could not adequately express in the language of social science. He was more interested in sociological questions than he was in the answers that could be produced using the tools of the discipline.

Fiction was not social science with window dressing, anecdotes, and bon mots; in Stegner's mind, it was superior and operated on a level that the writers and readers of social science simply failed to acknowledge or appreciate.[23] Stegner's eventual rejection of sociology resulted in a renewed commitment to the insights he was capable of achieving in each form that the book included. As historian Aaron Sachs writes,

> He knows his memory is flawed; he knows the documents are limited in scope and reliability. . . . What someone like Stegner does for us, when he is included in the ranks of historians, is force us to think explicitly about writing as a problem rather than a given, and especially to think about finding a form that is appropriate to our content. He suggests to us that form itself can convey meaning. . . . He reminds us that the effective combination of content and form, as practiced by poets for millennia, has the power to leave readers not just intellectually impressed but also aroused, moved, transformed.[24]

The Intelligent Layman Confronts the Incantations of Social Science

Sachs's assessment of the finished product makes the actual story of the creation of *Wolf Willow* that much more interesting, as it very easily could have taken a much different form. Aside from the "hypothesis" he formed in *Second Growth*, the research that led to *Wolf Willow* started in 1953 with funding from the Wenner-Gren Foundation for Anthropological Research and continued during a 1955–1956 fellowship year at the Stanford CASBS. "Project no.: #796," as *Wolf Willow* was first known, is categorized briefly at the bottom of a December 18, 1953, memo from Paul Fejos, the former film director and by then the director of research at the Wenner-Gren Foundation. Project #796 was granted "to aid research in Vermont, Saskatchewan, and Denmark on three forms of village democracy, by Dr. Wallace Stegner."[25] At the time of the memo, Stegner had completed his research in Saskatchewan in June of 1953 and his research in Vermont later that same summer. In his reply to Fejos, Stegner described his plans to head to Denmark in March of 1954.[26]

In a November 12, 1954, update after his trip to Denmark, Stegner opened the letter with an apology and expression of guilt for his delayed reply (this would be a pattern, as he never actually completed the project as designed but nonetheless continued reporting to Wenner-Gren up until 1959). Stegner had used the extra three hundred dollars added to his research funding to hire Kaare Svalastoga, "the only practicing sociologist in Denmark," to conduct a survey of a "country-wide sampling of Danish character and opinion and attitude."[27] In a preview of what he would later write more explicitly, there are hints that Stegner was growing suspicious of the value of sociological insights. Summarizing the process, Stegner wrote, "In general, his preliminary results corroborated my own unscientific impressions, but I await the final tabulations and summary before letting my impressions petrify too hard."[28]

A December 10, 1954, memo from Stegner fleshed out the project more concretely in the only surviving document that really indicated his original goals for it. The project was too ambitious, as he later realized. He described his goal as an examination of three places "in as intimate way as possible" through both individual lives and "some definition (however proximate) of the 'social character' of the people concerned." First, he wanted to study Eastend, Saskatchewan, a "Canadian village on the very last farming frontier, a village hardly more than a generation old, with all its institutions and its people in the midst of that flux and adjustment and process of trial and error and adaptation that has characterized successive frontiers on this continent." Next, Greensboro, Vermont: a New England village "settled by a homogenous population close to two hundred years ago, a village in which institutions have gelled and the local character has acquired a distinct and recognizable flavor." Third, Taasinge, Denmark: an "Old World village, as little changed as possible through as long a time of settlement as possible," with this village to be "used primarily to shed light on the two New World villages and on their formed or forming local character." Through comparative study of these three samples, Stegner had hoped to illuminate "characteristic patterns of human association" and "some of the effects of place and climate upon those patterns and upon individuals."[29] In another clue that he was perceiving the limits of his ability to pursue his ideas using the methods of midcentury social science, Stegner includes in his summary the statement that "I did not, in the beginning, specify a particular form that these studies were to take, or guess at the form in which they might eventually find publication."

The strange form of *Wolf Willow* was starting to crystallize. In his summary of his research completed thus far in Saskatchewan, he wrote, "It does not seem to me that the book I want to write about this village will be like any other book I know of. I am approaching it as if it were possible to mingle social history, fiction, and autobiography.... I should remark here that the approach is absolutely experimental, and I would be the first to admit that it may not work." But he was confident that he was onto something nonetheless: "If it will work, I think the combining of several genres into a single volume focused upon a place ought to provide a richer mixture than fiction alone, or autobiography alone, or history alone, or sociological essays alone." As he envisioned the book, Stegner hoped it might "make clear the emotional as well as the sociological effects of the country and the village and the forming institutions of both." It was forming in his mind as something like the New England town studies that appeared in the social history of the 1960s and 1970s, but with emotional force and the demand for an aesthetic response.[30]

He had little to report about Greensboro, other than that he had started his research into the town's "history and institutions" by collecting photographs, "lore," maps, "and other data." He had not started writing about Greensboro by that point. Denmark required more explanation. Wallace and Mary Stegner spent April of 1954 in Copenhagen, and from May until August split the remainder of their time in Copenhagen and Taasinge, an island of twenty-seven square miles southwest of Copenhagen, with a short trip to Norway and Sweden interspersed.[31] Stegner reported that the island gave him "the opportunity not only to study farms and villages of a very old type, but to observe the effects of modern subdivision of the Waldemarslot lands into small freeholds according to a pattern prevalent all over Denmark." He reported that his "informants" included "several of the farmers and planters, several of the retired sea captains and traders, the village poetess, the librarian, the veterinarian, many children and housewives, and so on." Both in person and through archival work, Stegner studied the town's institutions—"the modern welfare institutions of the parishes; the schools, old people's homes, hospitals"—and then went as far as to consult with an archaeologist who had worked on the island, Axel Steensburg of Nationalmuseet.[32]

In a very qualified initial assessment—"It would be futile to attempt at this stage to summarize conclusions which are still only intimations or suspicion"—Stegner reported that he was at least confident that the three places were "well-chosen" as each proved "revealing of characteristic patterns of human association" and the "effects of place and climate upon those patterns and upon individuals." His conclusions about the three villages were not sanguine. Eastend, he wrote, "has as yet no local character" and "institutionally it reflects not so much the formation of new patterns as the successive demonstration of the inadequacy of old ones," whether "native institutions" or farming methods unsuitable for land in Palliser's Triangle. The two men who were the town's original "pioneers of learning" are now "hasbeens of learning," with one "pottering around making a paleontological museum in the basement of the school, keeping alive the faint light of this rural Athens," and the other dead, "leaving behind him his home-made observatory into which no villager ever goes and about which curiosity is dead." Rather than fostering attachments and possibilities for community, the one "characteristic institution" that the town produced, commuter farming from larger towns to fields thirty to forty miles away, was, Stegner believed, likely to lead to the town's extinction. As he duly reported: "Climate and transportation have thus combined to produce a new community pattern."[33]

Stegner had done his research in Saskatchewan incognito, adding another element of complexity to the process. He later explained the decision to Corky Jones, the resident of the town who helped him most (and who was described as "pottering around" in his paleontological museum—he would be described in a more dignified way in *Wolf Willow*). He wrote that he was "afraid I made some people mad by pulling that fool incognito act." He regretted it and explained the decision as being "on account of my father's probable reputation in the town" at one level but, closer to his research, as being connected to his desire to "come back and look it over without anybody's memories except my own to interfere."[34]

Greensboro was also forming new patterns due to the turn to mechanized farm equipment that marked what became known as the Green Revolution.[35] It was losing population, and without summer residents, of which Stegner was one, the town "would be unable to collect the taxes to maintain the old community life." Stegner reported that the "characteristic Vermonter is still present, but fading," unable to remain in the town due to the mechanization of farming. "Farms get larger, small villages smaller, large villages slowly larger, with stronger infusions of non-natives . . . at the expense of the old agricultural Vermonter homogeneity." In his study of this transition, Stegner wrote that he wanted to "make the changes in this town meaningful partly by approaching them through the emotions of the people affected."[36] While Stegner's discussion of "non-natives" and "Vermonter homogeneity" is disconcerting, it is also fair to read this as Stegner's attempt to defend communities that have enough resilience to impress a distinct stamp on their members. Stegner was well aware of the dangers of cultures without any capacity to grow or to welcome diversity, as is evident in his rejection of restrictive covenants in the 1940s and the themes he explored in *Spectator Bird* (1976).

Stegner was even more cautious in his summary of Denmark: "Because I do not talk well in the lingo of sociologists, and do not always believe the lingo to be justified, I find it difficult to summarize even tentatively what I may do with this little Danish island." Qualifications aside, Stegner's initial impressions focused on the distinctive lack of competitive ambition. Referring to Svalastoga's research and his own observation, Stegner noted that a "surprising number of rural and smalltown Danes, though materially pinched and without many of the goods we would think essential" were "contented with their lives and willing to do them all over again the same way." He thinks that they have "scaled down their desires" and reconciled themselves to Denmark's economy of "'distributed scarcity.'" At the end of the summary, he again pointed to his real interest in the research, even if he also promised to keep trying to work in his original line of research. He wrote that he wanted to use "anecdotes and stories" to illustrate periods of change, but then also hastened to add that he was still "committed to some sort of analysis of the present social and economic and cultural patterns of the island."[37]

Stegner ended with another plea for patience regarding the fact that he was not writing a standard sociological or anthropological account. Including a similar plea in the cover letter, he apologized for his disciplinary transgressions five times in six single-spaced pages; the genre problem was clearly on his mind. After acknowledging that his inclusion of "personal feelings" and "autobiographical incident" might be unjustified, he wrote that he hoped the "total effect" would prove "richer and more flexible because of the personal interpolations, and because of the attempted welding of sociology, history, and fiction."[38]

By the time he was asked to report on the progress of the project in 1956, Stegner had begun to indicate that he did not foresee the possibility of finishing the project as he originally defined it. In a January 17, 1956, letter to Fejos written in the middle of his fellowship year at the Stanford CASBS, Stegner wrote that his time at the center had made him realize "how brash and bold I was to bite off such a mouthful. That was a life-work I undertook." By the end of his correspondence with Fejos, Stegner had sent him copies of articles that formed the basis of *Wolf Willow*, with promises that *Wolf Willow* was almost done. All he could report on Denmark was "half a manuscript plus a great many notes," and he had only notes to show for Greensboro. Mercifully for Stegner's conscience, the correspondence appears to have concluded with that letter.[39]

Stegner was less apologetic and generally more suspicious of social scientists in his correspondence regarding the Stanford CASBS. He held a fellowship there for a year, the year in which he did most of the work on *Wolf Willow*. In a March 7, 1956, letter to Preston Cutler, the associate director of the Stanford CASBS, Stegner complained, "My participation in the seminars and work groups has been limited by my imperfect education. All those groups proceeding by primarily statistical methods have been outside the range of my antennae." After this initial expression of his own perceived inadequacies, he indicated that perhaps these other antennae were only picking up noise, and that his own antennae might have been tuned to more significant frequencies: "On occasion [the meetings] have degenerated into windiness and fairly often I have been unimpressed with the quality of the 'science' brought to bear upon problems of human behavior. Some of the things around which argument has raged have seemed to me primarily word-magic or the incantations of epistemology." There are also indications that Stegner thought his own intellectual perceptions were not being treated with respect, as "none of the intent and preoccupied behavioral scientists in residence are particularly interested in anything I am capable of contributing."

In a 1956 letter to Bernard DeVoto, his good friend and fellow castigator of entrenched academics, Stegner was more cutting, while also allowing that there was some benefit to his work at the CASBS. Of the "Behavioral Sciences," Stegner wrote,

> They appear to differ from the social sciences in the way you cut the pie. If you cut it into psychologists, anthropologists, sociologists, political scientists, and all their dichotomies and mitoses, you are thinking in terms of social sciences. But if you cut it with the New Look into Communications Theory, Games Theory, Organizations Theory, and—best of all—General Systems Theory—then you are a Behavioral Scientist, dizzily enthroned.[40]

At this stage of the project, the shape of his arguments was not entirely clear; it was only clear that he was frustrated with the limits of discourse in the social sciences.[41] Overall, he seemed to think the social scientists of the day promoted either false certainties about human cultures or verifiable certainties about trivial matters. While he claimed begrudgingly to have learned from the social scientists, he gives the impression that the social scientists merely thought him quaint. He is useful to them as an object of analysis, a model "intelligent layman." He is more a sample for their studies than a colleague.

To summarize his reflection on the places themselves: each place seemed on the verge of disaster, whether from failing or nonexistent institutions in the case of Eastend, a failing economy as in Greensboro, or stagnation and disappearance in the case of Taasinge. Based solely on his formal reports, it seems as if Stegner would have had little choice but to write a study that would warn of the failures of rural villages to survive, much less sustain democracy. The reports are focused primarily on rural responses to the Green Revolution from Denmark to Saskatchewan. His later work revealed more subtle arguments about the value of each place and its effect on its inhabitants.

Wolf Willow

By the time Stegner had published *Wolf Willow* in 1962, he had advanced from the rather dismal description of his former hometown, Eastend, to a more hopeful assessment. He had also committed to the vision of the book that had proved so enticing to him. Due to its unorthodox structure, a brief description of its organization is necessary. It is divided into four main sections. It starts with Stegner introducing the landscape of the town as the actual subject of the book, and as the place where he spent his childhood. Stegner as narrator indicates little about his present life in the text itself other than that he is a "middle-aged pilgrim" returning to a town he last saw in 1920.[42] The narrator works through his memory of the town for three chapters before turning to the second part, which is designated to be history. Following nine short chapters of history, the narrator turns to a third section that starts with a return to memoir and then shifts to a novella followed by a short story. The last section brings the narrator back to his own lifetime, where memoir is checked against history in four more chapters. An epilogue posits educated guesses about the town's possible future.

In one indication of the notion that he was writing something that was operating in the interstices between history, memory, and fiction, Stegner tells his readers that he will "call" the town "Whitemud" in the book.[43] Just as in his decision to revisit the town incognito, he maintained the ambiguity of the project and placed himself awkwardly as both observer and subject. The structure of the book maintains this ambiguity. Of the landscape itself, however, Stegner's emotions are fierce: it is "one of the most desolate and forbidding regions on earth," where he "would not for a thousand dollars an hour return to live."[44] But it is also a place of remarkable beauty, where the "mystery of nights when the stars were scoured clean and the prairie full of breathings from a long way off" lingers.[45] It is the place where he "bent [his] entire consciousness upon white anemones among the white aspen boles." The anemones were "flowers whose name I did not know and could not possibly have found out, and would not have asked, because I thought that only I knew about them and I wanted no one else to know."[46] In sum: though terrifying, "there was never a country that in its good moments was more beautiful."[47] But he explores Whitemud itself and its characteristics with an ambivalence that is not resolved by the end of the book. More precisely, of the town itself he is ambivalent, but in his reflections on the reasons for his ambivalence, he indicates his sense of values regarding place and community in the West.

Stegner depicts himself walking the village in an agitated and absent-minded fog, testing childhood memory with adult perception. He tacks from childhood memory to historical context to rich description of the landscape to immediate perceptions of change and continuity. He is pleasantly surprised, disappointed, and flummoxed in his search. Finally, a scent gathers him. After handfuls of mud and several chewed leaves, he finds that it is the smell of the shrub known as wolf willow. With the scent, "a contact has been made, a mystery touched. For the moment, reality is made exactly equivalent with memory, and a hunger is satisfied. The sensuous little savage that I once was is still intact inside of me." This moment of recognition that establishes a personal continuity gives Stegner a double vision of the place, one that he then supplements with research and corroboration with other members of the town.

In this, Stegner's search for the past in Whitemud is almost exactly the opposite of historian Richard White's mode of research. In *Remembering Ahanagran*, a 1998 book that explores similar themes as *Wolf Willow*, White describes a scholarly epiphany except that his epiphany crystallizes when his past becomes strange to him:

> Any good history begins in strangeness. The past should not be comfortable. The past should not be a familiar echo of the present, for if it is familiar, why revisit it? The past should be so strange that you wonder how you and people you know and love could come from such a time. When you have traced that trajectory, you have learned something.[48]

The contrast is illustrative. Just as he was not searching for the same kind of knowledge as his colleagues at the Stanford CASBS, he was likewise not searching for the same form of historical knowledge as White. Stegner was searching for contact with a past that had eluded him. White was searching for the scholarly distance necessary to see a past distinct from the present. For Stegner, the problem he confronted as a child was knowing "as little of our intense and recent past as if it had been a geological stratum hidden underground." His effort was, therefore, to establish a connection against "an uncrossable discontinuity."[49] He wanted to understand "the strings by which dead men and the unguessed past directed our lives."[50] Stegner was trying to engage the past in a way that demands a response; he was interested in a living, possessed past. Like his mentor Bernard DeVoto, Stegner was writing a history in which "proportion, relationship of parts, emphasis, and the evocation of a personal response are all part of the conception, to be reconciled in any way possible with the facts of history." It is history in which "response, not mere comprehension, is the goal."[51]

In his search for corroboration of his memory and connection with the place and people who were also a part of it, Stegner starts with his recollection of what he knew about the town when he was a child. He concludes that he grew up without history. This is not to say that the place was without a past; it was to say that Stegner had no connections to either the past as preserved through the oral traditions of the First Nations peoples of the region or as preserved in written historical accounts. The most significant historical institution he can recall is the town dump. It is the only place he can remember that preserved a continuity and made human time visible.

The dump, Stegner writes, was the "kitchen midden of all the civilization we knew." It "gave us the most tantalizing glimpses into our neighbors' lives and our own [and] provided an aesthetic distance from which to know ourselves." The dump "was our poetry and our history."[52] (It is possible to argue that Stegner failed to accurately interpret the extent to which children prefer museums and other educational opportunities to town dumps. As a woman writing from California told him, "It seems to me, as I watch a great many little savages being led from one kind of lesson to another, music, art, riding, swimming, etc etc etc, that a great deal of your kind of invaluable [I think] freedom is lost.")[53]

Stegner's rhapsodies about the aesthetic experiences available at a town dump are genuine, as anyone who has explored a dump can attest. Nonetheless, he ends the chapter with the modest proposal that he should have known more about the past of his town than he was able to experience in illicit boyhood adventures at the dump. He grew up with only the teases from the dump, but there was more to learn and it should have been otherwise. The chapter ends, "If anyone had known that past, and told us about it, he might have told us something like this:"[54] This colon that ends the chapter indicates further that Stegner was not exactly after history as literal record, but after history as personal inheritance or debt. It would prove to be both.

Wolf Willow and the Frontier Thesis

The historical interlude in *Wolf Willow* is read best as a brief entry in the extended conversation sparked by Frederick Jackson Turner's "The Significance of the Frontier in American History," both contemporaneous to Stegner and following after Patricia Limerick's reinterpretation of it in her field-defining *The Legacy of Conquest* (1987).[55] Stegner had read Turner while in Turner's "backyard" during his years in Wisconsin while working on *Mormon Country* (1942) and *The Big Rock Candy Mountain* (1943).[56] His relationship with the thesis was complex, as is the thesis itself and its voluminous historiographical legacy.[57] In his early encounters with the frontier thesis, Stegner took it up eagerly as a way of explaining his own past to himself. In the light of the frontier thesis, his father made more sense as a man who had not received the memo that the frontier had closed in 1890. He was an anachronism like Henry Adams, trained for a world that no longer had any use for him. It is perhaps the case that without the frontier thesis, Bo Mason would have been a much less sympathetic character and therefore less complex.

Stegner accepted the idea that the experiences of people in places that were in the process of transition, that were without long-settled institutions, created the vigorous, Bo Mason–like character traits that Turner memorably described as characteristically American:

> That coarseness and strength combined with acuteness and inquisitiveness; that practical, inventive turn of mind, quick to find expedients; that masterful grasp of material things, lacking in the artistic but powerful to effect great ends; that restless nervous energy; that dominant individualism, working for good and evil, and withal that buoyancy and exuberance which comes with freedom.[58]

Turner describes the frontiersman as having an "antisocial . . . antipathy to control" that is also a very fitting description of Bo Mason. Further, "movement [is] the dominant fact" on the frontier for Turner and for the Mason family in *Big Rock Candy Mountain*, and the list of connections could continue.[59] Crucial to Stegner's interpretation of Whitemud is the idea that it was a frontier that outlived the extinction of the frontier as it was proclaimed by Turner in 1890. It was a place that slipped through the cracks of history and then had rushed to catch up. Naturally, a man like Bo Mason was attracted to such a place, as in his character traits he had similarly fallen outside the process of history. Frontier processes were thus put into hyperdrive in Whitemud; history would eventually win and Whitemud would take up residence in the modern global order.

Stegner also accepted the idea that the frontier proceeded in stages and that it was more or less inevitable that it would be eclipsed by the modern world. The processes take on an air of inevitability in Stegner as in Turner. In several instances, Stegner watches, like Turner, from the Cumberland Gap as the waves of settlers go by, confronting "savagery" with "civilization." Stegner did not take on Turner's definition of "savagery," however. He condemned without equivocation the treatment of First Nations peoples in the American-Canadian borderlands at the hands of the settler-colonials from whom he descended: "No one who has studied western history can cling to the belief that the Nazis invented genocide. Extermination was a doctrine accepted widely, both officially and unofficially, in the western United States after the Civil War."[60]

He was also decidedly unromantic about what he called the "ferocious virtues" that characterized the "experienced plainsmen" of the Medicine Line. Though perhaps "necessary for survival," such virtues created "men who lived freely, wastefully, independently," and by "killing—animals as a rule, men if necessary." Further, "if any of them were thoughtful men, which is not likely, they may have conceived of themselves as the advancing fringe of a civilization, an indispensable broom sweeping clean the Plains for white occupation."[61] If there is an air of inevitability about this assertion, it is also clear that Stegner was not minimizing the violence at the roots of the settler-colonial American West at its worst. He did fall, however, into the pattern of erasing the continuing presence of First Nations peoples in the West. Elizabeth Cook-Lynn's critical reading of

Wolf Willow is guilty of faulty selection that misrepresents Stegner's work and fails to honor any good intentions on his part, but her criticism of Stegner's falling into "nostalgic lament" for the "vanishing Indian" who is safely buried in the past and not an active presence in the present is fair and does reveal a significant flaw in the book.[62]

In general, the adult Stegner finds himself looking back with regret on what he had failed to learn as a child in his town. The past he was able to discover was a past worth knowing and one that might have given him that elusive "conviction of belonging" and, even better, might have spared both the place and his family the failures that befell them. He wrote,

> I wish I had known some of this.... I might have felt as companionship and reassurance the presence of the traders, *métis*, Indians, and Mounties whose old cabins were rectangles of foundation stones under the long grass, and whose chimneys crumbled a little lower every year. Kicking up an arrowhead at the Lazy-S fort, I might have peopled my imagination with a camp among the bends of the Whitemud and had the company of Sitting Bull, Long Dog, Spotted Eagle, Walsh, Macleod, Léveillé—some Indian Summer evening when smoke lay in fragrant scarves along the willows and the swallows were twittering to their holes in the clay cutbanks and a muskrat came pushing a dark-silver wedge of water upstream. I knew the swallows and the muskrats, and was at ease with them; we were all members of the timeless natural world. But Time, which man invented, I did not know. [It] was an unpeopled and unhistoried wilderness, I possessed hardly any of the associations with which human tradition defines and enriches itself.[63]

Here Stegner is seeking to be counted part of human time—and, it should be added, a human time that included First Nations peoples— not just geological time.

Stegner transitions to the years just before his family made it to their own Whitemud (Eastend). The section starts with an epigraph from Joseph Conrad's preface to *The Nigger of the 'Narcissus': A Tale of the Forecastle* (1897) in which Conrad describes his vision for fiction. It is a particularly powerful declaration of intent for the goal of *Wolf Willow* and

Stegner's journey into the past of the American/Canadian borderlands, or the "medicine line."[64] Stegner selected the following from Conrad:

> To snatch in a moment of courage, from the remorseless rush of time, a passing phase of life, is only the beginning of the task.... In a single-minded attempt at that kind ... [o]ne may perchance attain to such clearness of sincerity that at last the presented vision of regret or pity, of terror or mirth, shall awaken in the hearts of the beholders that feeling of unavoidable solidarity; of the solidarity in mysterious origin, in toil, in joy, in hope, in uncertain fate, which binds men to each other and all mankind to the visible world.[65]

With Conrad's statement marking the transition, it is clear that Stegner's shift to fiction in the middle of the book is meant to be perceived as something more than what has gone before or what comes after. The fiction is not just an attempt to render a moment, but in that rendering to make visible the links that bind people to each other through the imaginative description of the visible world. This vision of art is one that recurs in the story itself.

"Genesis"

Stegner's novella "Genesis," introduced with a short biographical reflection on the frontier culture that Stegner had inherited in Whitemud, was one of the only stories he wrote that included characters who were cowboys. He criticized the Western and its most important character often, but rather than reinterpret it with more complexity—as did Walter Van Tilburg Clark in *The Ox-Bow Incident* (1940) or Oakley Hall in *Warlock* (1958), to cite two early examples—Stegner most often simply preferred to write stories about other westerners in the attempt to open exploration of other experiences in the West. The reflection is one of his attempts to sift through the western culture that most marked him as a young child. Having already established that it was imported, Stegner writes that it was the horseback culture of the cowboys working the "belated" Canadian range that "impressed itself as image, as romance, and as ethical system on boys like me."[66] The ideal crowded out all other possibilities, regardless of fit.

In Stegner's account of the version that shaped his childhood, it was "an inhumane and limited code, the value system of a life more limited and crude than ours in fact was."[67] It "permitted the cruelest and ugliest persecutions" against any form of difference, especially racial; "the strong bullied the weak" and the weak attempted to prove themselves otherwise or deflect attention to another target.[68] At the same time, Stegner argued, the cowboy culture at its ideal was "as noble as it was limited" for how it "honored courage, competence, and self-reliance." The "comradeship" created by a "rough and dangerous job" fostered a life "calculated to make a man careless of everything except the few things he really valued."[69]

Before turning to the novella, Stegner informs the reader that the protagonist was some mysterious combination of himself, Corky Jones, and the composites of people that he had read about in his research and remembered from his life. Based on the limitations of his evidence—that the historical actors who experienced the event subscribed to a "manner of recording" that "is laconic, deceptively matter of fact.... They do not tell their stories in Technicolor; they would not want to seem to adorn a tale or brag themselves up"—fiction will yield more insight into the moment itself. It is conjecture, but in that, not different in kind from interpretations holding to more strict recordings of the available evidence. Stegner argues that he understood the context well enough to read past the reporting in the evidence and in building a story based on that research, yield a past as it "essentially was."[70] The result is a western bildungsroman condensed into a single, terrible winter, the winter of 1906–1907.[71] Stegner's imagery is beautiful and haunting, and it is widely admired as one of his best stories.

Lionel Cullen, rumored to be the second son of an earl, becomes Rusty upon his arrival in Saskatchewan. Arriving from England at the right time, he has become part of a cattle drive and is exhilarated. He sees himself from above: "They carried no lances or pennons, the sun found no armor from which to strike light, but in the incandescence of being nineteen, and full of health, and assaulted in all his senses by the realization of everything splendid he had ever imagined, the English boy knew that no more romantic procession had ever set forth."[72] Within the first few pages, it is clear that the story will be one of romance dashed against reality; what is less clear is what kind of reality will present itself. Rusty is hungry for experience and for a testing: "He watched every minute of every day for the vivid and the wonderful, and he kept an alert eye on himself for the changes that were certain to occur. He had the feeling that there would be a test of some sort, that he would enter manhood—or cowboyhood, manhood in Saskatchewan terms—as one would enter a house."[73]

Rusty's eagerness for assured, casual belonging with the other cowboys makes him a target and camp life just reinforces his as-yet-unachieved masculinity. He injures himself and receives no sympathy. He begins to hate Spurlock, the cowboy who most delights in pointing out what Rusty worries is true. With time, "adventure" becomes simply a frustrating "job."[74] When winter begins to set in, the job becomes something more like a useless waste of time. Rusty oscillates between the desperate desire to belong and a growing bitterness towards the whole futile enterprise of herding the "impenetrably stupid" Canadian cattle.[75] Chopping through an inch of ice to get water, Rusty watches water well up through the hole "like some dark force from the ancient heart of the earth that could at any time rise around them silently and obliterate their little human noises and tracks and restore the plain to its emptiness again."[76]

Rusty develops the ominous feeling that he is going to be tested, but not in a way that would yield him the masculine proofs he desires. He would suffer but without any hope of reward. The job "called only for endurance" and promised "very little of the quality of the heroic" that he had anticipated. Filled with visions of Victorian exploration, he begins to see the job as merely skill development for the real testing that now lay in the future, when he would "challenge the country alone," facing an ordeal difficult enough to reveal with "certainty ever afterward . . . what one was."[77]

But the ordeal comes, and it comes in waves. The temperatures drop too early and the circumstances decline over several storms. Goals dwindle until eventually just the survival of the crew is going to be a success, much less any of the cows they had been hired to drive. Rusty grows "furious at their violent effort" to herd a "bunch of cattle who would be better off where their instinct told them to go."[78] Eventually they are forced to walk their way out of the blizzard on frozen riverbed to shelter miles away, linked to each other by lariats.

To Rusty's ashamed relief, Spurlock begins to fail first. It is so cold that Spurlock's muffler freezes to his beard, nearly suffocating him. He stumbles and falls and needs to be cursed into movement by Rusty and another cowboy, Panguingue. A hundred yards from the cabin Spurlock falls, his eyes "frozen wholly shut with teardrops of ice on the lashes." In their exhaustion, Rusty and Panguingue cannot carry him. In what Stegner portrays as necessity more than courage, Rusty volunteers to stay with Spurlock while Panguingue goes to the cabin for potential help. Rusty drifts in and out of a dream state and then awakes to see Spurlock's corpse-like face with a flash of terror. In a frenzy of helpless activity, he throws himself into attacks on Spurlock and somehow gets him to his feet. They make it several steps and then fall. Rusty's hopeless shouts for help are "strangled and obliterated" like a "shout up a waterfall." The "wilderness howled at him in all its voices."

He drops Spurlock and rasps at his own face, clearing enough of the ice to see the dim outline of the cabin and Panguingue on his way to carry them back. His relief is "such pure bliss" that he is "rendered imbecilic" and eventually he finds himself in the cabin, his ears "swollen red-hot fungi," rubbing his frostbitten extremities with snow among the rest of the crew.[79] (One reader's response suggests that Stegner imagined this world well. A woman from New York wrote to Stegner to tell him the circumstances in which she found her husband reading *Wolf Willow*: "On coming in with an armload of groceries one afternoon I found him huddled in a bathrobe downstairs by a fire he'd built—and to my questioning look he said with a sort of belligerent sheepishness, 'I got so Goddam cold reading about that blizzard I had to build a fire.'")[80]

The cabin is masculine heaven, with the men suffering "each in his own way the discomforts of the outraged flesh," but bonded to each other by the "mystic smells of brotherhood."[81] Discussing their frostbite and lack of whiskey, and the probable death of their herd, one cowboy deadpans, "'There's no business like the cow business to make a man healthy and active. There's hardly a job you can work that'll keep you more in the open air.'"[82]

Rusty has changed. In paragraphs that seem too didactic in a contracted reading but are more fitting in the context of the whole story, Rusty has actually learned something. It is not so much a lesson, as from a McGuffey Reader, as a frank statement of fact. Contemplating the matter that no one has thanked or praised him for sticking with Spurlock, and his own realization that he does not seem to desire such recognition, he comes to see that it was simply the expectation: "To have done less would have been cowardice and disgrace. It was probably a step in the making of a cowhand when he learned that what would pass for heroics in a softer world was only chores around here."[83]

Despite Stegner's general resentment of the cowboy culture, it is strange, then, that his only real cowboy story was one that ultimately emphasized its virtues. It is still something of a revisionist story in theme, however, and one that is rare. Most revisionist variations on the cowboy story revel in merely destructive rather than the regenerative violence of the mythic West, as in John Williams's *Butcher's Crossing* (1960). Stegner's revisionist story attempts to highlight a western ordeal by weather that could only be endured by an association of men who become, only if briefly and in desperation, something like a community. In countless cinematic set pieces and stories, the open spaces of the West foster visions of solitary communion with nature. In this open space, however, a man would have been obliterated by a ride off into the sunset.

The novella is followed by a short story, "Carrion Spring." Readers are informed that the warm chinook winds that the Saskatchewan cowboys counted on to help their herds survive the winter came only briefly enough to thaw out snow and turn it into an even more impossible sheaf of ice. By May, all they can do is "skin out the dead."[84] Turning from Rusty, Stegner explores the aftermath of the winter through the eyes of Molly Henry. She has weathered the winter in a cabin by herself with only a few visitors while waiting to see what will become of her husband of only a few months, Ray Henry, who is also Rusty's foreman. When the thaw finally comes, the revelation is bleak: "Matted, filthy, lifeless, littered, the place of her winter imprisonment was exposed, ugly enough to put gooseflesh up her backbone, and with the carrion smell over all of it."[85] One cow is even suspended in a tree, having been stranded by a receding drift.[86] Ray returns haggard and under the orders to sell everything and move along; "the country had rubbed its lesson in."[87] She and Ray promptly depart the cabin as if from a funeral, with all but a dirge to accompany them. Though they have survived a horrible winter, their ride back to Molly's hometown of Malta, Montana, is marked by a mutually incomprehensible tension.

Finally, it is revealed that Ray wants to buy out the ruins of the T-Down Ranch, the outfit that he had just served as foreman. He had thought Molly understood the opportunity herself, but she can only wait to get out; there are "better things they could do than break their backs and hearts in a hopeless country a hundred miles from anywhere."[88] Ray has a different vision and sees the ruin as a golden opportunity for buying up land at its cheapest before the Canadian Pacific Railway brings towns and wealth for those who got in early. The story ends ambiguously, with Molly looking at him, "sick and scared," and saying, "'All right.... If it's what you want.'"[89] Each of them is skilled and each is capable, but it is entirely unclear that their sticking will be rewarded.

A Community Responsibility

All the boomers of the pre-1906 wave having fled for better opportunities, and only a few stickers remaining to found the town and its first institutions, Stegner has deposited a layer of history and story on the unhistoried place where he spent his childhood, and begins to work his way back through a combination of memory and history. The town's first Village Council and Stegner's family arrived in the same year, 1914, with the population just over one hundred. Within the year, the town built plank sidewalks and streetlights, opened its first newspaper, church, and school, and cheered a declaration of war.[90] Old and new arrivals sort into roughly three categories: sober farmers with a Populist tinge, the boosters and land speculators or "priests of Progress," and the gamblers. While Stegner's mother would have been happy to join the first category, his father moved freely in all camps, and Stegner notes that the land for their gabled house, one that remains in the town as of 2021, was won in a poker game, according to the family legend.[91]

Other than the shared space, what unites them all is a resolute commitment to "Progress": "It is impossible not to believe in progress in a frontier town.... In the shadowless light before sunup, no disappointments show. And everybody, everybody, is there for the fresh start."[92] But, as historian, Stegner has the benefit of hindsight: "Failure was woven into the very web of Whitemud"; it is "the inevitable warp, as hope was the woof, of that belated frontier."[93] Failure in Whitemud is no respecter of persons, as the town's richest and poorest, men and women, from all three categories, suffer. The Great War took some and then the 1918 flu epidemic took more. Drought hit the farmers; the town was flooded and its bridge ruined. Each year, one after another, "the resources on which it had proposed to build the future went flat"; the town seemingly had as many catastrophes as people.[94] By the end of the war, only four years from the auspicious founding of its central institutions, town members were defecting with regularity, with each defection diluting the town economically and psychologically.[95]

Though they lived in town during the winters, the Stegners were in Whitemud to grow wheat and also maintained a small homestead on 320 acres. Their fate was little better than the town's. The year 1915, their first growing season, was a complete success, with wheat grown high enough to hide Stegner's six-foot father. Adding twenty acres of flax to the thirty of wheat, the following crop started off to a wonderful summer only to be destroyed by rust. Then 1917 and 1918 brought them little more than seed, and then in 1919, the "blistering hot winds" were so terrible that they did not even harvest whatever remained. They were among those who left and are gone by 1920. In hindsight, surveying the imported agricultural practices they brought with them, completely unsuited to the semi-arid plains they inhabited, Stegner renders his verdict: "It was not a farm, and we were not farmers, but wheat miners, and trapped ones at that. We had flown in carelessly, looking for something, and got ourselves stuck."[96] Their life on the homestead was "written in wind" and "began as it ended—empty space, grass and sky."[97]

The epilogue brings Stegner to the present, evaluating the Whitemud that survived and attempting to assess its future. The boy who had once wantonly killed gophers, survived the harshness of homestead life, and suffered the humiliation of being bookish in a town devoted to horseback myths is now a man who directs the prestigious creative writing program at Stanford University. Since leaving Whitemud sweltered by his father's angry failures, he has taught at Harvard, traveled to countries across Asia on the largesse of the Rockefeller Foundation, and written books that have been read by thousands of people he never met. What does he see?

Attempting his answer without the "scorn of a city intellectual" or the "angry defensiveness of a native son," he finds more to the town than the institution of commuter farming that he mentioned in his report to

Paul Fejos, but the review is generally a sobering one. A sports culture built around local records tied to feats of strength, speed, and endurance, has been reduced to curling, which Stegner describes with unveiled disdain as "a cross between bocce ball and sweeping the front porch."[98] The arts also suffer, with no local library and "young people" who "borrow cultural collapse from the United States, and read comic books."[99] Even as deprived as it was during the Great War years of his childhood, Stegner notes that they had local musicians and sold out for a Chautauqua that came through; surveying it in 1953, he finds that "even the hope of an eventual Balkan color" is dead due to radio and access to mass entertainment.[100]

The hopeful signs are modest but Stegner paints them poignantly, especially considering his initial view as described in the letter to Fejos. It is not clear whether Stegner wanted to be aspirational for the town once he made it to print or whether he changed his mind. The first assessments in the chapter are quite dismal, so it is not as if he was dishonest about his misgivings. Corky Jones becomes a model pioneer in that he does not "scorn learning," is "always willing to try importing it," and, if it fails to "take root" does not tire of hunting for "native varieties that will."[101] Even if his collection of fossils preserved in the basement of the school is generally ignored, Stegner enlists it as an remnant of "knowledge being loved for its own sake" that might be enough to ignite the curiosity of a future town resident.

Another resident, Jack Wilkinson, died after finishing an observatory with an eight-inch telescope and Corky Jones rallies the town to form the Whitemud Astronomical Society, dedicated to "'further the study of the stars and perhaps someday to help develop a budding Newton.'"[102] But the "most humane institution" Stegner finds in the town is the "Farm Wives' Rest Home." Seeing its small size, disheveled surroundings, and poor upkeep, Stegner first considers it "quintessential Whitemud" for being a "human institution, born of compassionate and humane impulse, and tailored to a felt need" but "falling so far short of its intention" as to inspire snickers if considered without context. But the context is what matters. Considering that there is, even in 1953, no plumbing in Whitemud, no library, and no service stations, Stegner sees it as a modest attempt to make life less miserable for the farm women in town with nowhere to go on errand day. The institution matters because it is an acknowledgement of a "community responsibility."[103]

Reader Responses: An "Epidemic of Reminiscing"

A contemporary review of *Wolf Willow* was titled: "Stegner's Book Trig-gers Epidemic of Reminiscing." The author of the review, which was generally positive despite the cheeky title, started the review with the observation that *Wolf Willow* had "set off a chain reaction of I-remember-whens." Hal Borland and Robert L. Perkin, the author notes, "revealed much about themselves in their reviews" but seemed reserved compared to A. B. Guthrie, who "went all out" and "devoted about 80 per cent of his review" to "recollections of his own childhood on a ranch at Choteau, Montana."[104] The review is even more prescient with hindsight, as Steg-ner's memoir of the rural West, even if itself never a bestseller, can be considered a crucial moment in the move towards a new literature of the American West, memoir being one of the more prominent modes.[105]

Patricia Limerick offers one explanation for this trend. She argues that baby boomers were soaked in visions of the West from an early age and have turned to the West since the 1980s for a variety of therapeutic reasons, but perhaps above all, because it is where they can feel young: "Time passes, ordinary logic reverses, and the Old West ages into the New West. This, any baby boomer would have to agree, is a heck of a good deal."[106] She argues further that the great expansion in Western fiction since the 1980s is at least partially rooted in the notion that the "inherited tensions of conquest" are partially relieved by "the idea of whites at home in the West" even if American Indians and Chicanos have been notable participants in the boom in Western literature.[107]

Had the reviewer seen Stegner's letters, he would have had even more evidence for his epidemic of reminiscing. A woman who, like Stegner, was born in 1909 wrote to tell him: "How true it is that we were never taught anything of the history of the region!" She moved from the region to New York in eighth grade and had an experience of feeling "inferior and inef-fectual" in town, as Stegner did. She had the same ambivalence as well: "But somehow I have a sense of the land from reading your book that I have not found in a long time, and the urge to tell you that looking back to the years when I was an unprepossessing small girl suffering some of the same mental tortures that you seemed to, I figuratively wave to you across the prairie miles that lay between us. You have used your back-ground well—the prairie and I are proud of you."[108] Another reader who had experienced the winter of 1906–1907 wrote to tell him that he had done a "masterful job of weaving the country's past and present together." He also expressed ambivalence: "Like you, I love the land dearly—its grandeur gets into the blood, but like you, I wouldn't live there for a thousand dollars an hour."[109]

Many letters came from others who had grown up in a rural area but left. A reader who grew up in Saskatchewan but moved to London wrote:

> Professor Stegner, I just wanted to say that in my estimation it is the most moving and accurate account of that god-forsaken piece of earth that I have ever read. I pass it on to friends of mine so that they will understand what growing up in a free, wide, wild, untamed space does to a kid and why when once marked by that plain that mark never changes or fades.

Another native of Saskatchewan wrote from Texas to say, "Thank you for giving me back my childhood—a time remembered as dull and drab—but revived in joy in the perfume of 'Wolf Willow.'"[110] A woman who grew up in Montana but wrote from California said, "When one lives in California, it's good to go back and take a good look at your origins." Of her parents, in their seventies, she wrote, "They are still strong and sturdy, conservative of course, and a little outside the stream of American life today, but as you said, that's my seedbed, and I'm proud of it.... And frankly, I wouldn't trade it for anything. More than anything, that country gives me the ability and the resources to be alone, and that of course, is something city people never have the chance to even experience."[111]

The theme of western and/or rural exceptionalism, present above, came out even more strongly in others. Writing about the book in 1975, a retired Canadian farmer and hotel owner told Stegner, with references that are eerily contemporary:

> I first read *Wolf Willow* in Kindersley, Saskatchewan, where I then lived on my farm, and felt it was by far the best book on a prairie boyhood I had ever read. Nothing that has been published since has altered that opinion.... Our homesteaders were much more interesting than their offspring.... And when it

came out that Nixon had described our Prime Minister, Trudeau, as an asshole, he was using exactly the same words my father would use, and the same accent. For our Trudeau is a rich man's son, an intellectual who never had to worry about grocery bills, or machinery breakdowns, or sick horses, or even serving in the armed forces during WW2.[112]

Mostly readers thanked Stegner for helping them to recover their pasts in a meaningful way. One of his readers from a non-western but rural place, the Uwharries Mountains in North Carolina, felt kinship with him: "And how often have these sudden hills renewed my spirit and granted me that joyous, soaring gratitude to be able to live—here, and now.... May you touch others as you have touched me, and may you realize how fortunate you are to have such a power in an age of cheapness and disillusionment."[113]

Another reader credited the book with bringing him out of a "psychological breakdown." He had grown up on a farm near Hanna, Alberta, and read *Wolf Willow* in his mid-thirties. Looking back on that moment from twenty years later, he wrote,

> The past came alive, became part of the present. My father came into focus, living in his historical place and time, and I came into focus, too, in my proper place and time.... I can not revisit my hometown with an easy heart, and walk the old paths through my father's cow pasture with a joyous step.... It was once my home, and I found my way back to it, thanks to you.... That book changed my life, perhaps even saved my life.[114]

Conclusion

These responses suggest that Stegner achieved the goal that he had set for himself in writing a blend of memoir-fiction-history that brought people into a deeper connection with their pasts, as well as people and places that they had once shared a past with. The comparative town study he had started to write would probably not have provoked a note that gave him any credit for saving a life, as in the letter immediately above.

Taking the objections of Richard White and Elizabeth Cook-Lynn into consideration, what are the limits of such approaches? Are personal and possessed pasts necessarily exclusive of others seeking their own possessed past, even if not meant to be so? Is the search for that form of belonging inherently dangerous? As the following chapters suggest, Stegner was not really able to resolve these tensions.

Once Stegner stopped writing reports to Fejos in 1959, Greensboro, Vermont, and Taasinge, Denmark, faded away from his awareness as places to be subjected to formal scholarly projects. They did not disappear, however, and subsequent chapters explore the ways that his studies of those places shaped his later work. In between, he was devoted to the attempt to better understand his own neighborhood of Los Altos Hills. In those hills, he would struggle less with the complex inheritance of the horseback culture. There he would meet a new variation on a standard western theme and work through another sensibility whose basic impulses seemed just as destructive of the personal and possessed past that he sought.

Chapter 3
Community, and Its Consequences

Who in the world today, especially in the world of culture, defends the bourgeoisie?

—Daniel Bell[1]

Bohemia could not survive—once businessmen started hanging nonobjective art in the boardroom—Bohemia was deprived of the stifling atmosphere without which it could not breathe.

—Michael Harrington[2]

It all reads like one great cliché. But maybe love and sorrow are always clichés, ambition and selfishness and regret are clichés, death is a cliché. It's only the literary, hot for novelty, who fear cliché, and I am no longer of that tribe.

—Wallace Stegner[3]

Almost as if consciously coordinated, Wallace Stegner's *All the Little Live Things* (*Live Things* hereafter) was published on August 7, 1967, just as the Summer of Love was slipping into the mists of nostalgic memory for some and a nightmare of bad trips, regret, and even violence for others. *Live Things*, Stegner's first attempt to reckon with the California counterculture in fiction, was released to the public just a couple of months before the Diggers staged their mock funeral for the hippie marking the "official" end of the Summer of Love in early October.[4] Stegner's Bay Area neighbors had in 1967 alone witnessed two happenings that continue to reverberate in American culture.

On January 14, Allen Ginsberg, Tim Leary, and Jerry Rubin led the tribes gathered for the Human Be-In. This event, advertised by the San Francisco *Oracle* as a "union of love and activism," featured music, meditation, and messages in various media, not to mention high-quality LSD created specifically for the occasion by the underground chemist Owsley Stanley.[5] On June 16–18, the tribes gathered again for the Monterey Pop Festival. Up to sixty thousand people flocked (with flowers in their hair, as is obligatory to note) to hear performances from Bay Area local legends Country Joe and the Fish, Jefferson Airplane, and the Grateful Dead, not to mention acts from farther out: the Animals, Janis Joplin, Otis Redding, The Byrds, Simon and Garfunkel, and Jimi Hendrix in his first major American performance.[6] In between events, thousands and thousands of would-be hippies, reporters, and curious observers converged on San Francisco. The epicenter of it all, the neighborhood around the intersection of Haight and Ashbury Streets, was located about thirty-eight miles northwest of Stegner's home in Los Altos Hills via Interstate 280. For Stegner, then, the Summer of Love was both a local, national, and international event.

The Summer of Love happened after *Live Things* made it to press and therefore was not part of Stegner's past as he planned and wrote the book, but the coincidence of its publication date ensured that it would be read first as a novel about the increasingly prominent "generation gap" of the 1960s.[7] There were good reasons for this reading of *Live Things*, as a brief summary of the book suggests. Like most of Stegner's fiction, it is built around a revelation more than a plot.[8] It begins with a rumination that is something like a thesis for the book.

Joe Allston, the protagonist and narrator, is a newly retired literary agent from New York City who has moved to the middle of the San Francisco Peninsula with Ruth, his wife. They live on a five-acre spread in a wooded rural exurb on the verge of becoming a suburb.[9] Not yet completely adjusted to the place themselves, the Allstons soon welcome to the neighborhood Marian and John Catlin, a couple with one young child and another on the way. Joe and Ruth find out that Marian has recently been treated for cancer but is in remission. Marian and John hope that it will last long enough for her to withhold further treatment for the sake of the baby she is carrying.

More pertinent in the context of the Summer of Love, the Allstons welcome another newcomer to their neighborhood: Jim Peck. Peck is a student from the local university and convinces the Allstons to let him camp on their land in the woods down the road from their house. The exchange of ideas and filial affection that develops between Joe and Marian and, eventually, Marian's race to deliver her baby before her cancer takes over, shapes the central plotline. Nonetheless, biographer Philip Fradkin is correct to observe that the tension and eventual hostility that turns Joe and Peck against each other in one of the countless generation wars that marked the 1960s—in both fiction and history—"hijacks" the novel away from Marian and Joe.[10]

Even if Fradkin and other readers are justified in responses to the book that place Joe's confrontation with Peck at the forefront, that relationship was not the theme that Stegner himself thought to be central to the book.[11] In 1981, fourteen years after the book was published, Stegner told historian Richard Etulain in an interview that "the hippie [Peck] is the least important thing in that book, to me." Peck "just wandered into it by accident and became a rather half-witted Principle of Evil." He continued: the "hippie is only a kind of dumb bystander" modeled after the hippies he knew at the time "who didn't have any notion of what went on but thought they did."

Rather than it being about Peck, Stegner argued that "the book is about 'the little live things' and the relations one has to life." He had been reading the Roman Catholic priest, philosopher, and scientist Pierre Teilhard de Chardin and thinking about Teilhard's vision of immortality as well as the ecological problem of how people "maintain [their own lives] by the destruction of other kinds of life."[12]

These more existential themes forced themselves on Stegner in part because he and Mary Stegner had recently witnessed the death of four of their close friends to cancer. All were middle-aged and otherwise healthy women.[13] As was his lifelong habit and even compulsion, Stegner wrote his way through the difficulties of his life. This book was no exception; it was written at least in part to help him work through these terrible personal losses.

My close reading of the novel in this chapter explores both of these themes in the context of reader responses to the book as well as Stegner's more sustained intellectual engagement with the problem of community in the American West, California, and the Palo Alto suburbs in particular. *Live Things* is a novel and not a political tract or sociology monograph, but there is evidence in the book that Stegner had not completely abandoned the more formal scholarly questions he had begun studying earlier in his career with his Wenner-Gren funding and through the Stanford University CASBS. Through his fiction, however, he was still trying to understand the workings of society in a specific place, and the possibilities for community that might be present in it.

Live Things, and *Spectator Bird* (1976) after it, were in part his attempt to use fiction to imagine and comment upon his Los Altos society in an aesthetic whole that linked past, present, and a possible future. Stegner's novels promote the holistic mode of thinking that can be obscured by those shaped more by analytical habits of thought. Novels point readers towards the interplay of ideas, moral commitments, sensibilities, and emotions in each human life, and how all of these create a whole that is not easily untangled. In fiction, Stegner could raise and attempt to answer humanistic questions that were unasked or unanswerable in the social scientific milieu of the Stanford CASBS: What kind of life might Los Altos yield for its residents? What community was possible there? What would human flourishing look like in Los Altos?

The "formless non-community"

Stegner had published two short stories and a novella using Joe Allston as protagonist and narrator in the setting of Los Altos before he turned to the creation of *Live Things*. He had therefore already started to think through the eyes of his protagonist and begun building his setting. With the broader canvas allowed by the scale of a novel, Stegner had room to stage the characters and vignettes and tensions that he was observing in suburban California with more depth and intricacy. Further, he was able to start working themes into the book that brought generational scale into the chronology of the place.

In his interview with Richard Etulain, Stegner said he was disappointed that large swaths of contemporary fiction followed Ernest Hemingway's example by writing novels situated in the "absolute present" and populated only by "people between twenty and thirty-five, no parents, no children."[14] In another interview he argued similarly: "It seems to me that the real relationships, the things that last in life and that will probably last in fiction as well, are likely to be related to parents, children, courtship, marriage, and children, in turn."[15] Stegner, who had experienced a

West devoid of a felt sense of the past, wrote stories that sketched western places that seemed to foster commitments to the connections binding the past, present, and future. In other stories, the absence of a felt sense of the past or a meaningful future is made obvious. In either case, he did not want to simply reify an American West that was marked primarily by lives lived in the "absolute present" with stories about characters absent their generational connections. He generally tried to think in terms of at least three generations.

Stegner wanted to think about his suburban neighborhood as a dynamic space on the verge of becoming a place with the lived experiences of multiple generations accruing to it.[16] In undated notebook reflections on the novel, he included instructions to himself that indicated that when his characters take a walk in the neighborhood early in the book, he wanted to explore "the lack of shape, the lack of center or acquaintance or tradition—even a tradition of seasons known elsewhere" that marks the society. Several residents in the neighborhood are new. They are so new that they have not even experienced the cycles of the seasons enough to develop a sense of what is normal for their place. On another scrap sheet he describes the neighborhood as a "formless non-community." Yet another scribble points to a possible solution to the problem: "Where everybody is displaced, you may have to begin all over by loving one or two, and by rejoining life at large. Full humanity comes as a realized membership [underlining original]."[17] The questions about community had not left him.

In addition to the Allstons, Catlins, and Jim Peck, the neighborhood is fleshed out with several other families, two of which are consequential. Both of them are engaged in building projects. Tom Weld (of "Indoor-Outdoor Living"), who has been in the neighborhood for twenty years and sold the Allstons their land, is most often on his bulldozer, which is the favored tool of his teenage son, Dave, as well. Joe introduces him to the Catlins with a story about his general incompetence and specific failure to keep his dog from killing all the chickens in the neighborhood. Fran and Lucio LoPresti are engaged in a years-long remodeling project and in placating their sullen daughter, Julie, who favors her horse more than people. This cast of characters allows Stegner the space to think about this suburb as a western society like the nascent community in Eastend, Saskatchewan, which he explored in *Wolf Willow*. For Stegner, the suburbs were new iterations on an old western frontier tradition. As in other Stegner books, he was better at tracing continuities over ruptures in the western past.

This theme of the formless non-community and displacement and first steps towards membership is built and lent gravity through allusions to Shakespeare's *The Tempest*, the biblical narrative of the Garden of Eden, Voltaire's *Candide*, Thoreau's *Walden*, Dante's *Inferno*, regular observations of the flora and fauna of the place, and a structure set by all four seasons of a Peninsula California year. These allusions mostly enter into the text through Joe's ruminations. The point of the allusions is not for the reader to search for them—they are rarely hidden—but to keep them in mind, to use both the literary past and historical past to converse with Stegner about the more recent past as it is imagined in the novel.[18]

Joe and Ruth have retired, like Voltaire's Candide, to cultivate their gardens. They are two weary members of the metropole who have retreated to the provinces, or at least what seem like the provinces in comparison to New York City. They are jaded by the evil of the world and are at least hoping to reduce the scale of its impact by refusing modernity and seeking refuge in cyclical simplicity. They have attempted to "buy quiet" and escape history; they want to live in geological time rather than human time. Recounting their two years so far in California, Joe thinks, "It will hardly do to confess aloud, in this century, how little it took to content us. We walked, gardened, read: Ruth cooked, I built things. We simplified feeling, as we had already anesthetized memory. The days dripped away like honey off a spoon."[19]

This simplicity is bought and lived in a California Modern villa, simple but still beautiful and not exactly within reach of others. It is nonetheless simplicity of a certain kind.[20] Considered on its own, apart from any larger trends, the leisure wastes little, takes a minimal toll on exhaustible resources, and is closer to the renewable rhythms of wild nature than to the conspicuous consumption and planned obsolescence of the suburbs as they are typically characterized.[21] It is an attempt to live in concert with the tides of the past and the future, rather than the wasteful present. Readers find later in the novel that Joe is not completely unaware that his retreat is itself not as innocuous and divorced from modernity as he thinks.

The Tempest contributes the most to the shape of the novel.[22] Like the characters of Shakespeare's *Tempest*, the characters in *Live Things* are thrown together in a natural paradise seemingly detached from consequences in "history," suggestive of either utopian possibility or chaos or cyclical meaninglessness. Early in the book Stegner refers to their surroundings as "Prospero's island," but the primary allusion in the book is to Peck as Caliban. Though Stegner makes no direct reference to Marian as Miranda, the similarities of the names and personalities make this allusion meaningful. To a lesser extent, Joe is something of a Prospero.[23] These are two young people—Joe guesses that Marian is around thirty and Peck is in his early twenties—interpreting the "brave new world" of the 1960s for and against a cranky but sensitive skeptical observer.[24]

Jim Peck and the Generation Gap

Since the book is driven more by revelation than plot, the novel begins at the end, with Joe ruminating on Marian and the cancer that claimed her life. Before recalling the more pleasant memory of the first time he and Ruth met the Catlins, however, he wanders back in his mind to the first time they met Peck. The Allstons are walking across a path along a dry creek bed in the woods that surround their neighborhood and are startled to see Peck. He is sitting on his motorcycle in "orange helicopter coveralls bulging all over with zippered pockets," his suit "unzipped clear to his navel," with a hairy chest and dense beard: "Caliban," Joe thinks.[25] Peck smells like a "neglected gym locker" and is, Joe surmises, in his early twenties. Joe thinks he has him pegged: "If I ever saw the incarnated essence of disorder, this was it. He emanated a spirit as erratic, reckless, and Dionysian as his smell."[26] Just based on superficialities, Joe interprets Peck to be standing in contemptuous judgment of him and his bourgeois tastes, habits, and virtues. Most fundamentally, Joe interprets Peck as the embodiment of an attack on his desire to belong to the center of his culture.[27] Joe feels as if he is being personally repudiated, as if his ideals are being mocked and negated.

Ruminating over the situation in hindsight, he acknowledges that he was suspicious immediately, on superficial grounds, and wonders with some regret whether it was his animosity or Peck's that sparked the other's, and whether more generosity on his part might have led to a different outcome in their relationship. Stegner allows Joe to construct a whole set of assumptions about Peck's life before he has actually witnessed anything other than his appearance and demeanor. From a few superficialities, he constructs a whole identity, personality, and history for Peck. Stegner seems to allow that this is unfair and part of the seemingly irreconcilable generational animosity, but he also suggests that Joe has a right to this judgment due to his past experience. Further, his suspicions of Peck are generally proven accurate over the course of the novel.

Fitting with the reference to Shakespeare's Caliban, Joe senses in Peck a restless feeling of imprisonment by the past and the cultivation of an intense hatred for the civilization that preserves it. Early in *The Tempest*, Caliban damns Prospero for taking his island from him and imprisoning him on it by kind deceptions. Prospero challenges this account, saying that they lived together peaceably until Caliban tried to rape Miranda. Caliban agrees, saying without shame that he would have done it, and "peopled else / This isle with Calibans."

Miranda (or Prospero, according to some scholars) tells Caliban that he deserved it. Prospero and Miranda "took pains to make thee speak, taught thee each hour / One thing or other. When thou didst not, savage, / Know thine own meaning, but would gabble like / A thing most brutish, I endowed thy purposes / With words that made them known." Though Caliban learns from Prospero and Miranda, she says that his "vile race" had "that in't which good natures / Could not abide to be with," justifying his imprisonment. Caliban is unmoved: "You taught me language, and my profit on't / Is, I know how to curse. The red plague rid you / For learning me your language!"[28]

Though Stegner paints the two as being immediately suspicious of each other, Peck eventually asks a favor of Joe. He tells Joe that he has selected his land as a perfect spot for him to camp out for the indefinite future. He reveals that he is a philosophy student (the university is unnamed in the book). He feels too constrained by the available possibilities in Palo Alto, thus his desire to camp on the Allstons' property. Without context, it seems that there is no way that Joe will allow Peck to camp on his land. Unlike in the previous Allston stories, however, the novel begins to unravel their past. Their move to California, readers find, is not motivated only by a desire to avoid Joe's embarrassment of being seen in his aimless leisure by his former colleagues or to live in the California paradise.[29]

He and Ruth are actually retreating from the associations that their past had with their only son, Curtis, a troubled soul who had died three years before the action of the novel takes place. He was a lush and a pseudo-intellectual who mocked effort and discipline as merely the smokescreens of the bourgeoisie. After a lifetime of antagonism, Joe and Ruth are left only with questions about what level of blame they must shoulder for what they see as the waste of their son's life. This relationship, which is revealed in more depth over the course of the novel, is part of the explanation for Joe's hostility to Peck. It is also the explanation for why he allows Peck to camp on his land. While Joe is reminded of his failures as a father, Ruth sees another chance. She intervenes enough to force a conversation between Joe and Peck, and eventually Joe's objections are worn down and Peck convinces them that he should be able to camp in a wooded part of their land.

In his futile attempt to keep Peck from camping on his land, Joe first challenges the innocence of Peck's attempt to withdraw from the artificialities of the obvious choices for housing that, as a student, he could have taken. Peck has told Joe that he wants to withdraw for the sake of spiritual cleansing, to meditate and be closer to nature. Joe tells him that he will summarize his case against the "air-conditioned junkyard": "'You'd go into your spiritual retirement in a factory made, chemically waterproofed tent.... You'd go to and fro on a motorcycle built in Japan and brought to you by a complicated system of international trade.... The raisins you would live on would be mass-produced. Likewise the salted peanuts.... That's withdrawal?'"

Peck asks Joe why it bothers him. Joe asks him what he expects to teach the "junkyard" with his "phony retirement" and Peck replies that he doesn't expect to teach it anything, that he "only gets one life" and that it's not worth spending it "teaching lessons to a shitty civilization." Joe says that it takes a lot of mass-produced resources to support the withdrawal that he has so far indicated and ends with a challenge: "'You want your Walden with modern conveniences, is that it?'"[30] Peck says he is indifferent.

Joe finds himself wearied. He admits to himself that part of the reason for his frustration, in addition to bringing back painful memories of similarly circuitous conversations with his son, is that they are both in fact retreating from modernity and their contemporaries, and that their motivations are not as distant as he would like to think: "Yet he spoke some of my opinions, in his incomparably crack-brained way, and I was uneasily aware that in putting him down I was pinning myself. I had retired from our overengineered society as surely as he wanted to, and I lived behind a PRIVATE ROAD sign on a dead-end lane."[31] Were the western suburbs themselves just another form of utopian separation, separated only a few degrees from the communes that popped up all over the West in the late 1960s and early 1970s?[32] Would the Peninsula Housing Association, had it succeeded, been a different model?

In presenting this similarity, Stegner was adding complexity and difficult questions for both sides of the generation gap. He suggests that both the older generation and the younger were more like the side they detested than either would have liked to admit.[33] On the scale Stegner imagines here, the distance from suburb to rural commune is not so very far.[34] Both are attempting to evade history, though for different reasons.

Ruth and Peck eventually win. Joe concedes and the formless non-community gains a new resident. Joe and Ruth keep tabs on Peck as he proceeds to build himself a Swiss Family Robinson–style commune, ramshackle but adventurous and at times ingenious, which is periodically home to a rotating group of friends. Joe and Ruth adapt to Peck's presence on their property where he continues, without ever notifying the Allstons, to stretch out beyond the limits Joe set for him when he agreed to let Peck camp there. He builds a ramshackle shed for his motorcycle, and eventually taps into both the Allstons' electricity and water. His parties grow larger and louder and more consequential.

Peck is sometimes assumed to be a thinly fictionalized version of Ken Kesey, the one-time member of the Stanford Creative Writing Program, which Stegner directed. Stegner and Kesey had a tense acquaintance and then their relationship was severed for good when Kesey criticized Stegner in a 1963 interview. Kesey had just become the most prominent product of the Stanford Creative Writing Program with the publication of *One Flew Over the Cuckoo's Nest* (1962), a fact that undoubtedly galled Stegner. Mark McGurl surmises that the therapy meetings in the book are parodies of Stanford Creative Writing Program sessions and that, by implication, there is something of Stegner in Nurse Ratched's character.[35]

But the 1963 interview was the last straw. After praising Stegner's early work, Kesey said: "Then you try his later stuff and you find that he's not writing to people any longer, not to people he knows and loves, anyway. He's writing to a classroom and colleagues." Stegner had been institutionalized, in other words. He was writing for the Combine. After the interview was published, Kesey tried to make amends but Stegner would not meet and continued to refuse contact with Kesey up to his death. The closest Stegner came to forgiveness was an expunging of some of his harshest criticism of Kesey in his conversations with Richard Etulain.[36] Kesey never again disparaged Stegner publicly, however, and after Stegner died in 1993, he summarized their conflict as amicably as possible: "I liked him, and I actually think that he liked me; it's just that we were on different sides of the fence. As I took LSD, and he drank Jack Daniels, we drew the line between us there."[37]

Was Kesey-as-Peck payback for Stegner-as-Nurse Ratched in Kesey's *One Flew Over the Cuckoo's Nest*? In both cases, these suggestions only really work as abstractions of generational conflict. Stegner's notes do mention Kesey, but only to point out that he is not the model.[38] In his correspondence, he told people who suggested the connection that Kesey was not the inspiration for Peck. More specifically, the notes describe Vic Lovell and Ira Sandperl, two other lesser-known members of the Palo Alto counterculture from the Perry Lane neighborhood.[39] Lovell was the leading light of the Midpeninsula Free University, which was started in Palo Alto in January 1966 and had faded out by the summer of 1971.[40] Sandperl was the face of Kepler's Bookstore in Palo Alto, a political mentor to Joan Baez (whom he met at a Quaker service when she was a student at Palo Alto High School) and the cofounder, with Baez, of the Institute for Nonviolence.[41] In his draft notes, Stegner wrote,

> The Beat—model on Vic Lovell? Philosophical anarch [*sic*] whose anarchy is an expression not of philosophy but of instability and psychic failure? A repudiator of society whose whole repudiation depends on his use of that society—record player, water, light, liquor, pills.... He steals from the A&P, PG&E, Allston, Catlins. The world, in short, owes him his living. He is devoted to Ginsburg, Segovia, folk music, rebellious against any authority, ungrateful for favors.[42]

In another set of notes, Stegner wrote, "Peck a violent nonviolent man. Appears at all rallies and sitins, debates (a form of warfare), rides his motorcycle (a suppressed lust for action). He pollutes because he is impure. He isn't Kesey, he's Sandperl."[43] Suggesting the connections were legitimate, Stegner received a 1983 letter from a clerk at Kepler's who objected to Stegner's portrayal of his friends. A former student at Stanford from 1965 to 1970, he wrote that he thought Stegner had "caricatured certain people and ideas whom/which were close to my experience." But the next sentence, seemingly through the teeth, continued: "Now I find you are a stalwart supporter of the Sierra Club of which I am a member." He then closed with an offer to host an author's night for Stegner for his next new book.[44]

In addition to these Palo Alto locals, there were other examples from even closer to home. Stegner's son, Page, had allowed a motorcycle-driving friend to camp on his parents' property when they were in Europe. Another tenant who rented the Stegners' cottage with their permission, John McChesney, had at one point tried to grow marijuana on their property, very much without their permission. McChesney had been a student at Stanford in the 1960s and was a burr on Stegner's mind. In an undated rumination titled "Confessions of a Cultural Conservative: A Sort of Dialogue with John McChesney After Three or Four Years—Five Years Maybe," Stegner wrestled with the conflict between the two.

After summarizing in brief their overlapping ideals—opposition to the Vietnam War, support for the Civil Rights Movement, need for university reform—and their conflicts—"his direct action methods" and "revolutionary intransigence"—Stegner was still unable to come to terms. "We parted somewhat later, and he went off to Antioch to participate in more confrontations. . . . I have been conducting a dialogue with him ever since he first came to live in our cottage, because I couldn't understand him, and wanted to. He couldn't understand me, either, though I don't know whether he wanted to or not."[45] Yet even closer to home, Page's adolescence and early adulthood were marked by a long, simmering antagonism with his parents that, even if improved by 1967, was still raw.[46]

What is particularly revealing about Joe's conflicts with Peck (and similarly with his son, Curtis, described below), as well as Stegner's actual conflicts with Kesey, Lovell, Sandperl, McChesney, Page Stegner, and numerous others, is the pain, confusion, and hurt that are present in the accounts.[47] In the way that Stegner paints the conflict, the younger generation has simply broken contact and insisted that there is no relationship and no possibility for reconciliation.[48] While there is no shortage of anger in *Live Things*, Stegner's account of this relationship does more to highlight the sadness and loneliness of the parents.

A comparison of the public and private versions of this dispute is also revealing.[49] In print, Joe Allston is cranky and angry, but is also perhaps more confused, sad, and filled with guilt than he appears in Stegner's notes. In his notes, Stegner is more dismissive. While it is possible to read this as hypocrisy, Stegner's vision of fiction suggests another angle. "In fiction," he wrote, "I think we should have no agenda except to try to be truthful."[50] Perhaps the truth was that the sorrow was more deeply felt and lasting than the anger.

Marian Catlin and the Little Live Things

Interspersed with this slow-simmering conflict with Peck is a more pleasant meeting with the Catlins. It is a perfect California day and Joe and Ruth are working outdoors. Joe sees a gopher tug his tomato plant a few inches into the ground and goes inside to retrieve his shotgun. He is striding angrily out of his house with the shotgun right as the Catlins are walking up their driveway to introduce themselves. He is too far into the task to stop, so he puts his finger to his mouth to keep them from talking and blasts into the sod, killing the gopher. Joe digs out the gopher, a "twig of tomato vine in his grooved teeth . . . the Evil One," and hears Marian cry out in sympathy for the gopher.[51]

Joe's fierce hatred for gophers prevents him from identifying at all with sympathy for such a beast, and he is immediately prepared to dislike the person who would utter such a naïve sentiment. He is prevented from doing so by his first glance at Marian, "her eyes most alive, and her lips half-parted in a look that mixes pity for the gopher, and pleasure to meet me even if I *am* a brute, and delight simply at the way the sun pours down and the browned daffodils lie in a sheaf across Ruth's arm" [italics original here and in the following quotations].[52] It is immediately apparent to Joe that Marian's sympathy for the gopher comes from a deep well of love for life, and that this feeling more than moral superiority and judgment has inspired her exclamation. Her vitality makes Joe's heart rush. This does not, however, prevent a vigorous debate with his new neighbor about pests and perspective.

For Joe, the issue is straightforward—the gopher is a pest and it does not belong in the garden, and besides, "Did you ever look into a gopher's beady eye? ... *He* knows he's evil."[53] Marian is more attuned to her new habitat, even though she is more recently arrived than the Allstons. Responding to Joe's provocations, Marian plans to only grow native plants and refuses to condemn the gopher, or the tick that is its parasite, or the spotted fever germs that the tick carries, even as Joe tries to force her into tighter and tighter corners. Ruth tries to change the subject, but Joe cannot help himself. "'My dear child, it's one thing to be fond of little live things—who isn't?—but you have to remember that there's a struggle for existence going on. There are good kinds of life and bad kinds of life—'" Marian cuts him off: "'Bad is what conflicts with your interests.'"[54] Determined to enlighten her to the naiveté of her view, Joe launches into a discussion of poison oak, nettles, and wild cucumber, which he recently attacked. "'I dug up one last week, just to see where all that vile vitality comes from that can sprout these tentacles twenty feet long. You know what's down there? A big tumor sort of thing as big as a bucket, an underground cancer. I very much doubt that any of these things are the friends of man.'"[55]

John and Ruth shift uncomfortably and finally succeed in turning the mildly flirtatious debate back to conversation. John is an ethologist who studies whales and teaches at Stanford and tells the Allstons at one point that baby whales grow a ton a month, a fact that Joe says that he will be contemplating for a while: "What in *hell* is in whale's milk?"[56] Then all of them are interrupted by birdsong.

"For a moment," Joe thinks,

I have an acute awareness of how we look, quiet on the terrace in the bird-riddled afternoon, with the breeze dropped to nothing, the leaves still, the haze beginning to spread amethyst and lavender and violet. ... Marian Catlin's face tells me that she has the same perception. This is the way she feels everything in her life—hungrily. Sensibility that skinless is close to being a curse.

Joe thinks that Marian's eyes are "shiny with tears" as "the mockingbird pours on, unquenchable. '*Listen* to him!'" she says. Joe feels exposed by their emotional vulnerability and turns to humor. Mouthing the words, he says, "'He does it on a diet of worms.'"[57] Marian smiles, acknowledging his point and their camaraderie in debate, and Joe revels in his minor victory.

The conversation moves on again, and then as the Catlins are preparing to leave, Marian receives her own victory. Walking across the driveway, she sees little mounds in the pavement and demands everyone stop and look. They break the surface to find that the asphalt is being mounded by a "dinky mushroom." Eyes ablaze, Marian says to Joe, "Now, you see? You wondered what was in whale's milk. Don't you know now? The same thing that's in a mushroom spore, or in gophers, or poison oak, or anything else we try to pave under, or grub out, or poison. There isn't good life or evil life, there's only life. Think of the *force* down there, just telling things to get born!"[58] Joe is moved by her sincerity, and again makes a joke to cover his emotional vulnerability.

Marian is allowed the last word, and the couples head their separate ways. Ruth (who had talked with the Catlins earlier, but without relaying the information to Joe) tells Joe that Marian is both pregnant and recovering from a mastectomy due to cancer. Joe is deflated, and the conversation reveals itself to him in a new way. This dialogue was one that Stegner would wrestle with for most of his life. If the ideas are traced back to his essays, it becomes evident that this was a genuine internal dialogue for him. Like Marian, he argued against the idea that habitats and habits have no relation. He did not believe that people should be able to import species, tools, mores, and lifestyles without any respect for local geographic conditions and cultures. Like Joe, however, Stegner was not willing to follow idealism as far as Marian was, or, more fundamentally, to consider her commitment to life undifferentiated a proper ideal. It is probably the case that Marian is the only passionate idealist in all of his writing that Stegner actually seemed to trust and respect.[59]

Taken back one level of abstraction, the story also reflects Stegner's internal tension with his family's choice to make their home in the California semiwilderness. Rapid and chaotic growth was a problem that he was unable to resolve. The expansion of people into more and more wilderness troubled Stegner throughout his life, as his adopted home morphed from rural retreat to exurb to suburb to low-density city. As his former student Edward Abbey would later write, "Growth for the sake of growth *is* the ideology of the cancer cell" [italics original].[60] This tension with the growth that he contributed to in the Los Altos Hills perhaps accounts for the fact that Joe's guilt is one of the dominant themes of all of Stegner's Peninsula fiction.[61]

Stegner flashes forward again to Joe in his study ruminating on what the year has meant to him. Though a formless noncommunity, the neighborhood is nonetheless connected, and is a community of sorts in spite of itself. The members are entangled more than they realize. None of the people in retreat from their past or from society as a whole has actually managed to retreat or to be harmless. *Ahimsa*, whether imported or native-grown and called something else, is a fiction:

> None of us, surely, is harmless, whatever our private fantasies urge us to believe. Whatever any of us may have wanted in retiring to these hills, we have not escaped one another. The single-minded rancher anxious to capitalize on his remaining land, the Italian native son with the invalid wife and the sullen daughter and the narcotic adobe bricks, the threatened young woman desperate for continuity, the kook who lived in the birdhouse and this kook who lives at the top of the hill—whatever we wanted, we stumbled into community, with its consequences. And at the heart of our community was the Catlin cottage.[62]

Exploration of "community, with its consequences," and left unstated, the absence of community, with its consequences, is in some sense a summary of Stegner's lifetime intellectual labors.

In Joe's reflection, it is Marian's vitality and warmth that breaks apart the barriers, both intentional and unintentional, between the neighbors and elevates the formless noncommunity into something more, even if it is revealed to be fragile. He acknowledges that he and Ruth "have tended to protect [them]selves from people" and cherish their privacy, and that they are more likely to reject people peremptorily, as he did Peck, than "like them on sight." But Marian breaks through with them, and she does the same with Peck. Marian's generosity of spirit extends to Peck, and this forces the Allstons and Peck into company together. Several episodes unfurl, and Stegner stages them so that Peck is generally enthralling to everyone except Joe.

Peck is amusing and sometimes compelling to Marian and Ruth and thrilling for the Catlins' young daughter, Debby. He becomes a guru for the two neighborhood teenagers, the sullen Julie LoPresti, who, before Peck's commune starts, finds more companionship with her horse than anyone else, and Dave Weld, a pistol-toting outdoorsman like his father who eventually ditches the pistol and starts to grow his hair out. Marian attempts to help Joe learn to understand Peck and gives Peck the benefit of the doubt while also allowing Joe to rationalize and explain his suspicions of Peck to her.

Finally, Marian pries Joe's relationship to Curtis loose. Joe had been attempting to justify his reactions to Peck on an impersonal level, but Marian realizes that it is not quite that simple. Joe is not able to say what he wants to say in person, and instead composes a letter to Marian that goes unsent. I summarize it at length because it was such an outburst of emotion from Joe's creator, and also because it proved to be moving to readers. It is in some ways a rant, but one that is honest and not simply spiteful or completely unfounded. It encapsulated the personal losses, frustrations, and incapacities of a generation of parents as the 1960s wore on. It is also Stegner's dramatized indictment of the more facile versions of what he thought passed for freedom for too many Americans: a sense of being free from all previous associations, all pasts, all encumbering relationships.

"The obligation of the seed"[63]

The letter starts with the acknowledgement that it is possible that Joe is exorcising the ghost of his son Curtis in his hostilities with Peck. Joe has worked over his relationship with his son thousands of times and come no closer to a resolution. He knows that he could have been a better father but is unable to figure out what he could have done differently without ceasing to be himself. Curt, Joe says, "was modern youth to the seventh power ... crypto communist youth during the thirties, pacifist-internationalist youth in the forties, and overage beat youth in the fifties, and nothing very seriously ... he *wasn't* much of anything, he was simply against ... a rebel in uniform, [a] nonconformist who runs in packs and sings in close harmony with his age group." Though both he and Ruth tried to love him and persuade him of their love for him, they were incapable of doing so; Joe writes that "the only way to live with him in peace would have been to submit to his beliefs."

Ruth tried more valiantly than Joe, but Joe could not do it: "I believed, and I still believe, that some periods of human history are better than others.... Some codes are better than the codes that replace them," and that "this is a corrupt age because it accepts everything as equal to everything else, and because it values indulgence more than restraint."[64] Joe was "neither a good enough teacher nor a good enough example" to persuade Curtis, who thought of moral training for self-restraint as merely bourgeois: "Train yourself for what? ... To be a good corporation man? ... To contribute to this vulgarian's nightmare they call a civilization?" Joe, growing angrily impatient (the vice of his that he does forthrightly acknowledge), could not agree: "No, I would tell him, God help me, beginning to roar. To be a man. Isn't that enough? To be a man whose word is trusted and whose generosity can be depended on and who doesn't demand something without giving something himself."[65]

Curtis could not agree to Joe's midcentury masculine code.[66] Joe insists that Curtis "could have disagreed with us incessantly if we had felt in him some integrity that gave his disagreements weight." Without any principle, Joe argues, "the America he despised corrupted him, industrial civilization corrupted him with the very vices he thought he scorned in it. It encouraged him to hunt out the shoddy, the physical, the self-indulgent, the shrill, and the vulgar, and to call these things freedom."[67] With the luxury of a small trust fund from Ruth's family, Curtis cycles through various attempts to free himself from the shackles of civilization (too many to believe, perhaps, for his thirty-seven years) without finding anything that will stick.[68] He merely accumulates a "record of scorn for practically everything the human race ever thought worthy."[69]

Finally, at thirty-seven, he gives education one last chance at San Diego State College but ends up dropping out to live in a "motorcycle bohemia" in La Jolla with a girlfriend and a surfboard. He then drowns in a surfing accident that Joe surmises may have actually been suicide. Looking at Curt's face in the coffin, Joe feels a clutch in his chest and a "scald of tears at the total failure of his life and mine." At rest, his "face had given up all its poses and looked merely young, incredibly young, far younger than it had any right to look, the very face of kicks-crazy America, unlined by thinking, unmarked by pain, unshadowed even by years of scrupulous dissoluteness, untouched by life—or by death either—except for a slight discontented droop at the corners of the lips."[70] The description suggests Curtis is frozen in a present that has rejected both past and future, and not just because he is dead. Though they are not surprised, Joe and Ruth are devastated as they realize that, at the very minimum and without conscious thought, they "had counted on time" eventually allowing for reconciliation "and now time was run out."[71]

Ruth weathers the loss better than Joe, who sleeps in Curt's room as penance. He goes over and over their past again: "I tried to speak my heart, and I had the advantage of endless revisions; but the dead listened no more than the living had." Curt "would have none of my love unless it came unqualified and uncritical and in spite of every provocation. . . . It is not a kind of love I am ever likely to be able to give. I don't think any human being is entitled to it, and anyway I can't separate love and respect. Curt demanded what I couldn't give, I insisted on what he wouldn't accept."[72] In death and in life, they stared at each other across an abyss that neither could cross.

Having lost their most direct link to the future, Joe and Ruth are adrift. Joe is particularly weightless because he not only has no future but no past. His mother had been a Danish immigrant with little education and two dead husbands by the time Joe was six. She tended houses, and Joe's childhood is a "passage from vacuum to vacuum"—not a pun—no places are meaningful to him. Eventually through some luck Joe gets a scholarship but this distances him from his mother to his deep shame and regret. She later dies in an accident, falling down the cellar stairs at work, and is buried in Chicago. Summarizing her life, Joe writes, "It all reads like one great cliché. But maybe love and sorrow are always clichés, ambition and selfishness and regret are clichés, death is a cliché. It's only the literary, hot for novelty, who fear cliché, and I am no longer of that tribe."[73]

It is perhaps this sentence that best summarizes Stegner's long quarrel with the artistic trends of his era. He thought that the repudiation of what exists, and the search for the original, for novelty, for the escape from the past, was not just a repudiation of dead standards and cliché but a repudiation of humanity and any hope for basic decency. The escape and repudiation could not be so total without being dehumanizing. The fear of cliché required too much sacrifice and left too much collateral damage. Though in hindsight this letter has the ring of bitterness and is, at worst, almost cruel, it is also possible to see this as an honest quarrel with the cult of the avant-garde that shaped elite culture of that era. The avant-garde, Stegner seemed to be arguing, could lay claim to artistic novelty, but could it lay claim to much else? Without art capable of suggesting belonging, how would people imagine their connections to each other?

Joe found himself—and not by choice—where the fading avant-garde as it merged into the New Sensibility of the 1950s to 1970s seemed to want people to be, free in an absolute sense: without "any source, tribe, family, region, nation, tradition, gene pool, or anything else to which my wastage of a life could be called a loss."[74] For Joe, it is disturbing and dehumanizing: "I grew to hate the thin dispersal of my relatives, my mother in Chicago earth and my son in Buck's County, each alone among strangers. And here was I, random and now childless, making meaningless orbits in the Madison Avenue void."[75] Having no place to return to, Joe and Ruth make a new beginning in California, as myriad Americans, both in fiction and in life, had done before. This, Joe writes, is not "a radical act, in a way" but "a habitual one" that "conformed to twenty generations of American experience."[76] They left it all behind, expecting "to become less culpable by becoming more withdrawn."[77] The letter ends, but is unfinished, unsigned, and unsent when Joe finds it again in the present, rummaging through his office.

Reader Responses: "No One Cares Really!"

Stegner had experienced this form of freedom in the chaos of his early life following his father's death and rejected it. In Joe's words, it is a cry for the responsibility that each generation holds to the other through an exploration of the devastating weightlessness of a present without human links to the past or future. For some readers, it was likely a pitiful, tone-deaf attempt at justifying a corrupted generation to its rightfully jaded young. It is true that it is more self-indulgent than Joe (or Stegner) would likely be glad to admit given their understanding of themselves as moderate stoics. Nonetheless, it offers a window into the suffering of the parents who felt themselves cut off from their children in that decade. If it was not really successful in teaching his adversaries why they were wrong—and in fact Stegner was often incendiary in these cases—it did offer comfort to other parents who had gone through the same thing and could not express themselves with Stegner's clarity or depth of insight.

Marion Benasutti of Camden, New Jersey, noted the letter specifically as the heart of the book for her:

> It touched me so very much because it was literally a blow by blow description of the son I lost (by fire) several years ago after many long bitter years of trying to help him find his way. The bit about the books he read, especially, reminded me of my feeling about the very same thing. No, the books didn't do it but I am firmly convinced they helped. And while I do not believe in censorship I do believe that such books help such people over the edge, the wrong edge, of their thinking.[78]

Another correspondent, M. A. Arnold of San Francisco, wrote to thank Stegner for *Live Things* and told him that her only remaining son (the other son was killed at seventeen) disappeared and had been gone for seventeen months, presumably landing in Haight-Ashbury. The wounds were incredibly raw:

> Unless you are one [a parent with a missing child] and enduring this living Hell you cannot imagine—no one can—what it is. And do you know, that despite all the articles, publicity, broadcasts, talk, talk, talk, etc. that No one Really Cares? . . . No matter which way one turns—the police, clergy, law, friends, Hippies, etc. . . . you run into a Dead End. It is like a silent Conspiracy. A stone wall. And the very tragic heart of it all is . . . that No One Cares! Really![79]

Less raw, others appreciated him for helping them express or see what they could not. Paul Sanford wrote,

> Is there any way to meet the gap? I understand their yearnings for "nature undefiled." But the same ones who want it undefiled

leave a trail of bottles, cans, paper plates, cups, and fiberglass cigarette butts. I can answer their questions. They don't even try to answer mine. They grow numb, antagonistic. . . . They turn off at suggestions on attitudes, aspirations, desires. That is <u>my</u> generation gap. I do not press for answers. [underlining original][80]

Betty Hanson, a teacher from Ashland, Wisconsin wrote Stegner and introduced herself as the proud mother of a daughter at Stanford who served jail time with Joan Baez for the October 16, 1967, draft protest in Oakland. She told Stegner that the novel "shed light on the hippies" with "the most honesty anyone of our generation can."[81]

The Formless Non-community and Its Lonely Independence

Despite the bonds, however weak, that Marian fostered in the formless noncommunity, it fails to survive the summer. It all unravels at a neighborhood party on the Fourth of July. John Catlin is on a research trip, and the Allstons have planned to take Marian to the party. The party is a rural affair; in Joe's words, it is a "Renoir picnic on a construction site." The hosts, Fran and Lucio LoPresti, have been remodeling their house for a long time, and Fran is an artist who welds art from the building scraps. As Lucio is doing the construction for his own pleasure as much as to improve their home, the process is slow and they incorporate the building process into everyday life. The guests drink freely, shoot off firecrackers, prank each other, and gorge themselves on pit-cooked beef. Soon they find out that Peck is hosting his own party, one attended illicitly by Julie, the host family's daughter. By the time Joe is made aware of it, the formless non-community of their neighborhood has turned into a raucous chaos. Dogs are barking and music blares in connection with an experiment Peck is running that also involves the loud banging of culverts with people inside (an experiment in consciousness, obviously). The generations are at complete odds. Listening to Peck's party coming from down in the valley and imagining the worst, Joe summarizes the situation, bleakly:

> Was this all there was to do? . . . Did we come west for no better reason than to set shirttails afire and make brainless sport of

touchy friends, and periodically overturn habit, custom, order, and quiet in binges indistinguishable from those that went on down in the University of the Free Mind? Had we gravitated, despite ourselves, from suburbia to its cure, which is orgy? I had a considerable distaste for the good life as prescribed by Jim Peck, I disparaged his affection for the disorderly and irrational and his faith in chaos. But what better could I suggest? My withdrawal was more finicky than his, and I preferred alcohol to pot. There was the real difference. Pot, as I understood, did not leave hangovers. Maybe that was my total reason for repudiating Peck's brave new world. It is bad enough to live with yourself *with* hangovers.[82]

The "forces of disorder" are not extinguished yet, however, as after taking Marian and Debby home, the Allstons are asked by Marian to stay with her for a moment.[83] She reveals to them that her cancer has returned, that she only has a few months, and that she has rejected treatment in order to save her baby. The Allstons protest, but Marian has decided that since treatment would only delay the inevitable, she would rather carry the baby to term and not risk harming the baby with treatment. Joe and Ruth leave reluctantly, and as they return to their car they again hear Peck's party a hundred yards away, which has only increased in its intensity. Marian's situation fills Joe with indignant anger, and he resolves that Peck's party will end and that he will be kicking him off his property. He heads down with a flashlight, shines it in on the party, catches a couple—one of them Julie LoPresti—in "*coitus alarmus*," and tells them to turn off the music. There is a scuffle and whispered conversation about how severe the situation is, and Joe repeats his command. After they realize that it is a neighbor rather than the law, someone turns a flashlight on Joe and asks the immortal 1960s question, "'Who says?'"

There is laughter, and in a "time for quiet moral authority and the dignity of an elder," Joe loses it. This leads nowhere and eventually Joe has a showdown with Peck. Peck insouciantly keeps his calm against Joe's agitation and justifies his noise as a psychological experiment; it is fine in the country and within the realm of Joe's permission to live there. Recalling the incident in hindsight, Joe wonders whether he might have done better to have gone to the party, asked for a beer, and tried to understand the revelers, but that is not the route he takes. The conversation eventually ends with a recourse to the law and Peck concedes, but no one really wins.

Reflecting on his own moral impotence and Peck's impotence in the face of the law, Joe thinks: "I would much rather have been representative of something he had to respect for its manifest solidity and goodness, not for its power. And for that, who was to blame? Peck, with his compulsion to break all laws and deny all authority, or I with my emotional inability to accept anything he stood for?"[84] This statement is a powerful reflection of the standoff between the generations that so entangled the American public. It suggests that the older generations, for all their feelings of impotence, actually did hold most of the economic and political power. They ultimately pulled the strings. The young could not pull strings but could withhold respect and honor. In the context of the Vietnam War, these conflicts were life and death.

In an article written two years after *Live Things* that put the matter as directly as possible, novelist Kurt Vonnegut worked through an imagined conversation with Defense Secretary Melvin Laird, after being told by (his former high school classmate) Barbara Masters Laird that she wanted Vonnegut to join them for dinner because she had liked his just-published *Slaughterhouse-Five* (1969). After wondering what kind of conversation they would have, given his book's themes and her husband's occupation, he wrote: "But then I remembered high school, where all of us learned to respect each other's opinions—no matter what the opinions were. We learned how to be unfailingly friendly—to smile. So, maybe, the Secretary of Defense would be friendly about my pacifism and all that, and I would be friendly about the end of the world and all that." He then sarcastically imagined a polite and gracious exit, leaving with the thought that "I would have thanked God, too, that no member of the younger generation were along. Kids don't learn nice manners in high school any more. If they met a person who was in favor of building a device which would cripple and finally kill all children everywhere, they wouldn't smile. They would show hatred."[85]

Back on the Peninsula, neither Peck nor Joe could be satisfied with the arrangement. Their Fourth is over, and the formless non-community has declared its lonely independence. Whatever hope it had of being something more will die with Marian.

All Treadmill

Joe and Peck have one more conversation before Peck leaves. Peck drives over to the Allstons' driveway and Joe meets him outside having heard the motorcycle. Peck tells Joe that he wants to apologize "if we disturbed you" and make sure that Joe is not serious about the decision to make him move out. They argue, and eventually Joe thinks, "I understood him no more than I would have understood a Martian, but I understood the evil things he did to me, the way he had of making me be less than myself." Following their complete mismeeting of minds, Peck leaves with a spray of gravel and Joe is left in his driveway "baffled and unsettled and vaguely guilty."[86]

Joe has a much more difficult time saying his goodbyes to Marian, who has begun her own form of withdrawal. Since she has only limited time left, Marian is convinced that she needs to begin to distance herself from Debby in order to help her rely on John instead. She tells Joe that both of her parents died when she was young, and she does not want Debby to experience what she did, having nightmares about "being lost in some forest, or in a great bleak place like a tundra."[87] The cancer keeps advancing; "death and life grew in her at an equal pace" and the future is dismal, though Marian attempts to stay the course she has set for herself. One afternoon, walking home, Joe connects the forces of destruction. Tom Weld is landscaping again with a bulldozer and the resonance of the symbol is just too much for Joe:

> Full of the bitterness of being able to do not one thing for Marian, we took refuge in fury at that barebacked Neanderthal and his brutish machine. I associated the mutilation of the hill with the mutilations that Marian had suffered and was still to suffer, and I hated Weld so passionately that I shook. He was a born ugliness-maker, and he was irresistible and inescapable. . . . [W]e could no more resist the laws of property, the permit of the planning commission, and the Weldian notion that mutilation was progress, than we could stop the malignant cells from metastasizing through Marian's blood stream.[88]

Everything is at war in the place he has tried to make a home. There is no escape from history. The book culminates in a bloody final scene that is exceptionally vivid to the point that it is on the border of the fantastic.[89] At least one reader thought it was fitting, writing that it was "like a progression of chords whose notes are so right and unanticipated that you shiver."[90] Marian has told Debby goodbye and is headed with Joe and her husband to the hospital to die. They drive up a steep hill and are stopped due to the impromptu meeting of Peck returning to move his things, the now pregnant Julie LoPresti on her horse, and Dave Weld on his father's tractor. Joe stops on the hill and taps his horn, and Peck revs his motorcycle in response, planning to move out of the way. This spooks the horse. The horse rears up, and in the chaos, plunges its legs through the cattle guard at the top of the hill. This is a gruesome scene, with several of the horse's legs being broken—two of them broken off—a furious chaos, blood everywhere. John Catlin is the only one who can think in the moment and kills the horse with a sledgehammer before returning to the car to escort his wife to the hospital where she will die of cancer.

Joe is back where he started—Peck is gone, as is Marian. He is left with Ruth and his thoughts, attempting to make sense out of the world. It is a bleak ending. Marian dies "with John hanging to one of her hands and a nurse to another and the room full of her mindless screaming" and her baby is born a "blob of blue flesh that moved a little, and bleated weakly, and died."[91] Joe cannot accept Marian's affirmation of the goodness of life in the face of the evil she has had to endure, and that he has had to witness. He is "not reconciled." But this is not simply Joe playing Candide to Marian's Pangloss, and it does not mean he has not changed:

> She taught me the stupidity of the attempt to withdraw and be free of trouble and harm. That was as foolish as Peck's version of *ahimsa* and the states of instant nirvana he thought he reached ... by noise [etc.].... One is not made pure by ... retiring from the treadmill.... I disliked Peck because of his addiction to the irrational, and I still do; but what made him hard for me to bear was my own foolishness made manifest in him. There is no way to step off the treadmill. It is all treadmill.[92]

Joe-as-Prospero must return to Milan, absent his magical cloak and wand, reconciled to life where every third thought will be of death.

Joe-as-Candide must return from his gardens. History cannot be escaped and, as dehumanizing as the forces of modernity are, escape is worse.

But Joe does not consider this to be a failure. He ends the story reflecting on the forces of life they discussed in their first conversation: "One of the things that's in whale's milk is the promise of pain and death." But he asks himself: "Would I forgo the pleasure of her company to escape the bleakness of her loss? Would I go back to my own formula, which was twilight sleep, to evade the pain she brought with her?" The last sentence of the book answers his question: "I shall be richer all my life for this sorrow."[93]

It was admittedly a dark book.[94] In the end, one reading is that Stegner staged the conflicts in his novel to suggest that people like Marian were caught in a crossfire, collateral damage in the bitter war between two hostile and blameworthy generations. Though Marian has a loving husband and a caring friend to accompany her to the hospital, and another responsible friend to watch her child in their absence, she still dies in a place where she will not be remembered. Her husband and a couple she has known for only a few months, however intense these months of friendship have been, do not a community make. This is a suburban tragedy. It is a painful and unremembered death in a formless non-community.

Reader Responses: "Reverence for Life"

While there were more letters from parents who were relieved to have Joe help them work through their conflicts with their children, there were also a substantial number of letters from those who were moved by Marian's life and death and her effect on Joe. One came from Kirk Bundy of Palo Alto, a twenty-two-year-old graduate student in engineering who was introduced to the book by his wife. Bundy wrote that she "finished reading your book at about 3 AM one morning and came in to wake me up, hold me, and say that <u>Live Things</u> 'tore her guts out.' I was rather surprised since I've never been awakened at such a time except in emergencies or else to receive very bad news" [underlining original]. Bundy then read the book himself. Despite considering himself "fairly reserved emotionally," he found himself in tears after finishing the book: "I have never cried over a book before." The existential questions raised by Marian's death and the "reverence for life oozing from the pages" were thrown into his "consciousness with the force of a jackhammer." The book had "given me or rather evoked from me a new sense of the importance of life—breathing, biological life," he concluded.[95]

Rebecca Olsen, a younger reader from Salt Lake City, Utah, wrote to Stegner in 1987 after having read the book for the first time in 1982:

> My own mother died when I was 18 (I find no parallels with specific characters). In a meaningful way, your story reassures me. I am a thirty-four-year-old high school social studies teacher. I get awards and function alright, rather mentally fit on the outside, I think, but I feel like I can't "get over" losing my mother. Your book helps me accept what feels like an emotional inadequacy.... Thank you; not for "lessons of life," but for putting into words part of the human pain that I seem to be overwhelmed with.... Whatever you meant to say, I was deeply touched.[96]

Another reader from the 1980s, Nina Miller, writing of a book she had read "many years ago," described *Live Things* as a living presence in her life: "I was then a relatively young mother who had lost my own mother as a teenager. The book moved me so deeply that I woke weeping for weeks after I finished it. I think of everything I have ever read that book squeezed itself around and into my life more than any other." After praising other Stegner books, she continued: "Please share with that crotchety-but-tender narrator who is the voice in my very favorite Stegner novels that he has changed my way of seeing the world, and that I will carry him in my affections always."[97]

Conclusion

Since *Live Things* was published in 1967, it has faded into the middle third tier of Stegner's oeuvre; unlike several of his other books that have been reprinted as recently as 2018, *Live Things* has not been reprinted since 1991. On the surface, it is most historically significant now as the novel

Dear Mr. Stegner,

All the Little Live Things has been a double-fisted experience for me, and has caused me to write you this letter.

I first read the book when it was new. I didn't think much of it at the time, being a sort of female Jim Peck, myself. I found the author stuffy, tense and typical of the folks on the other side of the generation gap. I thought Joe Allston a fool for failing to appreciate the arrival in his woods of a cosmic creature. I found the novel a perfect blueprint of the pitiful manifestations of the middle class mind.

Now I am thirty-two years old and am taking the first college course I've taken in fourteen years ("Literature and Values," ENG 160 at Diablo Valley College), in which All the Little Live Things is a required text. What, that old chestnut?!, I cried. However, determined to get an A in the course, I set about re-reading the book carefully.

As Mark Twain (sort of) put it, it was amazing how much the old man had learned. I found myself agreeing with nearly everything Joe Allston thought and said, found myself crabby with Marian's love of everything in nature from weeds to weasels, found myself bitterly critical of Jim Peck and his lot. What transformation a few years hath wrought.

Anyway, I'm writing to tell you two things. First, I think you're a delight, a treasure, a sparkle, a literary treat, and I thank you very much for this book, especially the second time around. Second, as I worked on a mailing list in my office yesterday, I came across a Julie Peck living in Brisbane. Do you suppose Jim finally did the Right Thing?

Jody

Jody Johnson

P.S. So far, I am getting that A.

Figure 5. Letter from Jody Johnson, 1982. This letter from one of Stegner's readers captures humorously the generational conflict that kept *All the Little Live Things* in readers' minds. Courtesy Special Collections, J. Willard Marriott Library, University of Utah.

that made possible his award-winning novels from the 1970s. Its present status obscures, however, the ways that this book touched a nerve for Stegner's readers at the time and even through the 1980s. Some of the most poignant letters from his readers in relation to all of his books were written in response to *Live Things*.

This is the assessment of Stegner himself in his conversations with Richard Etulain and one that is also corroborated in the archives.[98] Even if *Live Things* was not a bestseller or a book that seems likely to survive the "slaughterhouse of literature," it did serve as a meaningful touchstone for a certain subset of readers.[99] This re-examination of it reveals ways of reckoning with the 1960s that have received less attention than the more dramatic moments that demand interpretation in most histories of the 1960s. The numerous letters—and many were from California—reveal the confusions and everyday family struggles of the 1960s.[100] They suggest a more ambivalent 1960s; Stegner's novel and the letters it inspired are a reminder that not everyone was able to choose sides and that some people were just confused, saddened, and left adrift by that momentous decade's events. Some people were torn apart by the personal and the political.[101]

The presence of the generation gap was and remains significant in both public memory and the historiography of the 1960s.[102] But *Live Things* and responses to it reveal a complexity and poignancy to this division that is less easily shunted into the shouting match between obtuse parents and alienated youths that it can so easily become. Further, *Live Things* marked a significant turning point in Stegner's moral and intellectual life. It records some of his most intense efforts to come to terms with the suburbs of Palo Alto and the new postwar West that seemed—in contrast to the Palo Alto he encountered when he moved there in 1945—to be developing along more permanent and unalterable tracks. With his choice to use as his protagonist and narrator Joe Allston, a retired literary agent and amateur birdwatcher, Stegner was allowing himself to look at the California he had helped create as a place in which he had an increasingly diminished stake. Through Allston he can only watch and comment; whether he is heard meaningfully is out of his control. A birdwatcher, he cannot build or shape. He can only observe with admiration, hope, curiosity, sadness, fear, disgust.

Since the latter three emotions tended to dominate Joe's series of observations, the book was also perhaps a way of coming to terms with the fact that the place he chose and that he had hoped to build had become dissatisfying to him, and that his life's work to build "a society to match the scenery" in California was likely to die out.[103] Joe is the first

Stegner protagonist of several who was situated in an "amputated present" and without a meaningful connection to either the past or the future.
In creating this character, Stegner set out a series of themes that would
guide most of his later work, including his Pulitzer Prize–winning *Angle
of Repose.*

Chapter 4

The Amputated Present

Strange memories on this nervous night in Las Vegas. Five years later? Six? It seems like a lifetime, or at least a Main Era—the kind of peak that never comes again. San Francisco in the middle sixties was a very special time and place to be a part of.... You could strike sparks anywhere. There was a fantastic universal sense that whatever we were doing was right, that we were winning.... And that, I think, was the handle—that sense of inevitable victory over the forces of Old and Evil.... We had all the momentum; we were riding the crest of a high and beautiful wave.... So now, less than five years later, you can go up on a steep hill in Las Vegas and look West, and with the right kind of eyes you can almost see the high-water mark—that place where the wave finally broke and rolled back.

—Hunter S. Thompson[1]

In my mind I write letters to the newspapers, saying Dear Editor, As a modern man and a one-legged man, I can tell you that the conditions are similar. We have been cut off, the past has been ended and the family has broken up and the present is adrift in its wheelchair. I had a wife who after twenty-five years of marriage took on the coloration of the 1960s. I have a son who, though we are affectionate with each other, is no more my true son than if he breathed through gills. That is no gap between the generations, that is a gulf.... My grandparents had to live their way out of one world and into another, or into several others, making new out of old the way corals live their reef upward. I am on my grandparents' side. I believe in Time, as they did, and in the life chronological rather than in the life existential. We live in time and through it, we build our huts in its ruins, or used to, and we cannot afford all these abandonings. And so on. The letters fade like conversation.

—Wallace Stegner[2]

Based on sales rankings, American readers have more often ventured back to the San Francisco Peninsula of the 1960s with Hunter S. Thompson's Raoul Duke from his hotel room scented with fresh weed-LSD-ether-mescaline layered over stale Marlboros in Las Vegas than with Wallace Stegner's Lyman Ward from the porch of the elegantly rustic Zodiac Cottage in semirural Grass Valley, California.[3] Both fictional observers drift in their imaginations across the Bay through a haze of regret, but for much different reasons. Raoul Duke saw the energy, hope, and promise of his generation collapsing from Woodstock to Altamont, from the Human Be-In to the Manson Family, from Birmingham to Watts, from Kennedy to Nixon. Lyman Ward just saw the decisive shifts of the decade as the eruption of a massive "gulf," a break from the past so decisive that it is better imagined as an amputation rather than a scar.[4]

Stegner bestowed his narrator, Lyman Ward, with sophisticated training that none of his other narrators possessed, and Lyman decisively shapes the ideas that Stegner explored in *Angle of Repose* (1971), the book that remains his most prominent. It is two stories woven into one. The first is set in Stegner's present-day California with Lyman as protagonist, and the other in various locations throughout the West of the 1870s–1890s, with Lyman's grandmother being the protagonist. With skill, Stegner works his way back and forth between these two worlds, but not primarily because he was meditating on the mysteries of form. It was time, the passage of time, and the interconnections of past and present that he wanted to explore, and that demanded this form for his novel.

Angle of Repose was Stegner's response to a public challenge he posed in "History, Myth, and the Western Writer," an essay published first in *American West* magazine in May 1967, and later republished in his first essay collection, *The Sound of Mountain Water* (1969).[5] In a concise review of the strange career of the Western in relation to attempts to write work of lasting literary quality in the West—western literature rather than Westerns—Stegner lamented the "amputated Present" that westerners inhabited.[6] "One of the lacks," Stegner wrote, "through all the newly swarming regions of the West, is that millions of westerners, old and new, have no sense of a personal and *possessed* past, no sense of any continuity between the real western past which has been mythicized almost out of recognizability and a real western present that seems as cut-off and pointless as a ride on a merry-go-round that can't be stopped" (italics original).

Stegner allowed that some might prefer to lose themselves in a "strident present," whether in Haight-Ashbury or in "an office in Denver or Dallas." Stegner hoped, however, that some western writer might discover a "historical continuity comparable to that which Faulkner traced from Ikkemotubbe the Chickasaw to Montgomery Ward Snopes." A Faulkner for the West? Stegner must have already had confidence that *Angle of Repose* was going to work: "Maybe it isn't possible, but I wish someone would try. I might even try myself."

In a sign of goodwill to his fellow westerners, Stegner ended the essay with a lariat. He believed in another alternative besides a past hidden by nostalgia combined with disgust for the present or an obliterated past overcome by a pulsing, consumerist present: "In the old days, in blizzardy weather, we used to tie a string of lariats from house to barn so as to make it from shelter to responsibility and back again. With personal, family, and cultural chores to do, I think we had better rig up such a line between past and present."[7]

Lyman Ward shares several similarities with Joe Allston of *Live Things*. Both are old enough to be curmudgeons, with Lyman being fifty-eight but seemingly older, and Joe in his sixties.[8] They are capable of "virtuoso grumblings," as one of Stegner's readers put it.[9] Lyman, for example, mutters to himself midconversation with his would-be hippie research assistant: "It happens that I despise the locution 'having sex,' which describes something a good deal more mechanical than making love and a good deal less fun than fucking."[10] Both are intelligent ruminators with discriminating tastes, and both are more emotionally sensitive than they are willing to acknowledge. They hold to similarly masculine, western stoic codes of honor, and both are gnawed by guilt and prone to almost secretly mystical reverence for nature.[11] Both have retreated to homes in semirural California and would likely enjoy riffing off each other about the damn hippies and the California counterculture that they observe from their semirural villas.

Judged by the letters Stegner received, many readers seemed to just meld the narrators together and think of them as thinly veiled versions of Stegner himself. This tendency annoyed Stegner, but the similarities that united him with these two cranky narrators are enough that he could hardly blame readers for not bothering to untangle the differences between Joe, Lyman, and himself.[12] There are significant differences between the two narrators, however, even if these are generally overwhelmed by the similarities. Where Joe is healthy and fit for his age, Lyman has been recently disabled by a debilitating bone disease that immobilized his neck and required the amputation of his right leg. Joe's marriage to Ruth is tested and strained, but generally loving and committed, and Lyman has just recently been divorced.

Most significant, though, are the differences between their respective families. Joe is born into poverty and unacquainted with any of his ancestors except his mother. His son is recently deceased but had been estranged from his parents—in Joe's account—for most of his life. The Allstons' home is one that they bought themselves in order to escape their past and was selected for its present charms alone. Lyman, on the other hand, is born into wealth and has also recently moved to a new house, but it is one "whose air is thick with the past."[13] Though Lyman's relationship with his father was complicated and his mother died when he was young, the house he inhabits was the home of the grandparents who took primary responsibility for raising him, both of whom he loved and respected. Lyman's relationship to his own son is affectionate but distant. In sum: though not as decisively pastless and futureless as Joe Allston, Lyman Ward is similarly adrift and straddling the tension between his desired form of withdrawal and a sense of obligation that seemingly demands a slow crawl back into the forms of belonging and the responsibilities still open to him.

There are other differences. Lyman is trained in a scholarly vocation, where Joe portrays his career as a literary agent as one that he took for pecuniary reasons exclusively. Lyman is imagined as not just a historian, but a Bancroft Prize–winning historian—"Coe Professor of History, Emeritus" at the University of California at Berkeley—whose scholarly habits are a crucial feature of the novel.[14] The training and skillset of his narrator allowed Stegner to experiment with layers of complexity that he was unable to achieve with Joe as his narrator. So while Lyman's story in the novel is, like Joe's, more revelation than plot, Stegner also embedded a plot-driven account of Lyman's historical exploration of his grandparents' adventurous lives into the novel as well. Lyman is comfortably retired and takes on his project with scholarly rigor but open-ended goals for its results. Readers are informed that Lyman eventually finds himself writing a novel rather than a history, and that he is doing so by recording his organized but still extemporaneous thoughts into a tape recorder which will then be transcribed.[15] Readers of *Angle of Repose* are ostensibly "hearing" Lyman's ruminations on the present interspersed with his rough draft of history as it reacts with and against memory and eventually becomes something closer to historical fiction.[16]

Having explored his own relationship to California as a newcomer with no past as Joe Allston, the creation of Lyman Ward as narrator gave Stegner the opportunity to think about California on a longer generational scale. He found it necessary to "borrow" one family's recorded past in order to build a fictional one that would be compelling. This choice to borrow a past would help him write what remains his most well-known book, a Pulitzer Prize winner.[17] This choice was also, however, the source of a controversy that has cast a pall over his literary reputation and status as the moral exemplar and "uber-citizen" of the West from his generation.[18]

Stegner's creation of the Ward family was built on his extensive research into the life of Mary Hallock Foote, a writer and illustrator who lived from 1847–1938. With her husband, Arthur De Wint Foote (1849–1933), an engineer who worked in mining and irrigation, Mary traveled across the West and from the 1870s to the 1890s lived in places as cosmopolitan as San Francisco and as remote as Leadville, Colorado. She wrote and illustrated as she went and was published regularly by one of the nation's premier periodicals at that time, *The Century*. Over the course of her life, she also wrote twelve novels and a memoir.

While the novel is filtered through Lyman's eyes, Stegner went to great lengths to see the West of the 1870s–1890s through Foote's eyes as well, and the novel should be read as the triangulation of Stegner's own vision filtered through the invented characters of both his narrator and his historical protagonist. Foote's life and work were well suited for an exploration of the issues that Stegner most wanted to think about regarding community, mobility, family, and place in the American West.

Like Stegner himself, his beloved mother, Hilda, and her fictional counterpart Elsa Mason in *Big Rock Candy Mountain*, Foote wanted to settle her family and begin building community in a place.[19] Like Stegner, Foote was a prolific and disciplined writer who wrestled with the strange dynamics of class, prestige, publication, and aesthetics on an East-West axis. Both were confident believers in the power of learning and immersion in cultural experiences, and sometimes disdainful of their western counterparts for their deficient cultural and intellectual sophistication, or at least for their lack of respect for formal learning. Neither were completely at home in the eastern literary centers of cultural power.

Each was simultaneously alienated by and a defender of what they perceived to be the cultural establishments of their time—though marginal, neither one could simply reject and stand superior to the cultural powers without rejecting crucial elements of their own aesthetic and intellectual commitments. By middle age, both Foote and Stegner found themselves straddling both West and East from California, where each eventually spent much of their adult lives. Further, Foote and Stegner shared a commitment to a nonsectarian but firm humanistic moral framework that made them seem stodgier than many of their contemporaries.

Finally, and crucially for later critics, Foote was a Victorian woman and Stegner a midcentury American man. Foote's life, then, was similar enough to Stegner's to spark recognitions and insights, but different enough that it allowed him to test his ideas and theories in a new context and with characters that he thought might add nuance to issues that he had already explored. Whether he had a right to explore his ideas through Foote's eyes in the ways that he did is still in dispute.

The controversy that erupted in western literary circles following the revelation that Stegner copied whole paragraphs from Foote's then-unpublished memoir and yet-unpublished letters still smolders, even if it is less passionately debated than it was from the late 1970s to early 2000s.[20] From the distance of nearly fifty years since it was published, the way that the controversy grew and the conversations it raised are so consistent with the themes of *Angle of Repose* itself that the irony is almost comic.[21] These ironies will be explored at the end of the chapter following my analysis of the book in relation to my primary focus on the themes of attachment, place, community, and time. *Angle of Repose* united more of the themes of Stegner's career in the mode of thought that most intrigued him, the novel, at the height of his power as a novelist and at a historical moment and place—the San Francisco Bay Area in the late 1960s and early 1970s—that was making local, national, and international history. Stegner's choice of a historian as his narrator allowed him to make an implicit and even imaginative argument about the study of the past and, more importantly, the value of a personal and possessed past.

Neither Lyman nor his Victorian grandmother were obvious choices for being raised as heroes in 1971, but Stegner seems to be arguing that a crippled and honest but broken and flawed historian and a prudish but courageous and persistent Victorian writer and illustrator were exactly the heroes that the 1970s might find necessary. Why did Stegner think it was important to look at his moment and Mary Hallock Foote's past through the eyes of a cranky, disaffected historian settled in an old estate in semirural Grass Valley, California? What did this character in that place help him see about the western past and its entanglements with the western present?

"The humanness of faces lost in time"

Stegner establishes Lyman Ward as a curmudgeon with the first sentence of the book: "Now I believe they will leave me alone."[22] Readers familiar with Joe Allston will immediately note that Stegner has returned to the theme of withdrawal and escape. Lyman has recently relocated with his library to his ancestral home in Grass Valley after arranging for its renovation and the accommodations making it possible for him to live there in his wheelchair. Also like *Live Things*, the book begins with a rumination that serves as a hypothesis of sorts for the rest of the book. Lyman is confident that his family history has something to teach him, but he is not sure what form the new knowledge will take or what it will require of him. It is framed as an escape from the present, but Lyman seems too honest and too intelligent to really believe himself when he says that.

True to his training as a historian, Lyman locates himself on the first page: "So tonight I can sit here with the tape recorder whirring no more noisily than electrified time, and say into the microphone the place and date of a sort of beginning and a sort of return: Zodiac Cottage, Grass Valley, California, April 12, 1970."[23] Lyman quite self-consciously tells the reader (listener, if strictly submitting to the framing device of the novel) that he is imagining his way into his grandparents' past for the purpose of escape from his present circumstances: "I'd like to live in their clothes for a while, if only so I don't have to live in my own."[24] Having "no future of [his] own" Lyman wants to see his grandparents' future as they saw it coming in real time, absent the distortions of what Lyman calls the "Doppler Effect of history." In Lyman's application of the scientific principle, the sound of an object moving towards an observer (a train, for example) is pitched higher than one going away, and, using his imaginative historical reconstructions, Lyman wants to "hear" history moving towards his grandparents rather than away from them.[25]

He allows that he is on an as-yet-undefined pilgrimage of sorts as well. He believes he can learn something meaningful from his grandparents. Professional historian that he is, he is on an existential mission and Stegner highlights the way that Lyman is driven by a vague but persistent "anguished question."[26] Having won his Bancroft and retired, he is under no pressure to write for anyone but himself and those who will hear him on his own terms. This search into the past is one that allows for wallowing, immersion, and selection at whim, even if it is also well organized into files and boxes and attentive to chronology. Stegner also makes it clear that, after a career dedicated to careful study, Lyman will not flinch from uncovering difficult truths once the parameters of the pilgrimage have been properly established.

Lyman is not committed to any kind of comprehensive history, and he does not know exactly what he hopes to learn in his immersion into the past of his grandparents, but he does have firm commitments regarding the value of the past, memory, and history. In contrast with Rodman, his patronizing sociologist son who sees Lyman's historical work as a merely antiquarian hobby for amusement rather than a potential source of revelation, Lyman believes in the value of history: "I can look in any direction by turning my wheelchair, and I choose to look back. Rodman to the contrary notwithstanding, that is the only direction we can learn from."[27] Lyman believes in the "life chronological" over the "life existential," and this commitment does not waver. He is committed to measuring himself and unsettling himself and his historical moment through his study of the past.

In what is undoubtedly an inside joke for his fellow writers, Stegner populates Lyman's study with a gun that is described in the first chapter. It does not go off in the second chapter or even by the end of the book, as Chekhov's famous dictum would demand. But it is not entirely irrelevant, as it is one of the objects Stegner uses to evoke the persistence of the past in the present throughout the book.[28] The gun hangs with a pair of spurs and a bowie knife in accord with the arrangement of his grandmother's that Lyman remembered from his childhood in her office. These items are totems that represent his grandfather, Oliver Ward (the fictional counterpart to Arthur De Wint Foote).

The rest of the office and his reflections on the past are shaped primarily by his grandmother, Susan Burling Ward (the fictional counterpart to Mary Hallock Foote). Her portrait hangs on the wall with framed letters from her correspondents, who ranged from Mark Twain to Henry Wadsworth Longfellow to Grover Cleveland.[29] These totems suggest the loyalties of the couple well. Lyman loses himself happily in the files each day and attends to his own needs by force of habit. Like Joe Allston, Lyman is wealthy enough to spend his retirement time in a semirural cottage in order to ruminate, but Lyman is more disciplined in his study and more thoroughly engaged by his stated objectives. Lyman's objectives are also pragmatic: in addition to escaping his present and attempting to learn from the past, he is also attempting to prove to his son Rodman that he is capable of living on his own. He does not want to be "led away to the old folks' pasture" at the retirement home in Menlo Park.[30]

Again, seemingly in reaction to his time at the Stanford CASBS, Stegner includes some criticism of the discipline of sociology. Lyman defines his approach to the past against his son Rodman and the crass quantitative form of sociology that he represents from the beginning of the novel. Stegner also introduces another young person into the story who allows Lyman to defend his commitments more humorously and vigorously. Where Rodman is patronizing, Shelly Rasmussen, the assistant Lyman hires to help him organize his files and to assist him with physical demands he cannot address on his own, is genuinely curious about Lyman's project, even if sometimes merely for her own amusement rather than for Lyman's lofty purposes. Rodman is a lost cause, but Shelly is a potential convert to Lyman's conception of a personal and possessed past. Her father is Lyman's property caretaker and her mother is Lyman's personal assistant, nurse, and confidante. By working for Lyman, Shelly becomes the third generation from her family to work for the Wards, and Lyman finds it appropriate that someone with a shared history of the place would become his research assistant.

But there are wrinkles. Shelly is at home hiding from her estranged "husband," a hippie that is her husband only for her parents and might as well be Jim Peck a few years removed from his experiences in the formless non-community depicted in *Live Things*.[31] Shelly is unthreatened by Lyman and brings her own set of questions for him, which Stegner depicts as alternately marked by playful teasing and honest curiosity.

Lyman finds himself, more than he had planned, explaining his methods and moral commitments to her throughout the novel. It is in part Shelly's inability to conceive of the past as real or significant that compels Lyman to even greater efforts to find the "humanness of faces lost in time" in the local and family history he studies. Lyman is interested in reconstructing persons who are recognizable as persons.[32] This is how he (and Stegner, especially in *Wolf Willow*) begins his search for a possessed past. Lyman knows that this is an imaginative process and one that requires diligence, curiosity, emotional range, empathy, and the capacity to perceive both continuity and change.

Rodman is more interested in history as entertainment. He wishes that Lyman would study "somebody interesting" like Lola Montez (1818–1861), the courtesan, dancer, and mistress of Ludwig I of Bavaria, as well as the most famous former inhabitant of Grass Valley.[33] (Given the themes of the book and the narrator's profession, it is surprising that Lyman never mentions the philosopher Josiah Royce—Stegner had read Josiah Royce and quoted him in *Wolf Willow*, published about a decade before *Angle of Repose*).[34]

Unlike Montez, whose "poor little gravel" has been "panned" by every "fourth-rate antiquarian in the West," Oliver and Susan are a "deep vein that has never been dug" and, more importantly, "they were *people*" [italics original].[35] While it is possible to view this as a degrading evaluation of Montez and her personhood, it can also highlight the ways in which accounts of the western past, whether fictional or historical, were, to Stegner's disappointment, obsessed with the more adventurous "local color" stories. Attempts to understand the western past had not been subjected instead to serious analysis about what kind of society was being formed there, and what kinds of long-term cultural, social, and political infrastructures were being built.[36] The West into which *Angle of Repose* was born was overshadowed by "regeneration through violence" stories, whether for the purpose of celebration or condemnation.[37]

Exile in the "Brutal West"

The first third (or so) of the book is expository. Readers are introduced to Lyman's theories of history, time, and place, and they are introduced to Oliver and Susan and a cast of minor characters. Lyman describes the early relationship that develops between Susan and Oliver and the gradual re-establishment of her relationship to Augusta and Thomas Hudson, the two people who share her deepest thoughts and who serve as her living embodiments of "the best that has been thought and said" in the Matthew Arnold Victorian ideal. Augusta and Thomas Hudson are characters built on the real historical figures of Helena de Kay and Richard Watson Gilder. Mary Hallock Foote maintained an extensive and nearly lifelong correspondence with Helena, and these letters were the most substantial feature of Stegner's research base (and the chief source of the controversy, as he copied the unpublished letters in paragraph-length sections with minimal changes in the text of *Angle of Repose*). Most of Lyman's insights come through the letters, which he reads and organizes throughout the novel.

Lyman portrays a genuine romance between Susan and Oliver, but one that is also marked by reservations on Susan's part that are even at times affirmed as legitimate by Oliver. Oliver is completely devoted and sees Susan through the same rose tints that filter Susan's vision of Augusta and Thomas. Oliver impresses but exasperates Susan. In their early years of marriage, she is more often impressed, but when exasperated, she lapses into evaluations of Oliver through the lenses of Augusta and Thomas. The Hudsons think Oliver has exiled her from her home, vocation, and cultural peers, and are incapable of seeing his work as being comparable to their own and to Susan's.[38] He is impressive in his own way but, nonetheless, forever a class below them. According to an old woman who serves a brief but prophetic role in the book, Oliver is "not a type [Susan was] trained to understand."[39]

A second major theme of the first third of the novel is Susan's reckoning with the new self she is becoming based on her residence in the West. Oliver has become western, but Susan still conceives of herself as someone on a temporary visit. She is not going west to a home but enjoying scenery and local color; she is essentially a tourist.[40] Her experiences are stories for her friends from elsewhere and they are to be interpreted on their terms. Observing a "Chinaman" working, one among many nameless others that inhabit Susan's world, Susan is incapable of any affection; in Lyman's description of her reaction: "The people here were not people. Except for Oliver, she was alone and in exile, and her heart was back where the sun rose."[41] With time, however, and in Lyman's description, imperceptibly, Susan changes more than she realizes.[42] Her demeaning assessments of her fellow inhabitants of the West are eventually challenged, and she also cannot prevent a change in her own sense of self.

In one instance, Oliver brings home a well-educated Austrian engineer who is conversant in art and aesthetics and who praises Susan's prints. He is a proponent of American regionalism and argues that American art can only be great if it deals with native subjects and places. The conversation is rejuvenating to Susan, and Lyman reports that "Grandmother had her identity back, having had the baron to reflect it for an evening."[43] But this reaffirmation of her identity that takes place in the West is shaken upon her return home to Milton, New York. After Susan returns to Milton and meets an old friend, "a wash of confused feeling went over her like wind across a sweating skin, for the identity that [her friend] took for granted and talked to and reflected back at her was not the identity it used to be, not the one that had signed all her past drawings, not the one she knew herself. Then what was it now? She didn't know."[44]

By the middle of Stegner's book, Lyman's Susan is strange to herself. What past will she be able to retain, and what present and likely future would she allow to be grafted into her sense of self? More, what *should* she retain, and what *should* she graft? How much does identity depend on place? What obligations does a person have to attempt to belong in a new place? What obligations to old places remain in effect for a person in a new place? Lyman clearly loves his grandmother and is sympathetic to her plight, but he is also not afraid to judge her choices and wish she might have done things differently. Her strangeness to herself is exacerbated by a life that demanded "constant uprootings and new exiles in raw unformed places, among people she tried to like but couldn't quite be interested in."[45]

Were the uprootings worth it? What would make them worthwhile? These are all questions that Stegner personally grappled with. Of course, he was also keenly aware that these were common struggles for many inhabitants of the West caught up in the migratory patterns of the twentieth century. In *Angle of Repose* he suggests that both the professionalized discipline of history and the personal, unprofessional work of memory that he explored in *Wolf Willow* are effective means for reconciling or at least addressing the tensions of selfhood by those westerners who found themselves drifting in and out of formless non-communities.

Stegner presents this struggle of identity and attachment as a form of testing, and a form of testing made more intense by the exceptional characteristics of the western landscape.[46] In her ride by horse-drawn carriage over a mountain pass into Leadville, Oliver and Susan are nearly run off a cliff by a stagecoach careening carelessly around the mountain pass. With a callous disregard grounded in a determination to save their lives, Oliver lashes the horses and manages to save himself and Susan. Two horses die due to altitude sickness on the rest of their journey. Susan is horrified by the "brutal West" exposed by Oliver's wearing out of the horses and heroic efforts to save their lives on the trip to Leadville, and writes,

> The mountains of the Great Divide are not, as everyone knows, born treeless, though we always think of them as above timberline with the eternal snow on their heads. They wade up through ancient forests and plunge into canyons tangled up with watercourses and pause in little gemlike valleys and march attended by loud winds across high plateaus, but all such incidents of the lower world they leave behind them when they begin to strip for the skies: like the Holy Ones of old, they go up alone and barren of all circumstance to meet their transfiguration.

Lyman interprets this passage as something more revealing: "I can't help reading that as more than a literary flourish; I want to read it as a perception of Western necessity, something deeper than scenery. Something must have told her, as they dragged over the summit and down to English George's, that character as well as mountains had to strip for the skies."[47] It is reminiscent of Stegner's account of Rusty's undoing in the brutal Saskatchewan winter in *Wolf Willow*, where he is stripped of all his preconceived notions of himself and tested to the point of his life.

"How marvelously free they are! How unutterably deprived!"

Another crucial shift develops by the middle of the book. Lyman's exploration of his grandparents increasingly becomes a project that is worked out in conversation with Shelly, rather than only a personal quest. In his interviews with Richard Etulain, Stegner noted that this element of the book was planned at least partly to tell a story about a different era in a way that made it possible for the uninitiated to see the continuities more clearly. When contemplating whether he would try to write a biography of Mary Hallock Foote or turn to fiction instead, his decision to write a novel was based in part on his sense that a traditional biography would not give him enough leeway to defend his subject and reveal the "humanness" of her face to a generation who would more likely find her merely amusing.[48] Shelly is, therefore, the devil's advocate Stegner needed in order to put the complexities of such differences in a more palatable and humorous form. It was a form that allowed the past to challenge the present, rather than merely vice versa. For Stegner, the historian at work was heroic in the 1970s, living as many did in the wake of the mantra not to trust anyone over thirty, and committed to Ram Dass's contemporaneous mantra, "Be here now."[49]

Where the first section of the book is filled with delightful hope and playful romance, even if interspersed with disappointments and occasional flashes of terror, the second half is marked by foreboding and doom. But the crucial move Stegner makes in this section is to look at the downfall of a marriage under a Victorian culture compared with the downfall of two modern relationships. This contrast is explored in the context of a Victorian accidental commune and a modern intentional one.

Lyman describes Shelly as a "card-carrying member of this liberated generation." Professor at Berkeley that he was, Lyman is not uninitiated and not surprised, but is nonetheless concerned "about the state of mind that holds nothing worth the respect of unhumorous suspended judgment."[50] Lyman's conversations with Shelly circle around similar issues as did Joe Allston's conversations with Jim Peck and his recalled conversations with Curtis. Because they are actually conversations rather than tense exchanges, they also recall Joe's conversations with Marian Catlin.

Juxtaposed with the conversations he staged between Joe and Marian in a book published only four years previously, the new variation on this theme seems even more poignant and even slightly pitiful. Was Stegner staging these conversations in fiction because they failed to occur in real life? Or were they just so prevalent that Stegner wanted to get them into fiction to test them and place them in an imaginative context?

Lyman begins to worry that Shelly is not just acting as his research assistant but is actually starting to study him. She has appointed herself his "confidential adviser, keeper, critic, teaching assistant, and lay psychiatrist."[51] Having decided that he is writing a novel rather than a history, Lyman includes some elements of his ancestors' sexual life. After a scene in Leadville, Lyman describes Susan and Oliver in sexual foreplay before "turning off the light" and moving on, but Shelly challenges this depiction after she has finished transcribing it. Lyman argues back to Shelly that, despite the fact that he is writing a novel, he is trying to be true to the people of the era and what they would have thought. Shelly is not satisfied and wants Lyman to explore all the "artificial restraints" and "hangups" that prevented the Victorians from expressing their sexuality more freely. She says that it is Lyman's inhibitions that are showing more than his ancestors' and that he should be more honest: "People nowadays understand things, they can sniff out the dishonesty when somebody tries to cover something up or leave it to the imagination. How would it be if every modern novel did it like Paolo and Francesca—'That day they read no more'?"

Lyman replies, "'O.K., so I haven't fooled you with my dishonest methods. . . . Just leave me there with old hypocritical Dante.'"[52] Shelly is glad to have the debate: "Earnest and pleased with herself, her brow bent against error, her lips touched with a live coal, she sat on my floor there and did her best to bring me into the twentieth century."[53] She asks Lyman what he would think about a gang bang she witnessed, where the participants were "just doing their thing, what they felt." Shelly sees it as "natural," just like a "Living Theater or something."[54] Bringing "old hypocritical Dante" back into the conversation, Lyman says that he thinks she is "describing a kind of hell. . . . You're talking about people who have become sub-human. Sub-mammal . . . I think our sickness has gone so far we aren't even sure it's sickness."[55]

Once Lyman is able to turn the conversation back to his preferred themes, Shelly asks why Susan was so disappointed to be traveling the West and so worried about making a home in it: "'What would be the matter with traveling around? When Larry [Shelly's hippie boyfriend] and I were hitching, I loved it. . . . I don't dig these home bodies.'" Lyman asks her why, if they loved traveling so much, they are not still on the road (or, implicitly, even still together as a couple). In what is probably the worst low blow Stegner imposes on one of his hippie characters, he writes

Shelly's humorous and unintentionally ironic reply: "'It did get a little hairy, sleeping in the washrooms of Canadian tourist parks in the rain. But I'd do it again. I mean, you're never that free again.'"[56]

It is significant that Stegner turns Lyman back to place after his discussion of sexuality, as these were clearly linked in Stegner's mind. As much as he was concerned with place and community, he was also concerned with sex; in Eric Bennett's accurate but overly cute summary of Stegner's oeuvre: "Never before had a novelist put his disinclination to philander on display with such intensity and pathos. He wrote at length about not sleeping with people."[57]

Stegner's choice not to write about sex (or, more specifically, to write about not having sex) was a considered choice that he defended on several occasions, including in his letters: "My reasons may be puritanical, and if they are I will have to accept the term. But they are also somewhat aesthetic. Sex as a direct and openly treated subject tends to become exclusive; it crowds out all other aspects of a character and all other interests that a reader might have."[58] Rather than a focus on the western "id," Stegner wanted to explore the western ego. William Bevis writes that Stegner "intended a moral vision; his public speech, his civic style were suited to exploration of the conscience, not of the unconscious, of conduct we can choose. What we can choose matters, his prose says in fiction, essay, history."[59]

From these unwelcome digressions, Lyman returns to Susan on a visit back to her hometown of Milton, New York, from Leadville, where Oliver has stayed to work on his mine. Milton offers a stark contrast to the formless non-communities of the West, in both landscape and experience of time and memory. Acknowledging the "rural picturesque" as a convention, Lyman nonetheless thinks there is something to the stereotype.[60] In Lyman's words, "Milton was dim and gentle, molded by gentle lives, the current of change as slow through it as the seep of water through a bog"; in Milton, "past and present were less continuous than synonymous."[61] Recalling Milton, Lyman wonders "if ever again Americans can have that experience of returning to a home place so intimately known, profoundly felt, deeply loved, and absolutely submitted to."[62]

Probably not: "We have had too many divorces, we have consumed too much transportation, we have lived shallowly in too many places.

I doubt that anyone of Rodman's generation could comprehend the home feelings of someone like Susan Ward." The transitions of the 1960s, as both a continuation of old western habits and a repudiation of Stegner's criticism of them, have eliminated the possibility of a whole range of emotional experiences—in this situation, such "homing sentiments" can only be sentimental nostalgia with no basis in reality. Lyman argues that his grandparents have been written out of the story of the West because so much of the focus has been on the "uprooted, the lawless, the purseless, and the socially cut-off." Women like Susan settled in the West much differently: it "was not a new country being created, but an old one being reproduced."[63]

What Stegner highlights here is that this kind of settler was not only being ignored in the historical depiction of the West, but in danger of being completely delegitimized by what he saw as the antihistorical commitments of the sociologists like Rodman and the hippies like Shelly and her boyfriend. It was a world of endless pioneering:

> The moderns, carrying little baggage of the kind that Shelly called "merely cultural," not even living in traditional air, but breathing into their space helmets a scientific mixture of synthetic gases (and polluted at that) are the true pioneers. Their circuitry seems to include no atavistic domestic sentiment, they have suffered empathectomy, their computers hum no ghostly feedback of Home, Sweet Home. How marvelously free they are! How unutterably deprived![64]

Where Joe is mostly angry and saddened by the generational division, Lyman actually feels something more like pity. His is a magnanimous detachment more than an angry and tormented anguish. This is where Eric Bennett's criticism fails. Stegner was less a denouncer than someone attempting to persuade his audience of the folly of their ways. He was concerned with arguments about wisdom and moral reasoning and discussion of human flourishing more than elaborations of ethical theory.[65] He tried to write fiction that was truer to human possibility and human frailty in an attempt to place desire in a longer chronological framework, where commitment might have more of a chance to look like the better option.

Reader Responses: "And Yet I Weep for These Kids"

Again, the reader responses were particularly poignant on this issue of the generation gap. One, a former student of Stegner's at the University of Utah (when Stegner was twenty-eight), and presently a mental health counselor at the Free Clinic in Laguna Miguel, California, expressed her conflicted feelings and confusion:

> It helped me clarify my own thinking as I weave my own way in and out of the fabric of today's crazy society, testing my own values against the new ones, discarding some, retaining some, embracing new ones. . . . What with L.S.D., Reds, Whites, Bennies, Speed, V.D. and unwanted pregnancies, we have our hands full. But it's hard to even get the kids to come in for counseling because they think they know everything. . . . And yet I weep for these kids, and see them destroying themselves like the lemmings because of the dramatic social change we are all going through.[66]

Others expressed similar feelings, including a woman who was a self-identified fourth-generation Californian: "I felt that you could express our generation's despair over the widening gap between ourselves and our young. (My husband and I are Stanford alumni, and we had a son there at that time—and a gap)."[67] A woman from Ohio wrote to tell him, "Your bringing together the elements of earlier generations with the contemporary scene, and a protagonist who must represent many people like myself, in my 50's, was beautifully and creatively accomplished. . . . We are those people who are puzzled, worried, concerned, angered, amazed by today's child, but not sure which attitude or set of values is the right one to believe in or to accept."[68]

Others wrote to tell him that he had given them more confidence to hold on to their convictions, rather than that he had helped them better understand their conflicting feelings. In the context of telling Stegner that he had helped her better understand a friend who had undergone an amputation, one reader wrote, "You have enlarged our understanding and our imaginations and, though it's very old-fashioned to assign any moral function to art these days, Mr. Stegner, you did it." She was sick

Dear Wallace Stegner,

I am one of a group of war veteran's who for various reasons are unable to enter societies mainstream. Many of us are remnants of the sordid Viet-Nam fiasco. Almost to the man we maintain a collective bitterness toward the bureaucratic bull-shit which has made shambles of so many lives that reside within my midst.

We read and study novels and even make feeble attempts at writing our own stories perhaps attempting to keep our sanity in an insane situation and thus read your 'ANGLE OF REPOSE'.

It is our fervent and common hope that you might do us the honor of autographing each of the 25 typescripts we have enclosed, so as to be distributed for each and all our members, as your work left a deep-seated impression on all of us.

Whenever a particular work meets unanimous approval and enjoyment, it's our intention to pursue this hobby.

Your the very first novelist whom we've written and we hope you'll be understanding towards our effort.

It's our hope that one sure-fire cure for writer's cramp is the good feeling you'll have knowing you are going to be loved by us for all-time.

Do what you feel is proper. There are 25 of us involved with this effort. Were you to sign only a few-we'll make do. Personally, I'd hate to see anyone left out in the cold. On the other hand--this is a lot of autographing for any one famous novelist.

We send our deep-seated thanks and admiration and truly hope for your sympathy in this matter.

Sincerely,

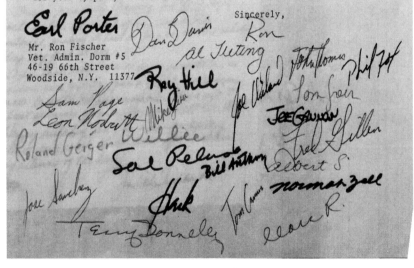

Mr. Ron Fischer
Vet. Admin. Dorm #5
46-19 66th Street
Woodside, N.Y. 11377

Figure 6. Vietnam Vets letter in response to *Angle of Repose*. This letter from a book club composed of Vietnam veterans illustrates well the appeal of Stegner's books to readers who had suffered under tragic circumstances. Courtesy Special Collections, J. Willard Marriott Library, University of Utah.

while reading the book and turned to it with gratitude rather than to her other option for "diversion," the radio or TV reports "chiefly featuring the trials of those delicious young Americans, Charles Manson and William Calley."[69]

A self-identified conservative reader (a repeat writer who sent Stegner several letters starting in 1961) appreciated Stegner's genteel characters—"I insist no other writer could create an absorbing and stimulating novel out of so many well-mannered and -intentioned people!"—but indicated that this appreciation did not result in the political convictions she had expected. Recalling a previous note where she mentioned "having such a strong feeling for Barry Goldwater," Stegner apparently wrote back to tell her that he was not a Goldwater supporter, as her note about *Angle of Repose* concluded with, "I'd like to ask you something about Nixon, but don't suppose I dare—after your 'Goldwater Rebuff,' I'm a little timid."[70]

He heard from readers on the other side of the generation gap as well. A reader who after her second reading of it said the book was "undoubtedly the finest novel I have ever read in my young life" told him, "In these times of such great confusion regarding choices of life styles and values, your book impresses upon me that there really is an order to life—or there was—and it removes some of the ambiguity which has to come from a life where bits and pieces are put together like a jigsaw puzzle."[71]

A younger reader from Iowa found *Angle of Repose* a "thoroughly enjoyable book" but wrote to defend her generation (and academic discipline, as she mentions she is a sociology student) to Stegner. Even though she was interested, "like Rodman," in understanding "the currents of change and the desire to measure the ebb and flow," she also valued "the experience of returning to a place which has not changed." She continued, "Perhaps it is a means of measuring our growth but more likely I believe it is a natural human seeking in a world that, at times, appears to be beyond the control of intelligent man." She concluded by saying that she refused to "believe that the collective mind of my generation has been completely molded by the TVs, super-highways, and instant freezer foods of progress."[72]

Another of Stegner's repeat letter-writers, an artist named Shelbee Matis, wrote to him in defense of the younger generation, though she also said the book "truly caught me." She mentioned that she is in her forties, "with teenagers, of the long hair variety (which, unlike Lyman

Ward, I love)." She thought "Lyman Ward's attitude about responsibility (Yours?)" was grounded in faulty anthropology: "In Susan Ward's time we knew a lot less about our inner needs and when they surfaced learned to suppress them. As a result our sense of responsibility was based on a lack of knowledge of what a human being really was."[73] She told Stegner that while she appreciated Lyman, she "felt the need to open him up a bit," and that his perception of the young people's "lack of responsibility" was better understood as a "search for meaningful responsibility. Or actually a fulfillment of their own—not society's."[74] A future letter suggests that they had a friendly debate over the issue and that Stegner stuck with Lyman's view.

Two Communes

Lyman delivers his most extended meditation on place and forms of community to Shelly. It is focused on two formless non-communities in the West: the Wards' Boise, Idaho, and a commune that is in the process of being formed near Grass Valley, which Shelly is tempted to join with her boyfriend. Stegner juxtaposes the two in a way that allows him to explore the dynamics of two western communities almost a century apart. Again, Stegner stages the conversation to reveal the similarities of the two positions. The results are complex.

Lyman has followed Susan and Oliver from New Almaden, California, to Santa Cruz, California, to Leadville, Colorado, and to Michoacán, Mexico; these trips are interrupted with brief trips to Deadwood, South Dakota, for Oliver and to Milton, New York, for Susan. But it is Boise, Idaho, where Susan and Oliver allow Lyman space to reflect for an extended period of time on the complex process of building place in the West. In all of these places Lyman has traced the ways that Susan and Oliver's relationship to each other and to their respective careers has formed based on their residence in each place. The addition of children adds another set of relationships.

Oliver is well respected in his work, but unable to find a position that will allow them to stay anywhere for an extended period of time. Susan is also respected and more consistently employed in her work, which is less place dependent. Age and children add to Susan's compulsion to find a place to stick, and this becomes more of a tension because Oliver, "addicted to the West," even (or especially) after less-than-satisfying experiences in mining, has developed the "incurable Western disease."[75] He has "set his crosshairs on the snowpeak of a vision, and there he would go," Susan feared, "triangulating his way across a bone-dry future, dragging her and the children with him, until they all died of thirst."[76] Oliver's vision is an ambitious plan to bring irrigation to the Boise Valley. Susan fears that it will not succeed and thinks she will be sacrificing her and their children's present for an ambiguous future.[77] Susan accedes, and at this point in their lives, Boise is "not an adventurous picnic" like New Almaden, Leadville, and Michoacán, but, in its seeming finality, merely "exile."[78]

Susan is apprehensive because she knows that this next trip West is the last she can take before becoming irredeemably a westerner and incapable of return to the life she once knew. On the cusp of Boise, Stegner situates both Susan and Oliver in dangerous places for each, especially if considered in the light of Stegner's understanding of western sticker virtues. The strands of criticism that have been most harsh on Stegner, especially since the revelation of his unattributed uses of Foote's writings, have tended to focus on Stegner's portrayal of Susan as a snob and the instigator of the downfall in her relationship with Oliver. But it is important to note that here Oliver takes on new shades of boomer vices that were absent in Lyman's earlier portrayals. Oliver has a gleam in his eye that blinds him to the consequences of failure and the costs of such failure on the lives of his family members. So even though Susan is the one who eventually breaks fidelity most visibly, Oliver's western "disease" is arguably the precipitating event that makes it more likely.

Oliver and Susan spend time in several "Wests" before arriving in Boise. Leadville and Michoacán are exceptions. Leadville's elevation made it impossible for the kind of settlement that Oliver and Susan were after, and Michoacán was a society that Oliver and Susan could have joined but barely influenced because it was already firmly established. Boise, in contrast, is a society in flux and one that Oliver and Susan take the opportunity to shape. It is another "formless non-community" in the process of change and becoming. What direction would it take?

In a letter to Augusta, Susan summarizes her initial reactions to Boise, which are decidedly in favor of the scenery over the society: "The country, as distinguished from its improvements and its people, is beautiful—a vast sage plain that falls in great steps from the mountains to the canyon of the Snake, and then rises gradually on the other side to other mountains. It is one of the compensations of being a pioneer that one may see it wild and unbroken."[79] It is, to Susan's eyes, a new country, one whose existing features are "no more than a scribble on the great empty page across which Oliver hopes to write a history of human occupation."

This perceived newness is not exhilarating to Susan, however, as it was to so many of her era. Based on her stage of life, it is only dismaying. The letter includes a sign of hope, however, as Frank Sargent, Oliver's assistant engineer and Susan's friend, will rejoin them in Idaho. This rejoining is an exception to the rule of the West and its hostility to social bonds, however: "there are even indications that the West which so lightly and cruelly separates and scatters people can bring them together again— that the binding force of civilization and human association is as strong, perhaps, as the West's bigness and impersonality."[80]

Susan, Oliver, and Frank are brought together in the Boise Canyon on the banks of the Boise River where Oliver has plans to develop an irrigation scheme that would, through the development of agriculture, "take a piece of wilderness and turn it into a home for a civilization."[81] They need to start with wilderness, however, and Susan finds herself living on a campsite in the canyon in the "tightest little society in all the West," a "Brook Farm without a social theory, and a melting pot Brook Farm at that," with "a Chinese cook, a Swedish handyman, an English governess, three Eastern-American engineers, two children, and a lady artist."[82]

The society is brought together by their need for shelter while they await more funding for Oliver's irrigation scheme. Though Oliver offers his employees the opportunity to move on to better opportunities, the employees choose to stick, and rather than stick by idly, to build a house out of the local materials. It is a Stegnerian dream, as it melds western nature and human civilization together in an original creation. Using stone from a nearby rockslide and homemade cement, they build a house with the dimensions of the Parthenon, twenty-one by thirty-five feet. Susan's apprehension disappears in her letter to Augusta: "Have you ever built a house with your own hands, out of the materials that Nature left lying around? Everyone should have that experience once. It is the most satisfying experience I know."[83]

Even Susan's racist apprehensiveness is challenged by this experience in her "wildest and sweetest" of "wild nesting places" as she admits that while "the sight of a Chinese" made her "positively shudder" after their first trip out West, now Charley Wan "is one of us," and that she believes "he looks upon us as his family." It is western community of necessity: "Is it not queer, and both desolating and comforting, how, with all associations broken, one forms new ones, as a broken bone thickens in healing."[84]

But they are there in their "little corner of Eden" waiting in preparation for the civilization Oliver plans to enable, not in an escape from it.[85] Eden eventually becomes true exile, however, as they are stuck in the canyon without necessary funding from 1883 until 1887. As financial pressure mounts, Susan and Oliver's marriage begins to deteriorate. Frank and Susan grow more entangled in their impossible Victorian romance and Oliver begins to drink. The wilderness exile is the undoing of the little community. Having reconstructed the "slow corrosion of the affection and loyalty that have held Oliver and Susan Ward together," Lyman finds himself challenged on several levels.[86] "Is it love or sympathy that makes me think myself capable of reconstructing these lives, or am I, Nemesis in a wheelchair, bent on proving something—perhaps that not even gentility and integrity are proof against the corrosions of human weakness, human treachery, human disappointment, human inability to forget."[87]

By 1888, the plan is stalled enough that Oliver and Susan separate for him to take a position with the U.S. Geological Survey under John Wesley Powell. Susan heads to Vancouver Island and Oliver follows the Survey, which adds strain to the marriage. By 1889, Oliver has received new backing and they start over in Boise. Without consulting Susan, Oliver has prepared for her arrival and bought her a house with a new lawn and the beginnings of a magnificent rose garden, his gift to Susan in an attempt to make the barren shelf more like home for her. But the wilderness has done its work. By July 4, 1889—another of Stegner's Independence Day culminations—the Victorian proprieties that have kept Susan and Frank apart are breaking down.[88]

Building the suspense and the contrast between Victorian and hippie customs, Stegner then returns the reader to Lyman and Shelly. Shelly has come to Lyman for advice about a commune she has been invited to join. While as idealistic as Stegner's own Peninsula Housing Association from the mid-1940s, the actual ideals are much different. Shelly hands Lyman the group's Manifesto. It begins: "We hold these truths to be self evident to everybody except generals, industrialists, politicians, professors, and other dinosaurs." The truths are a standard critique of the Establishment counterposed with an alternative vision. It ends with a call to join: "We invite there all who believe in people and the earth, to live, study, meditate, flourish, and shed the hangups of corrupted America. We invite men, women, and children to come and begin creating the new sane healthy world within the shell of the old."[89] This is not a commune built out of necessity and in preparation for a civilization, but one built in the attempt to escape from it.

Shelly wants to know what Lyman thinks, knowing that he disagrees, but Lyman tries to deflect the questions. Again, to think about why Stegner imagined a young braless hippie (and Stegner also describes Lyman's uncomfortable sexual arousal during this truth session) questioning a cranky old man so diligently and with such curiosity is somewhat pitiful, especially in light of Stegner's restless circling around these issues as recently as in *Live Things*. Having been patiently consulted even as Lyman is playing the curmudgeon, his first response is grounded in his study of history, with a list of failed communes from the Fourierist phalansteries to Brook Farm to the Oneida Colony. He summarizes the results: "'The natural tribal societies are . . . superstition-ridden, ritual-bound, and warlike, and the utopian ones always fail.'"[90]

Shelly is annoyed by the pleasure that Lyman seems to take in his confident predictions that the commune will fail:

> "It's one thing to think it's sure to fail, but you sound as if you thought it was *wrong*. . . . You can't think the society we've got is so hot. I *know* you don't. Haven't you sort of copped out yourself? What's this but a rural commune, only you own it and hire the Hawkes family to run it for you? . . . Is this manifesto so different from the come-on [Oliver] wrote for the Idaho Mining and Irrigation Company, except that he was doing it for profit? . . . All that big dream of his was dubious ecology, and sort of greedy when you look at it, just another piece of American continent-busting. . . . You admire your grandfather more than anybody,

even though the civilization he was trying to build was this cruddy one we've got. Here's a bunch of people willing to put their lives on the line to try to make a better one. Why put them down?"

Again Lyman tries to avoid answering, but Shelly wants to know. This time it goes beyond the professional and he starts, like Joe Allston, to "roar." Lyman finally lets loose:

"Because their soft-headedness irritates me. Because their beautiful thinking ignores both history and human nature. Because they'd spoil my thing with their thing. Because I don't think any of them is wise enough to play God and create a human society. . . . I want to make a distinction between civilization and the wild life. I want a society that will protect the wild life without confusing itself with it. You can't retire to weakness—you've got to learn to control strength."[91]

Shelly challenges Lyman's interpretation briefly, but Lyman has the floor and Stegner keeps him there for another round, this time in response to one of Shelly's points about Henry David Thoreau:

"What it suggests to me is that the civilization he was contemptuous of—that civilization of men who lived lives of quiet desperation—was stronger than he was, and maybe righter. It outvoted him. It swallowed him, in fact, and used the nourishment he provided to alter a few cells in its corporate body. It grew richer by him, but was bigger than he was. Civilizations grow by agreements and accommodations and accretions, not by repudiations. The rebels and revolutionaries are only eddies, they keep the stream from getting stagnant but they get swept down and absorbed, they're a side issue. Quiet desperation is another name for the human condition. If revolutionaries would learn that they can't remodel society by day after tomorrow—haven't the wisdom to and shouldn't be permitted to—I'd have more respect for them. Revolutionaries and sociologists. God, those sociologists! They're always trying to reclaim a tropical jungle with a sprinkling can full of weed killer. Civilizations grow and change and decline—they aren't remade."[92]

After this intellectual climax, Shelly is "indulgently smiling" at Lyman and the seriousness of the conversation is effectively dissipated.[93] Shelly then tells Lyman about the commune in terms that she thinks he will more likely respect, which he does, somewhat begrudgingly. She discusses going off to the commune or finishing her "stupid degree." Lyman tells her she can stay on as his assistant, but they laugh off the possibility. They part laughing, but the chapter ends with Lyman "looking out into the rose garden and across Grandfather's acres of lawn, and feeling, bleak, bleak, bleak."[94]

Lyman returns to another parting of ways in his historical account. Having allowed the affair between Susan and Frank to begin—Lyman is careful not to reveal the extent to which it was physically consummated—the two are caught in impossible circumstances. The evidence Lyman has to work with is spotty, but based on newspaper reports and the imprint of the events on his severe and taciturn father, among other things, he knows two very important facts: Agnes, the third child of the Wards, died tragically in a drowning accident in one of Oliver's canals; and her death was followed four days later by the suicide of Frank Sargent. In a series of guesses, Lyman surmises that Susan and Frank must have taken Agnes along as cover for an illicit meeting because either their feelings were "dangerously inflamed" or to say their final goodbyes and break off the relationship for good, as Frank was out of work and intending to leave.

Whatever happened and resulted in Agnes's drowning is less significant than a story that Lyman had overheard between his aunt and grandfather when he was a child. In a scene that most readers of *Angle of Repose* remember more vividly than any other, Lyman's aunt recalled watching Oliver walk out to their prized rose garden in Boise in the "very early morning," under a "sense of suspended time," and begin to tear out each rose bush "one by one, not yanking in fury, but tugging thoughtfully, almost absent-mindedly." He finishes the task, hands bloodied after uprooting the whole row of roses. He mounts his horse and rides off, having "not once looked at the house."[95] The event marks the end of Oliver's affection for Susan, and the beginning of his life as a merely dutiful husband.

1890 and After: Stegner's Fiction Versus Popular Myth

It is not until page 228 of 632 total pages that Lyman discovers for himself the anguished question that has motivated his research. Rodman is at Lyman's house checking up on his father and asks how the research is going. Lyman explains that Oliver is in Deadwood, and Rodman offers that Lyman should be sure to keep them there as long as possible to keep the story "interesting"—gold, shootouts with Wild Bill Hickok, saloons. Lyman explains that Oliver was working as an engineer building a mill ditch for the Homestake Mine and Rodman begins to lose interest. Lyman thinks: "He irritates me, he always does. Nothing is interesting to him unless it's bellowing as loud as he is."

In the context of Stegner's life work and especially essays like "History, Myth, and the Western Writer," this exchange encapsulated an argument about the stories of the West that dominated Stegner's lifetime, to his lasting discouragement. In Deadwood and elsewhere, Oliver is building infrastructure that will shape the lives and possibilities of thousands of westerners, but all people want are more cowboy stories. What happened in the West besides "regeneration through violence"? To Lyman's great annoyance, Rodman patronizes him again with a comment about how he is glad Lyman has found something that "interests [him] that much." But, forced to continue explaining himself, Lyman surprises himself by telling Rodman that what he is actually writing about is a marriage. In his mind, Lyman thinks: "What really interests me is how two such unlike particles clung together, and under what strains, rolling downhill into their future until they reached the angle of repose when I knew them. . . . That's where the meaning will be if I find any." Susan's sense of self in the West is central, but even more it is the way that her reckoning with herself and her husband, Oliver, in a series of new places, unfolds. Lyman is trying to understand a marriage of two people and, more abstractly, the webs that form to hold people and places together.[96]

Through this discussion, Stegner insisted to his readers that it is just as significant, and perhaps more important, to study sources of stability, continuity, and order than to study chaos, action, and disorder. Rodman stands in for countless numbers who dismissed the quieter stories of the West that Stegner thought were valuable and worth more in the long run.

He wanted people to study seriously infrastructure, aridity, geography, stability, custom. In the case of the cultural forms, he was arguing that they demanded attention to the value of cultural discourses in addition to ways that such discourses have served as tools of oppression. A classic midcentury liberal realist and a meliorist, he thought it was worth considering whether the brave new world might turn out to be worse than the actually existing one. As he puts it in an internal monologue about Shelly later in the novel:

> Somewhere, sometime, somebody taught her to question everything—though it might have been a good thing if he'd also taught her to question the act of questioning. Carried far enough, as far as Shelly's crowd carries it, that can dissolve the ground you stand on. I suppose wisdom could be defined as knowing what you have to accept, and I suppose by that definition she's a long way from wise.[97]

A crucial feature of the novel is that the profession of the narrator allowed Stegner to slip in short meditations on the distorting lens of the mythic western past, and the cost of such myths in the western present. But how effective was his attempt to combat western myth with western fiction? This problem was exacerbated by his use of Mary Hallock Foote's life and writings. In particular, his fictional depiction of Susan's affair with Frank Sargent and the subsequent death of her daughter Agnes introduced a persistent untruth into 1970s California. It was an untruth that distressed the descendants of the Footes.[98]

Another choice in his presentation of the past is very curious. Stegner often lamented that western historians stopped investigating the West after 1890, the date made significant by the U.S. Census Bureau's declaration of the end of the frontier, and made famous by Frederick Jackson Turner's frontier thesis. In his description of the aftermath of the affair and the death of Agnes, Lyman describes the story as one that is "all over in 1890." Nothing that happens after that is worth Lyman's notice; he has achieved his goals. For the Wards, it is just "year after irrelevant year"; they live through world historical events like World War I, but "through all those changes" there is "not a change in them."[99]

Why, given his criticism of history that stopped at 1890, did Stegner stop his fictional history at that very date? Stegner writes a first draft of the history of the 1960s and 1970s—a limited one, but still a history—in his book. While Lyman and Shelly are both proof that the Wards' historical legacy has lived on through the world wars and into their own present, there is still a notable gap. Was this an attempt to highlight that absence and illustrate just how much of a "presence" the absence was and is, along the lines of "positive negative space"?[100] Or was Stegner simply reifying the problem he had decried in so many different settings?[101]

Here it is ironic that Stegner did not find Oliver's and Susan's lives after 1890 more compelling, especially as he was interested in what kept them together after catastrophe. Presumably it was the cultural ideals that they held that would not allow for any other possibilities, given the level of their commitment to them. Perhaps he was being realistic and thought that there was no way he could write fiction about such quiet circumstances. The book is already long and he could have tested his readers' patience.

But the actual lives of the Footes might have inserted into western memory a set of stories that Stegner would have found valuable. Despite real tensions and a temporary separation, Mary and Arthur had managed to stick together and then, by some accounts, to thrive in their marriage.[102] Further, they were part of the creation of something of a western community in Grass Valley. Stegner explored this kind of quiet story in *Crossing to Safety* (1987), but perhaps he saw no way to write that kind of story at the time. Foote's reminiscences are structured similarly, with only a brief description of their lives in Grass Valley, so perhaps Stegner did not think he could invent plausibly without more of a record to ground him.[103]

In the novel, Lyman describes Oliver and Susan's failed marriage as one that is not a complete failure—to answer his own questions that he posed to Rodman upon his discovery of what he was writing about, cultural forms turned their marriage into something less than satisfying to them, but not one without its own benefits and unworthy of respect. Susan and Oliver are not intimate, but they treat each other with "a sort of grave infallible kindness."[104] They achieve something of what Susan referred to, making metaphor from a technical term, as the "angle of repose." After dismissing the angle as one that is simply inert and dead, a failure, Lyman continues:

> I thought when I began, and still think, that there was another angle in all those years when she was growing old and older and very old, and Grandfather was matching her year for year, a separate line that did not intersect with hers. They were vertical people, they lived by pride, and it is only by the ocular illusion of perspective that they can be said to have met. But he had not been dead two months when she lay down and died too, and that may indicate that at that absolute vanishing point they did intersect. They had intersected for years, for more than he especially would ever admit.[105]

Or is it something better? "I am sure she meant some meeting, some intersection of lines; and some cowardly, hopeful geometer in my brain tells me it is the angle at which two lines prop each other up, the leaning-together from the vertical which produces the false arch. For lack of a keystone, the false arch may be as much as one can expect in this life. Only the very lucky discover the keystone."[106] Even if it was not enough to give them as much joy as a more harmonious marriage, it still managed to build and preserve something. Lyman asks the reader to think in generational terms: would Oliver and Susan have been happier if they could have, without societal disapproval, freely rejected each other and chosen more compatible romance? Would they have built anything in that case? Would they have been able to forget each other? Or would they have just been a couple mounds of rubble rather than at least a false arch?

Conclusion

Of all of Stegner's works, *Angle of Repose* took on a life of its own to the extent that it could be said to have a "biography." The first ironic twist in the biography of *Angle of Repose* is the way that it was simultaneously cranky about the first rumblings of postmodernity while also itself postmodern in form and eventually adapted in ways that are plausibly postmodern.[107] First, it was turned into an opera by Andrew Imbrie and performed in honor of the American Bicentennial in San Francisco. The libretto for the opera was written by Oakley Hall, Stegner's near-contemporary and the author of *Warlock* (1958). He was also the father of Sands Hall, a playwright who would later produce a play about the book and the controversy attached to it. The opera was a choice of subject seemingly as odd as Lin-Manuel Miranda's choice to write a rap musical about Alexander Hamilton, but it did not inspire the same runaway success. Why would a novel with an immobilized historian as its protagonist inspire an opera?

The twisting of genres and layers of history in the Sands Hall play's production is particularly ironic because Stegner was so suspicious of the value of experiments in form that appeared to revel too much in the form itself rather than in representation of life. Despite protestations of the value of artistic freedom and his longstanding appreciation of the work of William Faulkner, Stegner never seemed to enjoy art that was more focused on formal questions than on the urgent moral questions that marked his commitment to realism. That his novel about the writing of a novel would inspire a play about his writing of the novel—and not only that, but a play written by the daughter of his colleague—is absolutely the kind of melding of art and history that the book evokes so well.

Stegner's depiction of the careful and significant historical work that Lyman does in Grass Valley was also fascinating in its irony because it inspired a renewed interest in the life of Mary Hallock Foote herself.[108] This is the kind of outcome Stegner might have deemed particularly successful, as it was evidence of Lyman's power to persuade his readers of the "humanness of faces lost in time," and the significance of past lives and the ways that they live on in the present. Stegner wrote to inspire a renewed sense of not just the cowboys of the past but the builders of infrastructure and community. It was his success in inspiring research into western lives like those of the Footes that led, in part—obviously the concurrent growth of second-wave feminism was more significant— to a renewed appreciation for Mary Hallock Foote's work and, in turn, a growing indignation about the ways that Stegner used it once Foote's work had been read with care and the plagiarized paragraphs noticed.[109]

Stegner's critics have often pointed to his responses to interview questions from Richard Etulain as evidence of his sexist disparagement of Mary Hallock Foote as a historical subject worthy of respect in her own right. It is interesting to compare Wendell Berry's praise of Stegner as a regional writer rather than a provincial one with the ways that Stegner described the process of writing his novel and his use of Foote's life and writings. Berry writes that Stegner was a regionalist who "writes about his region but also does his best to protect it, by writing and in other ways, from its would-be exploiters and destroyers." In contrast, Berry posits the work of "industrialists of letters" who mine "one's province for whatever can be got out of it in the way of 'raw material' for stories and novels."[110]

In his response to the question about Mary Ellen Williams-Walsh's article that argued the case for Stegner's unfair appropriation and even plagiarism of Foote, Stegner said,

> And I don't feel that I did Mary Hallock Foote any damage at all because, left alone, the papers would have been simply the raw material out of which a novel might be made. Molly Foote is raw material for Susan Ward.... As far as I'm concerned the Mary Hallock Foote stuff had the same function as raw material, broken rocks out of which I could build any kind of wall I wanted to—as poor Norman Foerster's ailments, which I borrowed for that wheelchair point of view.[111]

Without context, this certainly seems to place Stegner more in the category of "industrialists of letters" than in the category of a good regional writer (on Berry's scale of evaluation). And despite his respect for the Susan Burling Ward character and for Foote, which is evident elsewhere, he did not seem to understand why some of the descendants of Foote thought he might have treated Foote herself too much as mere "raw material." This coincidence of overlapping words in Berry's essay is particularly strange because Berry cites these very interviews with Etulain later in the essay. Later in the interview, Stegner lent some credence to the notion that his use of Foote was in part driven by some level of sexism. Some people—Stegner names George Washington and Clarence King specifically—are not meant to be "warped" by fiction but others are not bound by the same code, including Foote and Joe Hill. These lines seemed rather arbitrary.[112]

Despite his way of discussing Foote as "raw material" and its sexist undertones, there is also a definite and clear sense that he was fond and respectful of the Foote that he had met in the archives. One reader, a literary agent from New York City, wrote, "Among the criteria which one establishes as a reader, the one which has risen to the top of the heap, for me at least, is affection. . . . It is rare, it seems to me, to see the kind of affection for material that one finds in A of R."[113]

Finally, it was a book about human frailties and the effort to apologize and forgive and the consequences of failures to forgive. Stegner stubbornly refused to own up to the problems in his text once the situation changed and Foote's life and work became more public in a way that made her memory more complicated for Foote's descendants. Lyman's description of Oliver toward the end of the book seems almost a prophetic description of Stegner in relation to the history of his most famous book: "Nevertheless I, who looked up to him all his life as the fairest of men, have difficulty justifying that bleak and wordless break; and that ripping up of the rose garden, that was vindictive and pitiless. I wish he had not done that. I think he never got over being ashamed, and never found the words to say so."[114] It was as if Stegner himself was peering into the future at his own conduct in the scandal, writing words for what his own admirers were likely thinking.

Despite the ironies and tensions played out in the "biography" of *Angle of Repose*, or perhaps even because of them, Lyman's and Susan's parallel musings about place, identity, and history display some of Stegner's most compelling attempts to answer the pressing questions he posed to himself and his fellow westerners. First, Stegner is fairly explicit in his presentation of formal, disciplined history (in contrast to entertaining stories) and thoughtful memory (in contrast to sentimentality) as two effective forms westerners could use to achieve a sense of possessed past—and in so doing to build real places. A third resource is the land itself. Susan's awareness of the geographical distinctions of the West and her often reluctant reckoning with these distinctions were a significant part of what formed her identity and fit her for western community. Geography is another reconciling bridge to the possessed past. And finally in this quest for a possessed past, Stegner implies the essential importance of formal social institutions that oblige people to stick to other human beings, highlighting marriage and family as his primary examples. He would have agreed with his former student Wendell Berry when Berry wrote, "Form, like topsoil (which is intricately formal), empowers time to do good."[115]

Chapter 5

Growing Old in the New West

For the fact is, if it is the necessity of the young to challenge and risk, it is the obligation of the old to conserve, not only for their own sake but for the sake of the young who at the moment want anything rather than conservation. No society is healthy without both the will to create anew and the will to save the best of the old: it is not the triumph of either tendency, but the constant, elastic tension between the two that should be called our great tradition.

—Wallace Stegner[1]

Say not, "Why were the former days better than these?" For it is not from wisdom that you ask this.

—Ecclesiastes 7:10

Having explored a multigenerational West in Grass Valley, Stegner found himself beckoned back to Joe Allston and his "formless non-community" once more by the middle of the decade. In *The Spectator Bird* (1976), Stegner's Joe Allston is still "working" on his memoirs, watching birds, reckoning with his guilt, and cracking wry jokes. Ruth is still gardening and attempting to nudge Joe away from his darker musings. The California Midpeninsula remains beautiful if still marked by weather more perplexing than its reputation. The Allstons' neighborhood, however, has further revealed its formlessness and fallen apart. The LoPrestis are mentioned once as an afterthought, and Marian, John, and Debby Catlin are written about briefly only a few times.

At first glance, these erasures seem to be a concession to Stegner's desire to write books to address the events, images, characters, and ideas that he wanted to address, not for the sake of maintaining any kind of continuity in his fictional Midpeninsula universe. Whether intentional or not, however, the elimination of the old neighbors is also intriguing commentary on one of the central themes of the Peninsula novels, that of the transience and impermanence of communities in the suburban West. In *Live Things*, Joe notes that he and Ruth have been designated as Debby's guardians should John die. By the time Stegner chose to revisit the neighborhood in *Spectator Bird*, even the Allstons' relationship with John and Debby seems to have been extinguished by time and distance. With the Catlins gone, it seems fitting that no one else would remain either, and the formless non-community that was the Allstons' neighborhood in *Live Things* has been confirmed as such. It could not hold; the bonds that did exist were, for a variety of reasons, not possible to maintain.

The formless non-community that is revealed in *Spectator Bird*, however, is not explored on its own terms but against a much different society: Denmark in the 1950s. More specifically: Copenhagen, and Bregninge, Denmark. By writing what might be the world's only novel set in both Midpeninsula Bay Area California and Denmark, Stegner set up a new lens from which to explore the promise and peril of community in the American West. In doing so, he took another step towards the completion of the village democracy project he set for himself in the 1950s. Though not enough to form the basis of a social scientific study, Stegner finally had the chance to use his observations of Denmark gleaned on the trip funded by the Wenner-Gren Foundation. Rather than in comparison to Eastend, Saskatchewan, and Greensboro, Vermont, however, he explored Denmark in relation to his own Midpeninsula suburbs.

It is a novel of revelation more than plot, and it starts with Joe ruminating in his study, watching birds. The present-day action of this novel takes place in 1974 over the span of only about a week. After a brief update on Joe's ruminations and the reintroduction to the new variation of the formless non-community, Joe receives a postcard in the mail that sets the novel in motion. It is from Astrid Wredel-Karup, a woman that Joe and Ruth befriended during their trip to Denmark in 1954, right after their son Curtis's death.[2] The postcard sets Joe to rummaging for the journal he kept—uncharacteristically—during the trip. When Ruth catches him reading it, she insists that they revisit their past together through Joe's journals. Joe reluctantly agrees, and each night they read a section from the journal, with Stegner syncopating time and using documents to enliven the past in the present as he did in *Angle of Repose*. As they work their way towards a recognition of an unacknowledged secret in their marriage, their days in the Midpeninsula California present are poignant but darkly comic. Joe and Ruth are reckoning with their failing bodies, their relationships with younger associates, their terminally ill friends, and their own approaching deaths.

In the context of his exploration of community and place in Mid-peninsula California, *Spectator Bird* is the novel that most directly challenged Stegner's sympathies for place and stability by imagining it side by side with a European society marked by failures of community due to stasis. It was Stegner's most complex rumination on a society characterized more by stability than movement. In his exploration of Denmark, readers see Stegner imagining what it might be like to be trapped in a place that is stagnant and stultifying. More specifically, Stegner explored these themes in relation to age and what they might look like from the end of life rather than from youth. It takes a strange shape: Joe Allston is seventy, looking back on his life at fifty. What does a midlife crisis look like twenty years later?

The Clang of Bronze

The juxtaposition of scenes from daily life in both 1970s Midpeninsula California and 1950s Denmark allowed Stegner to work his way through some complexities in his thought about place and belonging.[3] In the fall of 1963, Stegner gave a speech to the Association of Greek Writers in Greece that he later related to Jackson Benson as the most significant day he experienced in all his travels. To his audience, Stegner had admitted his embarrassment over the notion that he, an American, might presume to be bringing culture back to the Greeks, but, to his surprise, the Greeks expressed great envy towards his situation.

His speech was reprinted in newspapers, and in Stegner's account years later, it was considered by the Greeks a "'revelation from the New World, where it seemed talents were not shriveled in the competitive glare of a great past.'" Stegner continued: "'I did not quite accept their view, but I had to realize how different my problems were from theirs.'"[4] While Stegner was enough of a midcentury liberal to condemn chauvinistic regionalism and to be aware of the failures of "closed societies," it seems that this moment was one that gave him his first genuine insight into people who felt oppressed by a thick conception of place and an overwhelming awareness of the past.

In his interview with Richard Etulain, he said of the moment, "It sprang out of my sense that growing up without history is a deprivation. I have no sense, or hadn't at least until then, and still really don't, of the obverse of that—how it might be to grow up with too much history."[5] His planning notes suggest that the comparison between Denmark and the United States, if not yet Midpeninsula California, was in the forefront of his mind as he was exploring his idea of the novel. The earliest notes, left undated but marked as "Early drafts for what became Spectator Bird," are built primarily around scenes from Denmark as observed by a yet unnamed American sociologist. Just as in *Angle of Repose* Stegner almost brought another Jim Peck into the story, in *Spectator Bird* he almost brings another Rodman into the story—fortunately he resisted the temptation both times. Stegner was committed early to the character that became Astrid, but not yet committed to writing about Astrid and Denmark from the narrative perspective of Joe Allston.[6]

From the earliest brainstorming notes, it is clear that he wanted to explore the intricacies of a relatively stable society from the perspective of an American without a strong connection to a personal past. In Stegner's early drafts, he describes how he wants to give the sociologist a chance to discover that the tradition he looks for, the thing he obscurely envies, being himself a maverick, has two sides. On the one side, the cooperativeness of the peasants, the industry, sobriety, democracy, of a place with nothing much but intelligence to sell; on that same side, the integrity and pride and noblesse oblige of the aristocracy, now without a function and without honor, but (as he sees it) sticking it out, making the best of it, being model farmers and estate managers. Little by little he finds the other side: the inbred arrogance, the caste consciousness, pride of place, incestuous exclusiveness.[7]

As he observes more of this decadence, Stegner imagined that the American would begin to see his "rootlessness" as a strength and begin to think that "his grandmother [who immigrated to the United States], taking off, had more vision and courage than those who stayed." But again, it is a tension more than an affirmation, as Stegner also reflects on the value of the migration and whether any such escapes are actually true escapes.

Where echoes of *The Tempest* lent gravity and thematic richness to the story in *Live Things*, *Hamlet* converses with this story, and not simply because it is set in Denmark. It is an existential reflection on a previous existential season. It is the closest Stegner wrote in relation to the Southern gothic tradition of William Faulkner, whom he praised, and Flannery O'Connor, whom he thought too excessive in her depiction of the grotesque.[8] Several more poetic forms shape the novel as well: Goethe's "Über Allen Gipfen," which is quoted in full by Astrid; Tennyson's "Ulysses" in a brief allusion; the old Anglo-Saxon poem, "The Seafarer" in the notes; Pascal's *Pensées*; and then finally, the Venerable Bede, whose words shape Joe's final moments in the book.[9]

Spectator Bird seems poised in the complex middle of the classic reflections on the wandering life as it concludes embodied in Tennyson's "Ulysses" and the old Anglo-Saxon poem, "The Seafarer." Both poems reward careful readings that emphasize the essentially tragic choice between adventure and security, but Tennyson allows for more heroism in his life of exploration while melancholy regret is more dominant for the old Anglo-Saxon poet. Tennyson's Ulysses affirms: "Tho' much is taken, much abides; and tho' / We are not now that strength which in old days / Moved earth and heaven, that which we are, we are; / One equal temper of heroic hearts, / Made weak by time and fate, but strong in will / To strive, to seek, to find, and not to yield." The Seafarer is more ambiguous: "Fate is aye stronger, / Measure mightier, than any man's thought."[10]

The Formless Non-community Revisited

Stegner reveals the rhythms of Peninsula life most fully with a party, one of the motifs that unites the three Joe Allston works ("Field Guide" and *Live Things* being the other two). Unlike the cooperative community planned by the Peninsula Housing Association (PHA), which included plans for several cooperatively owned businesses, leisure more than work or economic necessity brings the people together. Again, though not necessarily an intentional point from Stegner, this party is much smaller than either of the other two Midpeninsula parties. The party is staged so

Joe and Ruth have to observe their lives through the lens of a younger person, Joe's former client and Italian romance novelist Cesare Rulli, on two axes: age versus youth and country life versus urban life. Both Joe and Ruth "are fond of Cesare in spite of his books," which Joe finds "compulsive, theatrical, and decadent" even if Cesare is "the friendliest and best-natured of satyrs, far more fun than his books and far less repulsive than his audience."[11] He has "an interest in everything that moves; only quiet things elude him."[12]

This party also sets up a new contrast in that Joe is in the position of being judged. Rather than playing the role of the honored guest whose taste is being solicited, his own taste is being held up for inspection by a certified artist. Rulli's visit is last-minute—he is being hosted by an auxiliary from the State Department in San Francisco and has already exhausted their plans for his visit—and this throws Joe and Ruth into a frenzy of preparation. Joe explains their feelings about it and in the process reveals his own vision of suburban utopia:

> We had invented Eden and owed it a PR job. Probably we thought we were adapting to one of those illusions they call a lifestyle. We wanted our American plenty to show, but not too much. . . . We wanted to demonstrate that the rush out to the suburbs and the country, when conducted by the right people, could be an enhancement of civilization, not an evasion of it. . . . When we had Eastern or foreign visitors we watched them confidently for signs of envy. We wanted, maybe just a little desperately, to be thought terribly lucky.[13]

In this short description of Peninsula California, Stegner reveals his place as a suburb with layers of options for communities of choice. Joe acknowledges that they are in fact lucky, but that the feeling has become more desperate. The friends are much fewer, mostly due to death, and their place has taken on new meaning: "Eden with graves is no longer Eden."[14] Further, the hills have been invaded by junior executives and computer programmers whose tastes and pace of life cannot be trusted to sustain the villa style that Joe has set out for himself or to respect the lives that others have built for themselves in the place. In this sentiment, Joe finds himself allied with his housekeeper in a moment of cross-class solidarity forged by commitment to the place. Like her, Joe has little respect for the newly imposed "one-acre, one house rigidities" that have interrupted traditions where "land [was] lived on comfortably by people who respected it."[15]

In a scene that posits a nostalgia that contradicts Joe's testimony in the previous Peninsula stories, Minnie describes a world that seems too sweetly rose-tinted:

> Everybody helped everybody else, everybody went to the same Christmas and New Year's parties, there wasn't any difference except some people had a bigger house and maybe a couple horses in the pasture. And you *knew* people, you'd see things going on. Now everybody's behind a chain-link fence, you never see anybody even mowin' his lawn.... Them creeps with their subdivisions and their tax hikes and their zoning! My God, you can't even build a henhouse without a permit—can't even keep hens, for hell's sake.... Then that same woman and her phony husband that have sunk all they got, and a lot more, in this place they've made too expensive for anybody to afford it, they go on down to Town Hall twice a month and pass some more laws so their fancy address won't be hurt by dogs and chickens and cluster housing and black people and Chicanos and students and hippies and federallyfinancedlowerincomehousing, all one word.[16]

Minnie is exuberant because, on her way to the Allstons' during a downpour, she has observed that one such new couple has just watched their front yard slide away, a just repayment for hasty and ostentatious development in both her eyes and Joe's. It might seem odd to see Joe condemning those who would try to keep "hippies" out of the neighborhood, given his prior experience with Jim Peck. But the reference to social homogeneity reinforced by zoning laws recalls Stegner's experience with the Peninsula Housing Association.

The downpour forces Joe, Ruth, and Minnie to prepare hectically for Cesare's arrival with only intermittent power. The preparations are stalled and rushed, and Joe ends up greeting Cesare at the bottom of his driveway in his raincoat, trudging around in the muck. Though Joe waves, Cesare drives past the unrecognized man hidden in his slicker, splashing Joe in the process. By the time Joe sneaks in through the back, showers, and turns in to greet his guest, Cesare is already feeling restless. He has seduced his hostess from the State Department and their flirtations continue throughout the lunch, but he is not convinced that she and Ruth are an audience worthy of his monologues.

When Joe finally arrives, Cesare is effusive in his greetings to Joe, and compliments him for a beautiful place, with "views like Umbria." But it is not long before Cesare asks Joe why he is not living in San Francisco. He asks Joe who there is to talk to, where the cafes are for the literary people to meet together. Joe says that there is no literary world that Cesare would recognize, but that there are compensations. Cesare is not convinced, and to his hostess exclaims, "Look at him. He was once a man of the world, he had juice in him, he liked conversation, excitement, people, crowds, pretty women, literary discussion. Now he sits on a cow pad and consults the grass. . . . You are not fair to your wife. She is an angel, I adore her, she should be out where things go on." Cesare invites Joe and Ruth to join them at the Golden Gate Park: "You don't want to sit in this imitation Umbria and dig in the mud and struggle against uncivilized nature. That is the way to grow old."[17]

Cesare proceeds on monologues about the superiority of city life over country life. Even though Joe has joined the group, Joe suspects that Cesare still feels slighted by an insufficient audience, and he can tell that Cesare is looking for his first opportunity to leave graciously. He finds an opening and leaves full of well wishes and promises to return the Allstons to proper civilization should they ever visit him again in Rome. Joe, Ruth, and Minnie clean up, and Joe is deflated.

Cesare's "monologues were wasted on an empty house" and his eyes looked upon Joe and Ruth with pity, not the envy they had anticipated. He failed to comment on the lunch or the wine, and the conversation became tiresome to him. In sum, Joe thinks, "He has managed to make me feel ten years older than I was yesterday—out of it, self-exiled, and without the courage of my convictions, without the grace to be content with what I chose."[18] They are no longer the inhabitants of the Californian Arcadia that they saw themselves to be, but are instead human manifestations of the tombstone engraved "*Et in Arcadia ego*," a *memento mori* for Cesare and his vivacious friends to see, shudder at, and flee.

In 1982, Stegner was asked in an interview for the Sierra Club about his life in Los Altos Hills. His response reveals that Joe and Minnie were certainly speaking for him to some extent:

> We were here all during the time when the Santa Clara Valley was simply overrun and became Silicon Valley, and that was sort of demoralizing to see. When we came that was all a sea of blossoms in the spring. It was all orchards. It may be just as useful now, but it's very different.... And up here—we live, as you may have found out, on a kind of backward road. There were various eyesores and so on on the road that we applauded and wanted to stay, pig farms and things like that.... They're not here now. And when they went, and when water came into the hills, the whole place just exploded.... [and] real estate values were already heavily inflated ... which meant that the bank wouldn't lend on a cheap house for an expensive lot, so that the houses got bigger and more ornate and more vulgar ... so we're just full of these bloody seven hundred thousand dollar castles, with all these four-car garages.... This steepest and prettiest part of the Los Altos Hills, right around through here, has been developed in a way that would make a cannibal cry, I think.[19]

Stegner had seen too much development. The response above suggests that it was not just the effect on land that he deplored (and that is reflected elsewhere), but the fact that the places became less diverse and more oriented to progress as defined by the measures of Silicon Valley. Jason Heppler demonstrates that these environmentalist battles for open space did not simply stop destructive development; rather, more often the destructive development shifted elsewhere to places (usually populated by racial minorities) with less resources with which to defend against such steps.[20] In another 1982 response to these issues, Stegner deflected the charge of NIMBYism:[21]

> There is a cynical assumption in some quarters that those who fight for a degree of naturalness in the foothills are fighting to preserve for their own selfish benefit a place in which they arrived luckily early. I don't acknowledge that for myself and I

don't believe it of any Green Foothills member I know. Many who work hard to protect the hills don't live in them, and those who do live in them fight just as hard to protect Alaska wilderness or Montana grassland that they will never see. They want the hills protected for the simple reason that they love and respect the earth, know its value for other purposes than profit, and want to leave to their children and grandchildren a heritage that has not been dug up and paved over and—it is an ironic word—humanized.[22]

Again, Stegner is more confident here than in his novels, where he was more likely to pose questions that revealed the more tragic dimensions of how these legitimate and even noble attempts to preserve land in one place led to destructive policies in other places.

Growing Old in the New West

Joe knows the *"Et in Arcadia ego"* feeling acutely because he has been struggling against it himself when he sees his friends and neighbors. Joe and Ruth no longer associate with the owners of the bulldozers and the parents of young children, but with those who are, like them, living out the end of their days. In a particularly bleak metaphor of the loneliness of old age once all of the associational bonds have frayed and broken, he thinks, "I have no more to say to them than if we were refugees from some war, streaming along a road under air attack, diving for the same ditches when we have to, and getting up to struggle on, each for himself."[23] Is this self-pity too extreme in the suburbs of California? Perhaps, but this feeling of simply fighting to survive, alone, was not unique in the 1970s.[24]

Not that all of the neighbors approach aging in the same way: one neighbor, Ben Alexander, is a former doctor and is convinced that age is mostly in the mind, and that, properly viewed, old age can be a time of liberation. He is almost straight from the pages of Gail Sheehy's contemporaneous and bestselling book *Passages: Predictable Crises of an Adult Life* (1976). At the conclusion of a minilecture at the mailbox brimming with faith in modern medicine, he tells Joe that chicken tissues can be kept alive indefinitely in a nutrient broth. Joe's reply: "'You know, it's a funny thing.... I never had the slightest desire to live in a nutrient broth."[25] Ben is an achiever, and at seventy-nine, still growing and active. He serves on boards, checks up on former patients (including Joe), and tries to encourage others not to let themselves be beaten by old age. He is, Joe thinks, "one of those people, insufferable when you think about them, who have always been able to do exactly what they set out to do," but Joe also acknowledges that he goes out of the way to help his neighbors and is at least not wallowing around in self-pity like himself.

Ben thinks Joe is giving up and challenges him to leave more often the seclusion of his garden. Joe replies, "I never have needed many people around. I always had more than I wanted. A few friends are enough. There are lots of perfectly pleasant people whom I like, but if I don't see them I don't miss them. What kept me in New York was work, not people. When the work ended, most of the people ended, all but the handful that meant something."[26] Having experienced few whole-person relationships, Joe has little capacity for building bonds that are capable of surviving the end of the instrumental reasons holding them together.

Security Versus Life

Stegner stages several scenes that reveal the complexity of the search for roots that would become one of the great cultural trends of the late 1970s, especially after the success of Alex Haley's *Roots* (published the same year as *Spectator Bird*) and the broadcast of the miniseries based on the book on ABC.[27] At the beginning of their 1954 trip to Denmark after Curtis's death, Joe and Ruth encounter another couple headed back to the old country on their ship traveling across the Atlantic. Mr. Bertelson has not seen the Sweden of his birth since 1905, and he is taking his Minnesota-born wife to his old village to "live out their golden years" after having just sold the store that they operated in Minnesota throughout their adult lives. They are friendly but rigidly pious, and Joe observes that he is consistent with other immigrants (distinguished from political exiles) who have left the old country, whether for Minnesota or California: "The trauma of exile petrifies them. Forever they will love, and the old sod be fair. They bring it all with them, in its 1890 or 1900 version, and they plant it in America without modification and then spend the rest of their lives defending it against change, while in the old country what they knew changes so as to be unrecognizable."[28] Joe demonstrates to us that he is at least capable of seeing nostalgia in others, and that he will not spare himself if he begins to drift in this direction as well. The acquaintance does not last long.

Their ocean liner is hit by a storm of proportions fitting to *The Tempest*, and in the middle of it, Mr. Bertelson has a heart attack, dies, and is buried at sea in "unseemly haste." As the storm still rages, the crew takes Bertelson's body to send it to sea. They lift him and "there is no word for how instant his obliteration was."[29] Mrs. Bertelson is met by Mr. Bertelson's relatives in Sweden, none of whom speak English, and she vanishes out of the Allstons' life as well as what she knew as her own. The Allstons depart for Copenhagen, and Joe is chastened: "Not even the most foolish and bigoted member of Lutheran Christendom deserves to be wiped out like that."[30] Though there is an element of dark comedy to the story, it sets a foreboding mood, as if nostalgia is not just saccharine but poisonous. Neither places nor those who carry the memories of them are as stable as they might seem, Stegner appears to be warning his readers.

Since they are hoping for distraction from their past and immersion into the country, the Allstons board with Astrid, a Danish countess of around forty who has lost her privileged status for reasons that are revealed over the course of the novel. Joe and Ruth are both taken and perplexed by their hostess. She is beautiful and dignified, but still warm and engaging; nonetheless, she is virtually shunned by her community. After testing the waters to see if they will be merely lodgers or something more, the Allstons invite Astrid to the opera.

Though eyes follow them everywhere in the theater, no one greets her or speaks with her at all. They begin having some meals together, and after the Allstons tell her that Joe is planning to visit Bregninge on the island of Lolland, the birthplace of Joe's mother, Astrid informs them that her family is also from Bregninge, and that several of her relatives still live there in one of the most prominent estates. Delighted with the serendipity, they plan a trip even though Astrid is estranged from her brother and needs to arrange the visit so they will not cross paths.

Astrid also reveals that she is related to Karen Blixen (better known as Danish author Isak Dinesen). Wallace and Mary had actually met the author herself—her most well-known book was *Out of Africa*, published in 1937—when he and Mary visited Denmark in 1954. Slipping history back into fiction: both Joe and Ruth have long admired her books and they are thrilled to have the opportunity to meet her. Several days later, the more complicated revelations come out. Though Joe and Ruth have been trying to stifle their curiosity regarding the situation at the opera, Astrid eventually confesses that her husband was a quisling and Nazi sympathizer during World War II. Though she detested the Nazis and was proud of the Danish resistance, "he was my husband, what should I do?" Her husband had less regard for his marriage and his wife and left her after getting out of prison in 1947. When the Allstons meet her in 1954 she is still exiled in her hometown.[31]

On a beautiful day in early May, the Allstons and Astrid venture out to meet Karen Blixen, a revelatory trip. Once escaped from traffic, they stumble into a beautiful scene:

> We came to a stretch of beechwoods, and the light changed. Everything went from palely green to gold. Between the smooth gray trunks the grass was starred with white anemones or hepaticas. The leaves passing over our heads were tiny, delicate, tender as pale green flowers, a tinted mist that in a couple of days would be a green roof. Fairies must have been invented in spring beechwood.... Druidical magic.[32]

Joe takes a second loop through, and then a third. The countess expects Ruth to appreciate such beauty, but for Joe, she says, "'Mr. Allston is not the way Americans are supposed to be.... Why is he not loud and insensitive? Why does he not think all things can be bought for money? Why does he respond to beautiful things?'"[33] Joe is flattered. As in the previous Peninsula works, Stegner again allows Joe a sensibility that is contrasted with the artistic pretensions of the professional artists as well as Joe's own seemingly crusty demeanor. Stegner seems very concerned to suggest that emotional and sensual experiences of beauty are not reserved to artists alone, and that the suburban bourgeois should not be assumed callous philistines automatically.

They meet Karen Blixen in her garden and she shows them a rune stone that she has just found. They picnic in her garden and Karen speaks almost exclusively of her time in Africa, and Joe remarks on her love for it. She replies, "'It was life.'" Reveling in the beauty of her garden, Joe asks her what she calls her present place. "'This? This is safety,'" she replies. Joe tips his hand, asking, "'Is it bad to have a place to come back to? . . . An American, or at least one kind of American, would envy you. . . . He was born in transit, he has lived in fifty houses in fifteen places. When he moves, he doesn't move back, he moves on. . . . No traditions. A civilization without attics.'"[34] Karen replies that Americans also do not have rubbish piles, dungeons, or ghosts. Joe adds rune stones to the list.

Astrid remarks that they are headed in a week to visit Joe's mother's ancestral lands, to see if Joe can find his safe place. Joe is startled to see that Karen and Astrid have seen through him. By adding Blixen's *Out of Africa* to the story, Stegner again asks readers to consider the theme of place and community. In *Out of Africa*, Blixen escapes the stifling community of the Danish aristocracy and its restrictions on women's lives for the freedom of her coffee farm in Kenya (which was in turn a freedom dependent on British colonial subjection of Kenya). Joe has grown up with "freedom" and seeks security. Headed in opposite directions from each other, they have something of an understanding.

Driving home sunburnt and quiet, past beaches and other spring revelers, Joe's mind takes him back to Curtis's death and the futility of the attic he was preparing for his son, who would have nothing to do with attics. He is back in La Jolla to pick up Curt's things, reflecting again on what might have motivated him: "Intent upon what? Rebellions? Repudiations? Apathies? Boredoms? Fears, panics, terrors? Or just on Now, on the galvanic twitches of the eternal pointless present? What is that life style (that jargon term) except a substitute for a life?" Again, Joe is incapable of understanding or respect, but equally incapable of exonerating himself:

> Curt's repudiation let the air out of my confidence that I know what my job, my principles, my vote, my admirations, my friends, and my marriage are all about. I am as unsure of myself as I ever was of him. And I know why. In rejecting me he destroyed my compass, he pulled my plug, he drained me. He was the continuity my life and effort were spent to establish. I have been guilty of making first Ruth and then Curtis into barricades behind which I could take shelter. But why couldn't he have understood the

Figure 7. Wallace Stegner in a snapshot taken during the Stegners' 1954 trip to Europe. The country is not identified. Courtesy Special Collections, J. Willard Marriott Library, University of Utah.

Figure 8. Mary Stegner in a snapshot taken during the Stegners' 1954 trip to Sogn og Fjordane fylke, Norway, in 1954. Courtesy Special Collections, J. Willard Marriott Library, University of Utah.

hunger and love and panic, the trembling and cold sweats and the sleeplessness, the times when I looked at him sleeping, as a child, and was overwhelmed by my responsibility to him and his dearness to me? Who broke it, he or I?[35]

Joe summarizes their family history in two sentences. It is "the saga of an immigrant family, a succession of orphans, that began in flight on the island of Lolland in 1901 and ended fifty-two years later (in flight?) on the beach at La Jolla, on the western or suicide edge of the New World. Fifty-two years from wooden shoes and hope to barefoot kicks, fear, and silence; and in between, Joseph Allston, the bright overachiever, his mother's joy and treasure, his son's alien overseer."[36] Being in Europe, Joe places this futile cycle in historical context, wondering if it will ever slow down:

What did the Europeans gain by Columbus? The illusion of free-dom, I suppose. But did they gain or lose when they gave up the tentative safety of countries and cultures where the rules were as well known as the dangers, and had been tailored to the dangers, and went raiding in a virgin continent that was neither country nor culture, and isn't yet, and may never be, and yet has never given up the dangerous illusion of infinite possibility? What good did it all do, if we end up in confusion and purposelessness on the far Pacific shore of America, or come creeping back to our origins looking for something we have lost and can't name?[37]

Again, Joe is toying with a rejection of modernity and the mythical sense of progress. Karen had hinted at another secret to be revealed about Astrid's past, and it is at this point that Stegner turns back to testing safety, order, and nostalgia against life, chaos, and progress.

Astrid takes the Allstons to visit her family's estate. Though the trip has been carefully orchestrated to avoid revealing what Karen had hinted at, an awkward dinner ensues with Astrid's family. Then afterwards on a walk, Joe runs into Eigil, Astrid's brother. Eigil charms him into spending the afternoon playing tennis and touring the grounds. These grounds, which Eigil manages, are state-of-the-art in the 1950s, the most scientifically run in Denmark if not the world (in Eigil's opinion).[38] Joe sees hardly anyone, as Eigil has managed to mechanize most of the labor. After seeing the animals, all of which are scientifically managed "pure" strains of their kind, Joe comes full circle and plays Marian to Eigil's Joe. He says that the estate is magnificent but lacking "wild things.... Little cottontails or gophers or snakes ... that could breed in the hedges in spite of you. Holsteins and short-haired pointers are nice, but a little predictable."[39] Eigil remains unconvinced and they part on respectful terms.

The trip raises more questions, however, and Joe and Ruth are even more curious about Astrid's family after leaving. Eigil has told Joe that his father was a famous scientist, but "hounded" by his contemporaries.[40] Joe, unable to resist, investigates and hears disturbing revelations from the public affairs officer at the American Embassy, but the Allstons do not really get the truth until they have a long conversation with Astrid. They find out that Astrid's father was in fact a famous scientist during his lifetime. But there is a reason his fame became infamy. Her father committed suicide several weeks after her mother did the same in the wake of public revelations that he had quietly impregnated a peasant woman living on his land, and then later their daughter as well, in the hopes of developing a better understanding of human genetics. Though her parents died disgraced, Astrid's brother, Eigil, has decided to continue the experiment, and it is clear that, unlike his father as reported by Astrid, he takes more than scientific interest in it. The Allstons find this out only after they have visited the castle and sat through awkward silences and unintended introductions.

Given the historical moment and several references to Nazi atrocities, including eugenics and the obsession with racial purity, not to mention the direct connections via Astrid's estranged husband, this adds even more complexity to Stegner's theme of the formless non-community. Nostalgia for Gemeinschaft, and potentially even the actual resurrection of Gemeinschaft, is no easy solution to the loneliness of the California suburb.[41] Zygmunt Bauman's chilling metaphor of the "gardening state" comes to mind, in relation to both this theme and the significance of Stegner's pastoral themes in his explorations of the Midpeninsula.[42]

The Venerable Bede and the Midpeninsula

Back in the Peninsula, Joe closes the journal, having ended it with Astrid's revelations about her family and the horrors of Eigil's plans for continuing his father's genetic experiments. But Ruth is not convinced it is the end to their story. She insists to Joe that there must be more, as they were in Denmark for another month. She continues to prod, and eventually it is revealed that Ruth has always been suspicious that Joe and Astrid began an affair after the revelations about her family. Joe issues vague denials, and finally Ruth asks why both Joe and Astrid were missing from their rooms after their Midsummer Night celebrations, which they celebrated by taking a trip to one of Astrid's ancestral properties (reduced to a small cottage by a lake) near Helsingør, the location of Kronborg Castle and setting for *Hamlet*. After saying truthfully that he was unsettled by the celebrations and went for a walk and ran into Astrid, Ruth asks if that was all. Finally, shaking and on the verge of tears, Joe tells Ruth that no, that was not all: they kissed once. Joe then leaves the house in shame for a walk.

Joe is outside on a hilltop with stars visible as if on the deck of a ship, and he is forced to account for himself. "From up on that chilly platform you can look back down on your life and see it like a Kafka road dwindling out across the Siberian waste. You can raise your head and look into the infinite spaces whose eternal silence terrified Pascal."[43] His "absurd tears" dry quickly and Joe recalls the moment. He is back in Ellebacken at the cottage property with Ruth and Astrid. Joe and Astrid both leave their rooms independently and after running into each other and allowing their attraction to overcome their consideration of Ruth, take a walk near the lake. They are somber in recognition of both the stillness of the place and the Allstons' impending return to the United States.

Astrid asks Joe if he knows Goethe's "Über Allen Gipfeln," a "poem made all of whispers." Joe knows it but asks her to recite it. Stegner has her recite it in German without translation in the book. In English, however: "O'er all the hilltops / Is quiet now, / In all the treetops / Hearest thou / Hardly a breath; / The birds are asleep in the trees: / Wait, soon like these / Thou too shalt rest."[44] Astrid brings Joe to a rowboat and takes him to the small island where her father had shot himself and then was buried in a barely marked grave. Staring at the grave, their respective obligations are forced into the open. Joe tries to insist, stupidly, that Astrid should return to the United States to live near Joe and Ruth. Astrid knows better but Joe insists that she needs to escape the exile the men in her family have left her to rot under: "You don't owe anybody any duty except yourself. They've lost all claim on you. . . . Why haven't any of them helped you during all the years you've been in trouble? . . . You can't stay here and mold. You're too special." Astrid does not deny the legitimacy of Joe's assertion but will not accept it, and she also reminds him of Ruth. The romance of the impossible situation takes over for the moment and they share a kiss. Astrid pushes Joe away first and the affair is over. As Joe is getting the boat, he looks back and sees Astrid rising from a curtsy she had "dropped toward her father's gravestone."[45]

While the novel has been building up to the revelation of the brief affair, the curtsy just after the kiss was the crucial scene in Stegner's mind as he was planning the book. It was a scene that he repeated three times in his notes, and one that seemed nonnegotiable as it, unlike many of the other ideas in the notes, remained in the published novel. It is a particularly complex scene. Based on the notes for all three of the California novels, Stegner seemed to have started the novel with both a series of questions he wanted to explore, but also at least one dramatic scene that he thought would bring the ideas and themes together. It is not hard to imagine that he built the novels in order to make the dramatic scenes happen with maximum effect. The notes for *Live Things* reveal that the scene with the horse breaking its legs off in the cattleguard was an early feature of the novel, and the notes for *Angle of Repose* suggest that Oliver's tearing up of the roses after Agnes died in connection to Susan's affair with Frank was in his mind from the earliest stages.

The scene Stegner wanted to ruminate on in *Spectator Bird* is much less dramatic and in fact is fairly easy to miss because it is overshadowed by Joe's guilt over the kiss. In one draft, Stegner writes, "As for Karen [Astrid], her curtsy at the stone on her father's grave—that other sort of rune stone—is a gesture of defeat like Eveline's in Dubliners— an acknowledgement of the impossibility of uprooting. It is possible that I should make the American unstable enough and selfish enough so that the reader is not too upset to see her throw aside this one chance for escape, for he would know it was escape only into something just as bad, however opposite."[46] Though it was very prominent in Stegner's mind as he was exploring possibilities for the novel, the scene where Astrid curtsies to her father at his gravesite is swallowed up in the description of Joe's guilt and revelation of his infidelity. Joe and Astrid renounce each other, and that is the most prominent element of the scene. Because the novel returns to Joe and Ruth attempting to make sense of how the moment affected their life together, readers see that Joe's renunciation of Astrid was ultimately more of an affirmation of his commitment to Ruth.

Joe moves on to consider himself in the present. Was that renunciation a renunciation of life, or something else? Is Joe "one of those Blake was scornful of, who controlled their passions because their passions are feeble enough to be controlled?" He imagines his life written by Cesare Rulli, or others for whom "the highest reach of human conduct is expressed by the consenting adult." It is one of Babbittry and failure, milquetoast conformity and banality. But Joe decides he will argue back this time:

> I do not choose to be a consenting adult, just to be in fashion. I have no impulse to join those the Buddha describes, those who strain always after fulfillment and in fulfillment strive to feel desire. It has seemed to me that my commitments are often

more important than my impulses or my pleasures, and that even when my pleasures or desires are the principal issue, there are choices to be made between better and worse.[47]

It is a cathartic moment, one where Joe finally allows himself to win one of his internal arguments against his own conscience and interlocutors from Curtis to Murthi to Kaminski to Peck to Rulli. Ruth comes outside, and awkwardly they come back together in the warmest moment between them in all of the Peninsula novels. Joe apologizes for the moment in their past and his crankiness in the present, and Ruth apologizes for forcing the confession out of him. Joe tells her that he was smitten by Astrid, but that eventually he forgot her and that he has gone years without thinking of Astrid at all. Had the postcard not come he would not be thinking of her yet, which he acknowledges is sad in its own way. But that is not the end of the story: "I'll tell you something else. If I'd played the game the way people seem to expect, and jumped into the Baltic, all for love and the world well lost . . . I couldn't have forgotten you that way. I'd have regretted you for the rest of my life."[48]

Ruth says that she was angry and offended by what she had imagined, but not enough to risk the end of their marriage. They affirm their love, kiss, damn the cold and their joints, and head inside. If he has not changed much, this moment has affirmed at least the life he and Ruth have built together:

> The truest vision of life I know is that bird in the Venerable Bede that flutters from the dark into a lighted hall, and after a while flutters out again into the dark. But Ruth is right. It is something—it can be everything—to have found a fellow bird with whom you can sit among the rafters while the drinking and boasting and reciting and fighting go on below; a fellow bird whom you can look after and find birds for; one who will patch your bruises and straighten your ruffled feathers and mourn over your hurts when you accidentally fly into something you can't handle.[49]

It is a fittingly avian ending to a series of stories about the suburbs that began with "Field Guide to Western Birds" and a miserable towhee slamming his head into the sliding glass door.[50] Ultimately, it is belonging, whether cliché or not, that is worth fighting for. It is the least worst of the available options, and sometimes even good.

Reader Responses: "Adrift in a World I Can't Understand"

Stegner's warm account of Joe and Ruth's marriage resonated with his readers. Most of the responses spoke to that theme and the theme of aging. One of the more surprising responses to *Spectator Bird* came from a younger reader who read the book with her new husband on her honeymoon and appreciated the book because "it captured a very real part of my relationship with my husband and felt that 'it' would be a part of this relationship always."[51] Another reader also thought it might be valuable for marital therapy: "I tried to assist friends in keeping a marriage together by loaning them The Spectator B. It didn't work, but I still think it's a damn good book."[52] A social gerontologist at New York State Psychiatric Institute enjoyed it and also found it useful in her teaching: "I am tasting The Spectator Bird so that I should not come to the end too quickly. To say that it is poetic–marvelously sensitive–heartwarming, seems somewhat pedestrian. But I have no other words. I am recommending it to others, and I shall use it in teaching."[53]

Several other readers found the book valuable for its reflections on aging as well. A rabbi from Rochester, New York, wrote to thank Stegner for "helping me pass through this period of my life with some modicum of dignity and humor."[54] Another reader who appreciated Stegner's meditation on aging wrote, "In a culture obsessed with youthfulness, whose most fervent endeavor seems to be the prolongation (physical, mental and emotional) of the attributes and appearance of youngness, I, as a middle-aged mother, acknowledge the passing of the years with its inevitable physical deterioration and inescapable signs of changes yet to come, have been inspired by your book." Ultimately, she found it hopeful, probably more than Stegner might have been himself, as suggested by her description of Joe Allston as "a man attempting to reconstruct his life, evaluating his life-experience, coming to terms with himself, coping with the sorrows, accepting and finally celebrating his life."[55]

Other readers responded to the book as a welcome respite in a world that left them confused and lonely. A woman from California wrote,

"The book left me with questions, but a good novel should. I am so glad to be able to identify with the people you write about. So many things I read lately make me feel alienated, adrift in a world I can't understand."[56] Another letter from a member of the Classic Book Club of Bloomington, Indiana, with "33 ladies" as members, wrote to ask Stegner a question: "Many of the ladies are getting older and are eager to know how you would have handled this situation had Joe Allston not had a loving companion to soften the pain of illness, loneliness and aging. Because of the statistics—a similar final story is often faced alone."[57]

Similar, but with a more critical edge, were readers who praised the book as too exceptional: "It seems that these days what is being written are non-books by non-writers for non-readers," one frustrated reader from Palm Springs, California, wrote.[58] Watergate seemed to be on the mind of another reader from Virginia:

> Mr. Stegner, much of your work suggests a special respect for the heroic virtues of the common man. Yet, such characteristics seem more and more difficult to locate in the uncommon man, that man or woman squarely in the public view. Does America no longer have room or need for heroes ... or are we turned away from the traditional hero toward the anti-hero ... and can a people maintain a lasting spirit and integrity without public heroes upon which to depend for guidance and leadership?[59]

Another reader who identified *Live Things* as his favorite of several Stegner books wrote to tell him that he was grateful for Stegner's artistic vision: "Sufficient to say, the books are cherished as literature, as thought, as substance in a wasteland (that is mockingly littered with such as Mailer's mind-wipings.) ... We are a thoughtful and charitable people, not pugnacious boors. I believe this. From your works I gather that you believe it too, and I rejoice that you have been so busy spreading the word."[60]

Conclusion

Perhaps because Stegner had caught up to Joe in age, the book was decidedly more meditative about aging than any of the other books. Joe and

Ruth find themselves confronting dying friends, physical ailments, emotional regrets, and the fear that they have already become invisible to the rest of the world. If Joe learns that he cannot retreat in *Live Things* but does so anyway, he learns in *Spectator Bird* that his retreat has come at a cost, and that, having retreated successfully, he has in fact been left alone by any broader public. When he is not being left alone, he feels he is being chased into the grave.

By the end of the book, which community has won: the formless non-community, or the safe harbor for lonely seafarers? Astrid curtsies to her ancestors and acknowledges that she must stay in Denmark, despite her internal exile. When the Allstons receive her postcard, they pity her but not completely. There is an acknowledgment that her effort to sustain her connections to her place and her obligations—both inherited and chosen—are worthy of respect. Joe has no ancestors for whom to bow and he will be forgotten by his community once he is dead. He will have no place to be buried. But he does have Ruth. In his affirmation of Ruth and their marriage, Stegner is starting with the one bond present when no others can be found.

Conclusion

The Geography of Hope?

We simply need that wild country available to us, even if we never do more than drive to its edge and look in. For it can be a means of reassuring ourselves of our sanity as creatures, a part of the geography of hope.

—Wallace Stegner[1]

California, it should be said at once, is not part of the West.... California is a nation of in-migrants, and its writers are in-migrants too, either writing about the places they came from or frantically scratching around and reading Sunset *to find specifically Californian patterns to which to conform.*

—Wallace Stegner[2]

Of all the phrases Wallace Stegner wrote over the course of his life, none have remained more resonant than "the geography of hope." These were the last four words of his famed "Wilderness Letter." Thus far I have only alluded to Stegner's famous phrase. At the end of my survey of his life and work in California, it is worth coming back to this phrase, which he revisited throughout his life. Did the "geography of hope" include Los Altos Hills, California?

The letter was written on December 3, 1960, to David Pesonen, a lawyer for the Wildlife Research Center who was working on a report on wilderness recreation sponsored by the Department of the Interior.[3] It was (and is) most often evoked as a nonsectarian spiritual defense of the intrinsic values of wilderness lands. Most celebrants of this phrase conjure images of Stegner's beloved Canyonlands in Utah, Yosemite, or Yellowstone when thinking about the geography of hope. More dedicated readers might think of the stark prairies of Saskatchewan where Stegner spent his early years.[4] The geography of hope as conceived by Stegner was

THE GEOGRAPHY OF HOPE? | 171

more than these majestic wilds, however. Wilderness was also hopeful because its existence demonstrated that Americans were still sane enough to "apply some other criteria than commercial and exploitative considerations" to the land they inhabited.[5] In other words, wilderness was a source of hope in itself, but its presence was also hopeful because it had been set aside and, in a sense, created through democratic processes by a people who could have instead chosen to turn the "last virgin forests [into] comic books and cigarette cases" and push "paved roads through the last of the silence."[6]

On the eve of the Kennedy administration—in which he briefly served as special assistant to Stuart Udall, Secretary of the Interior—Stegner was as hopeful as he would ever be, even if his hope was generally more modest than most of those who found his writing so powerful.[7] Wilderness, and a political order dedicated to protecting it, he argued, might be one necessary step toward a better society, even if not sufficient in itself.[8] By 1964, two years after the Cuban Missile Crisis put "our sanity as creatures" through one of its more severe tests, the Wilderness Act had made Stegner's hopes a reality by enshrining in statute a version of this vision of American wilderness.[9]

Five years later, at the end of a decade that vexed him, he was still capable of hope for the West. Stegner concluded his introduction to *The Sound of Mountain Water*, published in 1969, with this affirmation and challenge: "Angry as one may be at what heedless men have done and still do to a noble habitat, one cannot be pessimistic about the West. This is the native home of hope." Should the West learn "that cooperation, not rugged individualism, is the quality that most characterizes and preserves it," the West might have a "chance to create a society to match its scenery."[10] Though Stegner's own writings suggested that "cooperation" did not actually "characterize" the West very consistently—even if it might best preserve it—these words rang true for many westerners of the time.[11] Such statements and the essays of that volume as a whole could almost be described as the foundation of a political and cultural program for a certain population of the West.

Nearly two decades later, in 1986, Stegner returned to this most durable phrase of his in a lecture series. While delivering the William W. Cook Lectures at the University of Michigan Law School, Stegner referred to the "reckless moment" in which he called the "western public lands" the "geography of hope."[12] And then in 1988, he doubled down in his despair. In the early, giddy stages of the academic boom that was the "New Western History," one year after the publication of historian Patricia Limerick's *Legacy of Conquest* (but a year before the Trails Conference in Santa Fe), Limerick invited Stegner to deliver a keynote lecture at a conference named for another of the key phrases he introduced into the public vocabulary of the West.[13] Held at the University of Colorado, the conference was "A Society to Match the Scenery: Shaping the Future of the American West."

While still capable of "native enthusiasm" in the presence of western wilderness, Stegner told the audience, he was less hopeful about the people of the West—those same people he had once hoped might be wise enough to protect wilderness areas.[14] Could westerners be counted on to recognize the value of their places and build healthy societies capable of engendering the loyalty of three generations or more without destroying them?[15]

No. The end of his lecture suggested, at best, a grim realism more than anything like hope. In a dryly humorous preconference planning letter, Stegner admitted to the "pretty pessimistic" tone of the Michigan lectures. He then promised Limerick that he would see if he could, "without emetic results, inject a little Reaganism into [the address] and send people home happy." By the time he delivered the address, however, he could not bring himself to end on a cheery note.[16]

Philip Fradkin surmises that the geography of hope phrase came to Stegner's mind as an inversion of the "geography of despair" surveyed in Dante's *Inferno*.[17] Observing the American West in 1988—Stegner was an early critic of President Ronald Reagan and a vehement critic of his first Secretary of the Interior, James G. Watt—Dante's image had become more vivid in his mind than his own earlier phrase.[18]

After "calamity howling" about the destructive patterns of settlement in the West for most of the lecture, Stegner looked like a twentieth-century western Qoheleth, observing that "no boom seems to learn much from the previous ones."[19] The West, he believed, would only choose a better future if forced to do so by extreme circumstances. He ended with a challenge again but one terse and forceful more than aspirational. Incidentally, it came from Satan, via Mark Twain's *The Mysterious Stranger*:

"Dream other dreams, and better."[20] Surveying Stegner's relationship to what she calls "the hope trope," literary historian Krista Comer argues that Stegner had simply been chastened by the knowledge of not only too many boom-and-bust cycles but the recognition that "the West's history of settlement by conquest necessarily meant that one man's geography of hope was another man's geography of the *end* of hope" [italics original].[21]

This shift in his thinking did not go unnoticed. Donald Worster, whose *Rivers of Empire* Stegner had promoted just before it was published in 1985, wrote to Stegner to express his qualified surprise after reading *The American West as Living Space*: "It is a pretty pessimistic book, surprisingly so for someone who has generally come down on the hopeful side of life, and I can't help feeling a little personally guilty about contributing to your gloominess. Of course, you've seen that dark side of the region and the country long before I and a few others started sounding so radical and critical about it."[22]

There is one more twist to this extended conversation that Stegner had with himself about his famous phrase. Both the Michigan and Colorado lectures were included in his last essay collection, *Where the Bluebird Sings to the Lemonade Springs*, published four years later in 1992. The Michigan lecture series was reprinted without significant change, but his "A Geography of Hope" lecture underwent thorough revision.[23] Whether out of a sense of public responsibility, a belief in the power of aspirational description, or genuine honest conviction, Stegner ended his essay much differently. While not ignoring the lingering legacy of the "boomers" like his father whose "dream of something for nothing" led to a life that did "more human and environmental damage than he could have repaired in a second lifetime," he also wrote with the desire "that these essays do not say that western hopefulness is a cynical joke."[24]

Rather than turning to the advice of Mark Twain's Satan for his conclusion, he turned instead to a consideration of the most recent spate of western writers: the "Ivan Doigs and Bill Kittredges and James Welches, the Gretel Ehrlichs and Rudolfo Anayas and John Daniels, the Scott Momadays and Louise Erdrichs, and many more." Stegner wrote that he felt a "surge of the inextinguishable western hope" for the "civilization that they are building," the "history they are compiling," their "way of looking at the world and humanity's place in it." It was a culture he hoped he would be "around to see … fully arrive." These writers, he believed, were contributing to a western "civilization" of the "stickers," or "those who love the life they have made and the place that they have made it in." This generation of stickers might "work out some sort of compromise between what must be done to earn a living and what must be done to restore health to the earth, air, and water." Stegner's hope of seeing this new era arrive was not to be, as he died a year later.[25]

The question remains: did the geography of hope include Los Altos Hills? On the one hand, there is certainly a sense in which Stegner was hopeful for the West that includes Los Altos Hills, and for the cultures that were being built in that West by the writers he mentioned. He is still foremost in the hearts and minds of many as a defender of a humane American West. But I think it is also telling that *Spectator Bird* ends with a couple that has only each other at the end, as heartwarming as the love they share is. As I have attempted to show, they are still facing their deaths in a place that is a formless non-community. The dissatisfaction of this ending point to his California novels is made more poignant by contrast with Stegner's writings about Greensboro, Vermont.

Greensboro

Almost four decades after he first conceived of his village democracy study, Stegner revealed the hypothesis that he had started with but kept hidden at the time, in obedience to the dictates of social science. The revelation came in his introduction to a history of Greensboro published by the Greensboro Historical Society in 1990.[26] Granting that it was a small publication and that it was written to and for people who were his friends, the article is still interesting as a reflection of how the study remained in his mind and of how it looked from the distance of several decades. It is also revealing for what Stegner says about Greensboro in light of these explorations of several "formless non-communities" in the American West. Looking back on the origins of his Wenner-Gren project, Stegner said that he had contemplated writing a book about Greensboro as "a demonstration of how human beings learn to live amicably in groups, how they organize their lives for mutual helpfulness, for social stability, for order; how their arts and architecture, mythology, legends, characters, history, customs, laws, and institutions develop, change, and grow through the daily friction and wear of association."[27]

He thought of Greensboro, in other words, as a real place, and a real place that had managed to endure. But further, he thought of it as a "sort of ideal middle ground between stasis on the one hand and chaos on the other, as a model of formed and tested village democracy." He admitted his hypothesis: Greensboro would stand out as something of an ideal in contrast to Eastend—a place that was so new that it "forced the abandonment of most of the cultural baggage people had brought with them and the desperate improvisation of new patterns. . . . Where the old had all been thrown away and the new not yet developed"—and Taasinge, on the other hand, as an "isolated, inbred" village "too little invigorated by outside stimuli."

Reassuring his Greensboro readers that there was no need for alarm, that the "notes are long lost" and the project "abandoned," he said he was neither "historian enough nor sociologist enough" to write the comparative book. Further, and more importantly, he realized that Greensboro was "neither as simple nor as changeless as I once thought it."[28]

His recognition that it was not in fact changeless did not obscure the fact that it was still a place, one capable of producing a "local history," which he called "the home-grown, the best kind" of history. It is history written by the "people who made it," out of records kept by "the generations before them," or "generations with which the present has the most intimate familial and community relationship." It is a place that has survived at a generational scale; a place whose history "speaks from the stone walls that once bounded fields and now disappears into rank woods, and from the barn ramps and cellar holes of burned-out farms, and from the family names that appear as surely on the latest Grand List as on the earliest gravestones." It is a place with something close to an "unbroken record, which is also a promise, of continuity and tradition, and of change so slow that it appears to be changelessness."[29]

Coming himself from a "society that knew more about moving on than about settling down," Stegner wrote that Greensboro had what he "lacked and wanted: permanence, tranquility, traditional and customary acceptances, a stable and neighborly social order." It was a place that had endured long enough to produce members who "knew who they were and where they belonged."[30]

Stegner in California

Stegner broke many western hearts when it was revealed that he had decided to have his ashes spread in a grove of ferns in Greensboro rather than, say, in the prairies of Saskatchewan or the Canyonlands of Utah, two of the other places Stegner loved.[31] Though he lived in California for more years than in any other state, Stegner's complex relationship to the state—and Los Altos Hills in particular—has in some ways obscured the intensity with which he attempted to think about his place in it. In this study, I have traced the difficult questions that Stegner posed about his adopted state, one that he migrated to with much hope, but which eventually proved to be beyond his capacity to imagine as a place, at least on his terms.

Though he worked very hard to make it a place, it seems that Los Altos Hills was ultimately too similar to the Nevada City that Lyman Ward described in *Angle of Repose*: "Main Street, Anywhere, a set used over and over in a hundred B movies, a stroboscopic image pulsing to reassure us by subliminal tricks that though we are nowhere, we are at home." Lyman grumbles to himself, "Towns are like people. Old ones often have character, the new ones are interchangeable."[32]

Wallace Stegner possessed a particularly refined "homing sentiment." Searching for his home in *Wolf Willow*, Stegner wrote, "I may not know who I am, but I know where I am from."[33] Several decades and many, many words later, still unsure of who he was, he chose to articulate his sense of self, safety, and stability differently. It was, notably, not in terms of geography. In one of the most poignant lines from his last novel, *Crossing to Safety*—set in Greensboro—Stegner's Larry Morgan thinks, "I didn't know myself well, and still don't. But I did know, and know now, the few people I have loved and trusted."[34]

APPENDIX: Wallace Stegner's Books Listed by Date of Original Publication

Remembering Laughter. Boston: Little, Brown and Company, 1937.

The Potter's House. Muscatine: The Prairie Press, 1938.

On a Darkling Plain. New York: Harcourt, Brace and Company, 1940.

Fire and Ice. New York: Duell, Sloan and Pierce, 1941.

Mormon Country. New York: Duell, Sloan and Pierce, 1942.

The Big Rock Candy Mountain. New York: Duell, Sloan and Pierce, 1943.

One Nation. Boston: Houghton Mifflin, 1945.

Second Growth. Boston: Houghton Mifflin and Company, 1947.

The Women on the Wall. Boston: Houghton Mifflin Company, 1950.

The Preacher and the Slave. Boston: Houghton Mifflin Company, 1950.

The Writer in America. Kanda: The Hokuseido Press, 1952.

Beyond the Hundredth Meridian: John Wesley Powell and the Second Opening of the West. Boston: Houghton Mifflin, 1954.

This Is Dinosaur: Echo Park Country and Its Magic Rivers. New York: Alfred A. Knopf, 1955.

The City of the Living and Other Stories. Boston: Houghton Mifflin Company, 1956.

A Shooting Star. New York: The Viking Press, 1961.

Wolf Willow: A History, a Story, and a Memory of the Last Plains Frontier. New York: The Viking Press, 1962.

The Gathering of Zion: The Story of the Mormon Trail. New York: McGraw-Hill, 1964.

All the Little Live Things. New York: The Viking Press, 1967.

The Sound of Mountain Water. New York: Doubleday & Company, 1969.

Discovery: The Search for Arabian Oil. Beirut: Aramco, 1971.

Angle of Repose. Garden City: Doubleday, 1971.

The Uneasy Chair: A Biography of Bernard DeVoto. Garden City: Doubleday, 1974.

The Spectator Bird. New York: Doubleday, 1976.

Recapitulation. Garden City: Doubleday, 1979.

American Places. New York: E. P. Dutton, 1981. (cowritten with Page Stegner)

20-20 Vision: In Celebration of the Peninsula Foothills. Edited by Phyllis Filiberti. Palo Alto: Western Tanager Press, 1982.

One Way to Spell Man: Essays with a Western Bias. New York: Doubleday, 1982.

The Sense of Place. Madison: Silver Buckle Press, 1986.

Crossing to Safety. New York: Random House, 1987.

The American West as Living Space. Ann Arbor: University of Michigan Press, 1987.

Collected Stories of Wallace Stegner. New York: Random House, 1990.

Where the Bluebird Sings to the Lemonade Springs. New York: Random House, 1992.

On Teaching and Writing Fiction, with Lynn Stegner. New York: Penguin Books, 2002.

Marking the Sparrow's Fall: The Making of the American West. Edited by Page Stegner. New York: Henry Holt and Company, 1998.

NOTES

INTRODUCTION

1. Edward Abbey, *Desert Solitaire: A Season in the Wilderness* (New York: Touchstone, 1990), 1.

2. Stegner, "To a Young Writer," *The Atlantic* 204 (November 1959): 88–91.

3. The character Lyman Ward in Stegner, *Angle of Repose* (1971; New York: Vintage Books, 2014), 166.

4. John M. Findlay traces the first use of "Silicon Valley" to describe the Santa Clara Valley between Palo Alto and San Jose in a series of articles published by Don C. Hoefler in *Electronic News* in 1971. Findlay, *Magic Lands: Western Cityscapes and American Culture After 1940* (Berkeley: University of California Press, 1992), 145, 340n95. More broadly, see also Richard A. Walker, *The Country in the City: The Greening of the San Francisco Bay Area* (Seattle: University of Washington Press, 2007), and Jason Heppler, "Machines in the Valley: Community, Urban Change, and Environmental Politics in Silicon Valley, 1945–1990" (PhD diss., University of Nebraska, 2016).

5. See William DuBois, "The Last Word: The Well-Made Novel," *The New York Times Book Review*, August 29, 1971, 31; John Leonard, "The Pulitzer Prizes: Fail Safe Again," *The New York Times Book Review*, May 14, 1972, 47. DuBois damned by faint praise, but Leonard's review considered *Angle of Repose* a signal of the deterioration of the Pulitzer Prize. *Angle of Repose* was chosen by jurors "who ignore the living and dishonor the dead by settling for whatever is comfortable, tame, toothless and affectionate—a pet instead of a work of art.... We have obviously settled for pacifiers, and one hopes we choke on them."

6. Two well-researched biographies of Stegner are by Jackson Benson, *Wallace Stegner: His Life and Work* (New York: Viking, 1996), and Philip Fradkin, *Wallace Stegner and the American West* (New York: Alfred A. Knopf, 2008). I rely on both of them and challenge their interpretations throughout.

7. As Larry McMurtry wrote, "Though car wrecks happen everywhere, in the West death on the highway is as much a part of the culture as rodeos." McMurtry, "The West without Chili," *The New York Review of Books*, October 22, 1998.

8. Stegner, *Where the Bluebird Sings to the Lemonade Springs* (New York: The Modern Library, 2002), 6.

9. "Letter, Much Too Late," in *Where the Bluebird Sings*, 33. The essay is Stegner's most poignant reflection on his mother's life. Benson and Fradkin have supported Stegner's description of his mother, but the record is hard to corroborate. Fradkin, *Wallace Stegner and the American West*, 45–49; Benson, *Wallace Stegner: His Life and Work*, 16–21.

10. Benson, *Wallace Stegner: His Life and Work*, 17–18.

11. Stegner discussed his relationship with his father most directly with historian Richard W. Etulain in *Stegner: Conversations on History and Literature* (Reno: University of Nevada Press, 1996), 8, 42–43. The conversations took place in 1980 and 1981. Stegner described his father as "enormously entertaining" but "cursed with a wicked temper." He was alternately "very proud of him" and so frustrated with him that he would have "willingly strangled him." Later in the interview he said that his father bred in him a "kind of insecurity which may never be healed" and discussed his fiction as an attempt to "exorcise" his father.

12. "Former Mining Man Shoots Woman, Self to Death in Salt Lake Hotel," *Salt Lake Tribune*, June 16, 1939.

13. Stegner, *Where the Bluebird Sings*, 15.

14. Wallace Stegner, *The Sound of Mountain Water* (New York: Doubleday & Company, 1969), 199.

15. Stegner, *On Teaching and Writing Fiction* (New York: Penguin Books, 2002), 115. He encouraged others to practice writing-as-therapy as well. Mary Powell describes such a moment. She had been at a writer's seminar with Stegner and recalls how he helped her with more than the writing: "You talked to me as a friend, an understanding one, one who had been hurt in your youth as I myself had been, and later you invited me to use you as though you were a psychiatrist. . . . As a result, I cured myself, with your help, by writing to you how I had suffered." Her letters ran for many pages and took the form of psychoanalytic exploration of her past. Mary Powell to Wallace Stegner, November 14, 1949, box 9, folder 36, Wallace Earle Stegner Papers, University of Utah Library, Salt Lake City (hereafter Stegner Papers).

16. The image is from Ludwig Wittgenstein, trans. G. E. M. Anscombe, *Philosophical Investigations*, 4th ed. (New York: Wiley-Blackwell, 2009).

17. Stegner, *The Sound of Mountain Water*, 193.

18. Stegner, *The Spectator Bird* (New York: Penguin, 2010), 4.

19. Stegner, *Angle of Repose* (New York: Vintage, 2014), 6.

20. Stegner, *Spectator Bird*, 63.

21. Stegner's character Larry Morgan, also a writer, on writing characters in fiction: "They were people whom, having invented them, I rather liked. I didn't want to do them in, only to make them see a little better." Stegner, *Crossing to Safety* (New York: Modern Library Classics, 2002), 253.

22. On white middle-class angst, see Norman Mailer, *The White Negro* (San Francisco: City Lights Books, 1972), for as good an ur-text for this sensibility as any, and Grace Elizabeth Hale, *A Nation of Outsiders* (New York: Oxford University Press, 2014), for historical context.

23. See Gyorgy Lukács, *The Meaning of Contemporary Realism* (Talgarth, Wales: The Merlin Press, 1979), on the response to the question of angst being at the center of the modernist bourgeois novel. See also Trilling on the "escape from the middle class," or escape from society in general, as the dominant theme of modernist literature. Lionel Trilling, "On the Teaching of Modern Literature," in *The American Intellectual Tradition Volume 2: 1865 to the Present*, ed. David A. Hollinger and Charles Capper (New York: Oxford University Press, 2006). Mark Greif describes these themes as well in *The Age of the Crisis of Man* (Princeton: Princeton University Press, 2015).

24. Stegner, *Where the Bluebird Sings*, 223.
25. "The conviction of belonging" is in Stegner, "To a Young Writer," *The Atlantic*, November 1959, 88–91. The "formless non-community" is in Stegner, Notes on *All the Little Live Things* "Walk Around the Neighborhood," box 78, folder 1, Stegner Papers: "Purpose of this walk, to make visual and olfactory the setting, the formless non-community."
26. Stegner, *Where the Bluebird Sings*, 223.
27. Daniel Immerwahr's *Thinking Small: The United States and the Lure of Community Development* (Cambridge: Harvard University Press, 2015) demonstrates the pervasiveness of idealistic evocations of town life and small communities in the same era. The popularity of Norman Rockwell and the themes he represented during this era suggests the strength of the counternarrative toward home and place.
28. Jeffrey Bilbro, *Virtues of Renewal: Wendell Berry's Sustainable Forms* (Lexington: University Press of Kentucky, 2019), 72–79. Bilbro thoughtfully explores the potentially reductive qualities of these categories—most notably, that not all mobility is "boomer mobility"—in relation to Wendell Berry's use of them in his 2012 Jefferson Lecture, but emphasizes their value as a provocative challenge to a dominant sensibility in American culture. Stegner, *Where the Bluebird Sings*, xxvii.
29. Stegner, *Where the Bluebird Sings*, 201. In his classic study, geographer Yi-Fu Tuan offers two succinct definitions that align with Stegner's: "Space is transformed into place as it acquires definition and meaning.... Place is a pause in movement." Tuan, *Space and Place: The Perspective of Experience* (Minneapolis: University of Minnesota Press, 1977), 136–38. Both Stegner's and Tuan's definitions emphasize the simple point that place requires time, though Stegner's is more specific about the scale of time being more than one generation. Stegner argued on two levels for place: first, that it was desirable and its failure to develop or its loss should be regretted, and second, that place would not develop without time. The latter is a simple point, but one worth emphasis. On place in the West, see David Wrobel and Michael C. Steiner, *Many Wests: Place, Culture, and Regional Identity* (Lawrence: University Press of Kansas, 1997), and Dorman, *Hell of a Vision*.
30. Etulain, *Stegner: Conversations*, 132.
31. Stegner, *Marking the Sparrow's Fall: The Making of the American West*, ed. Page Stegner (New York: Henry Holt and Company, 1998), 118.
32. Mary Stegner wrote a detailed list of corrections for Benson that also included strong reactions to sections of the book that were critical of Stegner's books, particularly *Shooting Star*. See the 1994–1995 correspondence between Mary and Jackson Benson included in box 1, folder 3, Stegner Papers.
33. Fradkin, *Wallace Stegner and the American West*, 12.
34. I address other interpretations of Stegner's life and work where relevant throughout the book.
35. Stegner, *Where the Bluebird Sings*, 220. It is interesting that Stegner includes autobiography as a form of fiction. This issue will be explored further in relation to Stegner's *Wolf Willow*.
36. "Stegner's Diary, European Trip," May 13, 1976, box 1, folder 22, Stegner Papers.
37. See Michael Denning, *The Cultural Front: The Laboring of American Culture in the Twentieth Century* (New York: Verso, 1998), 57.

38. In Jackson Benson's account of the Sierra Club controversy that led to David Brower's resignation in 1969, Stegner turned against Brower after he had said on several occasions something to the effect that "novel writing was really rather unimportant when considering the fate of the planet." Stegner wrote a letter to the *Palo Alto Times* that asserted that Brower had been "bitten by some worm of power." He later regretted it and publicly praised Brower for his conservation work. Benson, *Wallace Stegner: His Life and Work*, 333–35. For Stegner's later reflections on Brower, see Stegner, "The Artist as Environmental Advocate," an oral history conducted in 1982 by Ann Lage, Sierra Club History Series, Regional Oral History Office, The Bancroft Library, University of California, Berkeley, 1983.

39. William Bevis, "Stegner: The Civic Style," in *Wallace Stegner: Man and Writer*, ed. Charles E. Rankin (Albuquerque: University of New Mexico Press, 1996), 255.

40. Stegner was harsh on various artistic trends, but also resolute in his commitment to artistic freedom. Near the end of his life in 1992, he declined a National Medal of the Arts in protest of the National Endowment for the Arts for its attempts to limit artistic freedom in the wake of the culture wars. In his rejection letter, Stegner wrote, "I believe that [NEA] support is meaningless, even harmful, if it restricts the imaginative freedom of those to whom it is given." Benson, *Wallace Stegner: His Life and Work*, 5.

41. Since the end of the "myth and symbol" school of American Studies and history, fiction has been marginal in intellectual history with several notable exceptions. Forrest G. Robinson offers a strong defense of the value of Stegner's intellectual labors—especially his fiction—for the study of the western past in "Clio Bereft of Calliope: Literature and the New Western History," included in Robinson, ed., *The New Western History: The Territory Ahead* (Tucson: University of Arizona Press, 1998). Recent books that have influenced my approach of the study of fiction in the discipline of history are Jennifer Burns, *Goddess of the Market: Ayn Rand and the American Right* (Oxford: Oxford University Press, 2009); Mark Greif, *The Age of the Crisis of Man*; and Paul Arras, *The Lonely Nineties: Visions of Community in Contemporary U.S. Television* (Cham, Switzerland: Palgrave Macmillan, 2018). On the history of sensibility and emotion, I have been influenced by Elisabeth Lasch-Quinn, *Ars Vitae: The Fate of Inwardness and the Return of the Ancient Arts of Living* (South Bend, IN: University of Notre Dame Press, 2020), and Daniel Wickberg, "What Is the History of Sensibilities?" *The American Historical Review* 112, no. 3 (June 2007): 661–84, and "Intellectual History vs. the Social History of Intellectuals," *Rethinking History: The Journal of Theory and Practice* 5, no. 3 (2001): 383–95. On moral history, I have relied on George Cotkin, *Morality's Muddy Waters: Ethical Quandaries in Modern America* (Philadelphia: University of Pennsylvania Press, 2013), and Jennifer Ratner-Rosenhagen, "The Longing for Wisdom in Twentieth Century US Thought," in Ratner-Rosenhagen, et al., eds., *Worlds of American Intellectual History* (Oxford: Oxford University Press, 2017), 182–202.

42. See Fradkin, *Wallace Stegner and the American West*, 109–61, and Benson, *Wallace Stegner: His Life and Work*, 151–70, as well as Eric Bennett, *Workshops of Empire: Stegner, Engle, and American Creative Writing during the Cold War* (Iowa City: University of Iowa Press, 2015), 117–41. Notable authors to come out of the Stanford program are often listed in these discussions of Stegner's legacy. Stegner himself was generally circumspect in his descriptions of his influence on the

program. He believed in modesty and that is certainly a factor, but it is also important to note that he taught on a rotating schedule and took fellowships that removed
him from the program for a year at a time. Nonetheless, from 1947 to 1971 he was
heavily involved in the administration of the program and the most significant
public representative of it. Wendell Berry is the most well-known of the writers
from the program to work consciously under Stegner's influence. He has written
some of the most thoughtful reflections on Stegner's work at Stanford. See *What Are
People For?* (New York: North Point Press, 1990), 48–57, and *Imagination in Place*
(Berkeley: Counterpoint Press, 2010), 39–47. Maggie Doherty's *The Equivalents:
A Story of Art, Female Friendship, and Liberation in the 1960s* (New York: Alfred A.
Knopf, 2020), describes Stegner's early discouragement of the poetry of Maxine
Kumin and her resolve to prove him wrong in his assessment (12–14).

43. For this tally and categorization of Stegner's work see Fradkin, *Wallace Stegner
and the American West*, 10. See also Nancy Colberg, *Wallace Stegner: A Descriptive
Bibliography* (Lewiston, ID: Confluence Press, 1990), for a detailed bibliography of
Stegner's publications through 1990. Colberg's bibliography includes print totals
from publishers and articles in obscure publications.

44. Timothy Egan, "Stegner's Complaint," *The New York Times*, February 18, 2009. Stegner defined his understanding of "the West" and explained the variations among the
subregions most clearly in the introduction to *The Sound of Mountain Water* (1969),
9–20. Stegner located the West using the hundredth meridian, west of which aridity
is the "ultimate unity," even if unable to account for the Pacific Northwest and other
humid regions. Stegner's basic working definition is the one that will govern this study,
though I will work through some of the complications throughout. Robert Dorman
uses the hundredth meridian to define a "nationalist West" in *Hell of a Vision: Regionalism and the Modern American West* (Tucson: University of Arizona, 2012), xii.

45. David Gessner, *All the Wild That Remains* (New York: Norton, 2015), 279. See Mary
Stegner and Page Stegner, eds., *The Geography of Hope: A Tribute to Wallace Stegner*
(New York: Sierra Club Books, 1996), for the most personal collection of reflections on Stegner's life and work. Rankin, *Wallace Stegner: Man and Writer*, is more
scholarly and critical but still generally celebratory. Most but not all of the writers in
the volumes are identified with the American West in some fashion. Public figures
who contributed to either of the collections (some contributed to both) include
Bruce Babbitt and Stuart Udall, each of whom served as Secretary of the Interior
(under Presidents Bill Clinton and John F. Kennedy, respectively); historians Patricia Limerick, Arthur Schlesinger Jr., Elliott West, Dan Flores, and Richard Etulain;
and writers Terry Tempest Williams, Barry Lopez, Gretel Ehrlich, Nancy Packer,
Ivan Doig, and Wendell Berry.

46. Dorothy Bradley, "Contemporary Western Politics of the Land," in *Wallace Stegner
and the Continental Vision: Essays on Literature, History, and Landscape*, ed. Curt
Meine (Washington, DC: Island Press, 1997), 206.

47. Mark Fiege, "A Country without Illusions—Wallace Stegner in His Time and Ours"
(lecture, Montana State University, October 2016), accessed March 29, 2019, https://
www.youtube.com/watch?v=DJTuuqQIsvA.

48. David Foster Wallace's parody of the exercise of describing literary reputation is
worth recall. See "Death Is Not the End," in *Brief Interviews with Hideous Men*
(Boston: Little, Brown and Company, 1999), 1.

49. *Angle of Repose* (1971) was published under the Modern Library label in 2000, and *Crossing to Safety* (1987), his last novel, and *Where the Bluebird Sings to the Lemonade Springs* (1992), his last collection of essays, were reprinted as Modern Library Classics in 2002. Several others of his books were reprinted as Penguin Classics in the 1990s to early 2000s. Within the last decade, five of his novels have been reprinted under the Vintage Books imprint by Knopf-Doubleday. Two of his essay collections and his biography of John Wesley Powell, books published in genres that typically age out of circulation more quickly, continue to attract readers. Nancy Colberg's *Wallace Stegner: A Descriptive Bibliography* lists publication runs of all of Stegner's books up through 1990.

50. Stegner requested that his name be removed from the fellowships following an administrative dispute over a faculty hire that he interpreted to be a rejection of his vision for the program. Several years of requests eventually wore him down and he relented. He also removed his papers from Stanford and had them placed at the University of Utah. See Fradkin, *Wallace Stegner and the American West*, 281–83. He later gave a keynote address at Stanford's Founder's Day centennial in 1991, but the Stegner legacy at Stanford remains complicated. See box 2, Stanford University Founder's Day Collection, Stanford University Library.

51. The University of Utah's S. J. Quinney College of Law hosts the Wallace Stegner Center for Land, Resources and the Environment and Wallace Stegner Professor in Law, in addition to the Stegner Young Writing Scholars Institute in the College of Education. The Wallace Stegner Environmental Center occupies the fifth floor of the San Francisco Public Library. The Peninsula Open Space Trust in Palo Alto, California, hosts the Wallace Stegner Lectures annually, as does Montana State University's Department of History, Philosophy, and Religious Studies, and Lewis-Clark State College in Lewiston, Idaho. Stegner's childhood home in Eastend, Saskatchewan, was restored by the Eastend Arts Council and sponsors a residency program for artists, the Wallace Stegner Grant for the Arts. The Geography of Hope Conference, an annual literary festival in Point Reyes Station, California, takes its name consciously from one of Stegner's most famous lines and invokes his name prominently on its website. Geography of Hope, a program sponsored by The Road Less Traveled, sponsors educational outdoor experiences for underserved schools and claims Stegner as an inspiration for its vision. The Wallace Stegner Academy, a public charter school located in Salt Lake City, Utah, opened its doors in 2016. The Quivira Coalition, an organization dedicated to building a "radical center" for ranchers and environmentalists in the West, cites Stegner multiple times in its manifesto and works consciously in the same vein as Stegner did.

52. In addition to Benson's *Wallace Stegner: His Life and Work* and Fradkin's *Wallace Stegner and the American West*, see Forrest G. Robinson and Margaret G. Robinson, *Wallace Stegner* (Boston: Twayne Publishers, 1977), and Robert C. Steensma, *Wallace Stegner's Salt Lake City* (Salt Lake City: University of Utah Press, 2007). Of the dissertations, Ruth Newberry's "Wallace Stegner's *Wolf Willow* and 1960s Critical Essays: Renarrativizing Western American Literature for the West and for America" (PhD diss., Duquesne University, 2011), is most relevant to this book.

53. Krista Comer, *Landscapes of the New West: Gender and Geography in Contemporary Women's Writing* (Chapel Hill: University of North Carolina Press, 1999), 38–59.

Comer argues that the Stegnerian spatial field is "representative of western literary history's dominant spatial field at its most dynamic and sophisticated," even if limited in its capacity to account for gender inequality. See also, for example, Anthony Arthur, ed., *Critical Essays on Wallace Stegner* (Boston: G. K. Hall, 1982); Mark McGurl, *The Program Era: Postwar Fiction and the Rise of Creative Writing* (Cambridge: Harvard University Press, 2011); Elizabeth Cook-Lynn, *Why I Can't Read Wallace Stegner and Other Essays: A Tribal Voice* (Madison: University of Wisconsin, 1996); and Nathaniel Lewis, *Unsettling the Literary West: Authenticity and Authorship* (Lincoln: University of Nebraska Press, 2003).

54. David Gessner, *All the Wild That Remains* (New York: W. W. Norton, 2015).

55. Aside from Stegner's attention to aridity, Jennifer Ratner-Rosenhagen inspired the hydrological metaphor: "Ideas are never frozen in their time and place, nor are they vapors that float in some otherworldly, transcendent realm. Rather, they are historical forces that move—and thereby change—from one interlocutor to another, one place to another, and even one time period to another." *The Ideas That Made America: A Brief History* (New York: Oxford University Press, 2019), 5.

CHAPTER 1

1. Alexis de Tocqueville, *Democracy in America*, ed. J. P. Mayer, trans. George Lawrence (New York: HarperCollins, 2000), 536.

2. Quote by the character Lyman Ward in Stegner, *Angle of Repose*, 303. Suggesting the resonance of the metaphor, the recent Christopher Nolan film *Interstellar* (2014) includes a paean to pioneers and ends with a space colony.

3. Stegner to Phil Gray, April 23, 1944, box 15, folder 14, Stegner Papers. Written on *Look* stationery but presumably written from Massachusetts. All of the letters included in this chapter are quoted unaltered.

4. Kevin Starr, *Golden Dreams: California in an Age of Abundance, 1950–1963* (Oxford: Oxford University Press, 2009), 5–6. See also Findlay, *Magic Lands*.

5. Michael Redmon, "The Hammonds and Their Montecito Estate," *Santa Barbara Independent,* June 15, 2010, accessed March 29, 2019, https://www.independent.com /news/2010/jun/15/hammonds-and-their-montecito-estate/.

6. Page Stegner, ed., *The Selected Letters of Wallace Stegner* (Berkeley: Shoemaker and Hoard, 2007), 172.

7. Margaret O'Mara, *Cities of Knowledge: Cold War Science and the Search for the Next Silicon Valley* (Princeton: Princeton University Press, 2005), 103.

8. Wallace Stegner to Phil Gray, April 23, 1944, box 15, folder 14, Stegner Papers.

9. Wallace Stegner to Phil Gray, July 6, 1945, box 15, folder 15, Stegner Papers.

10. George Packer, *Blood of the Liberals* (New York: Farrar, Straus, and Giroux, 2000), 168–73. On Stanford, see Heppler, "Machines in the Valley," and Findlay, *Magic Lands*, in addition to O'Mara.

11. Mark McGurl, *The Program Era: Postwar Fiction and the Rise of Creative Writing* (Cambridge: Harvard University Press, 2009), 183–86. Eric Bennett, *Workshops of Empire: Stegner, Engle, and American Creative Writing during the Cold War* (Iowa City: University of Iowa Press, 2015), 5, 37.

12. "The Little Man with the Purchasing Power," *Delphian Quarterly* 25 (July 1942): 10–15; "The Naturalization of an Idea," *Delphian Quarterly* 25 (October 1942): 76–83;

"The Co-ops in Crisis," *Delphian Quarterly* 26 (January 1943): 15–18, 50; and "The Cooperatives and the Peace," *Delphian Quarterly* 26 (April 1943): 15–18.

13. Benson, *Wallace Stegner: His Life and Work*, 153, 195. See Herbert Ruffin, *Uninvited Neighbors: African Americans in Silicon Valley, 1769–1990* (Norman: University of Oklahoma Press, 2014), 75–79; and Heppler, "Machines in the Valley," 101–45, for an overview of the extent of restrictive covenants in the Santa Clara Valley during this period.

14. Stegner, "Four Hundred Families Plan a House," *'47 Magazine* 1 (April 1947): 63–67.

15. On *Shelley v. Kraemer*, see Jeffrey D. Gonda, *Unjust Deeds: The Restrictive Covenant Cases and the Making of the Civil Rights Movement* (Chapel Hill: University of North Carolina Press, 2015).

16. See Richard Rothstein, "De Facto Segregation: A National Myth," in Molly W. Metzger and Henry S. Webber, eds., *Facing Segregation: Housing Policy Solutions for a Stronger Society* (New York: Oxford University Press, 2019), 21. Rothstein also discusses the PHA in *The Color of Law: A Forgotten History of How Our Government Segregated America* (New York: W. W. Norton, 2017), 10–12.

17. *House and Garden*, August 1952, December 1952. Stegner's home was designed by architects Bolton White and Jack Hermann, and the landscape was designed by the firm Eckbo, Royston & Williams. Stegner's character Joe Allston describes the allure of this porousness: "I can think of nothing pleasanter than to be close to danger or discomfort, but still to be protected, preferably by one's own foresight and effort." Stegner, *All the Little Live Things* (New York: Viking Press, 1967), 27.

18. For the Bay Area, see sources above from Ruffin, Findlay, O'Mara, and Heppler, as well as Robert O. Self, *American Babylon: Race and the Struggle for Postwar Oakland* (Princeton: Princeton University Press, 2005), and Stephen J. Pitti, *The Devil in Silicon Valley: Northern California, Race, and Mexican Americans* (Princeton: Princeton University Press, 2004). For suburban history more broadly, see Kenneth Jackson, *Crabgrass Frontier: The Suburbanization of the United States* (New York: Oxford University Press, 1985); Thomas Sugrue, *The Origins of the Urban Crisis* (Princeton: Princeton University Press, 1996); and Lisa McGirr, *Suburban Warriors: Origins of the New American Right* (Princeton: Princeton University Press, 2001).

19. Robert Fishman, *Bourgeois Utopias: The Rise and Fall of Suburbia* (New York: Basic Books, 1987), 5–6.

20. Ibid., 155.

21. More recent scholarship on the suburbs focuses on the political definition of suburbs within broader metropolitan frameworks and emphasizes that suburbs cannot really be studied in isolation. Even if the ideals have shifted and suburbs take on more definitively urban characteristics, such as the blurring of the distinction between residential and commercial uses—the separation of which Fishman emphasized as a defining feature—suburbs are still places apart politically and competitive with urban and rural political entities. See Kevin M. Kruse and Thomas J. Sugrue, eds. *The New Suburban History* (Chicago: University of Chicago Press, 2006), 5–6.

22. Stegner, *Marking the Sparrow's Fall*, 113. For a critical review of this conception of white American masculinity, particularly in its western variation, see Gail Bederman, *Manliness and Civilization: A Cultural History of Gender and Race in the United States, 1880–1917* (Chicago: University of Chicago Press, 1995), 170–216.

23. Stegner, *One Way to Spell Man* (New York: Doubleday, 1982), 175–76.
24. Muir quoted in Roderick Nash, *Wilderness and the American Mind* (New Haven: Yale University Press, 2001), 128.
25. Stegner, *One Way to Spell Man*, 141.
26. Aside from his work with the Stanford Creative Writing Program, and the Peninsula Housing Association, Stegner also helped found a short-lived journal, *The Pacific Spectator*, and served as the coordinator of an attempt to establish partnerships with Asian writers following his travels there on a Rockefeller Grant in 1951. See Bennett, *Workshops of Empire*, for broader context for these efforts. Without dismissing the influence, Greg Barnhisel and Patrick Iber have argued against the more conspiratorial interpretations of CIA funding for art during this period, suggesting that artists used the CIA as well. See Barnhisel, *Cold War Modernists: Art, Literature and American Cultural Diplomacy* (New York: Columbia University Press, 2015), and Iber, *Neither Peace nor Freedom: The Cultural Cold War in Latin America* (Cambridge: Harvard University Press, 2015).
27. Walter Lippmann, *A Preface to Morals* (New Brunswick: Transaction Publishers, 1982), 19–20: "The acids of modernity are so powerful that they do not tolerate a crystallization of ideas which will serve as a new orthodoxy into which men can retreat. And so the modern world is haunted by a realization, which it becomes constantly less easy to ignore, that it is impossible to reconstruct an enduring orthodoxy, and impossible to live well without the satisfactions which an orthodoxy would provide."
28. Robert Dorman, *The Revolt of the Provinces: The Regionalist Movement in America, 1920–1945* (Chapel Hill: University of North Carolina Press, 1993), xii.
29. Ibid., xii–xiii.
30. Ibid., xiii.
31. Ibid., 25.
32. *The Delphian Quarterly* was a small publication that paid well. Stegner called it his "meal ticket" though he was never quite sure what the Delphian Society was. Benson, *Wallace Stegner: His Life and Work*, 112–13.
33. Stegner, "The Trail of the Hawkeye: Literature Where the Tall Corn Grows," *Saturday Review of Literature*, July 30, 1938.
34. Ibid.
35. Stegner, "A Decade of Regional Publishing," *Publisher's Weekly*, March 11, 1939, 1060–64.
36. Stegner, "Publishing in the Provinces," *Delphian Quarterly* 22 (July 1939): 2–7.
37. Stegner, "Regionalism in Art," *Delphian Quarterly* 22 (January 1939): 2–7, 18.
38. I read *Look's* bound-copy index and sampled articles from 1944–1945, and also sampled articles from *Life* from 1943–1945.
39. Stegner criticized this trend in "The Colleges in Wartime," *Delphian Quarterly* 25 (April 1942): 2–7.
40. Etulain, *Stegner: Conversations*, 38–40.
41. Walter A. Jackson, *Gunnar Myrdal and America's Conscience: Social Engineering and Racial Liberalism, 1938–1987* (Chapel Hill: University of North Carolina Press, 1990), 241. Stegner cites Myrdal prominently in both the introduction and conclusion of *One Nation* (Boston: Houghton Mifflin, 1945), 4, 329.

42. Stegner also cites McWilliams's *Factories in the Fields: The Story of Migratory Farm Labor in California* (1939). *Brothers Under the Skin* and *One Nation* are organized similarly, with a prominent focus on minorities in the West. Stegner, *One Nation*, 96.

43. Stegner, *One Nation*, 9–12; 220, for Smith. He also thanked a large group of scholars, agencies, and advocacy groups in his acknowledgments, even if few of these made it into the text itself.

44. Wallace Stegner, "Who Persecutes Boston?" *Atlantic Monthly* 174 (July 1944): 45–52.

45. Benson, *Wallace Stegner: His Life and Work*, 339–40, 144–50.

46. *Atlantic Monthly*, September 1944.

47. Fradkin, *Wallace Stegner and the American West*, 105.

48. This phrase is from Jackson describing American liberalism after the publication of Myrdal's book and seems to be an accurate depiction of the political setting in which *One Nation* was written. Jackson, *Gunnar Myrdal and America's Conscience*, 241.

49. Patricia Limerick also describes this emphasis in "Precedents to Wisdom," in Rankin, *Wallace Stegner: Man and Writer*, 108–13.

50. The choice of the photograph makes little sense, particularly because it was included in a *Life* magazine spread on the riots and there was another photo of the same three men that captured them fleeing from the attackers with fear rather than smiles on the faces of the two white men. In that case, it was obvious that the white men were actually helping rather than posing. The black man was also walking with support, rather than being completely supported. *Life*, July 5, 1943.

51. This tendency has been described by many scholars. Two of the most relevant in the era explored here include Mary Dudziak, *Cold War Civil Rights: Race and the Image of American Democracy* (Princeton: Princeton University Press, 2000), and Carol Anderson, *Eyes off the Prize: The United Nations and the African American Struggle for Human Rights, 1944–1955* (New York: Cambridge University Press, 2003).

52. Stegner, *One Nation*, 225.

53. Two famous incidents illustrate the general trend of the FSA photographs. The most famous of all FSA shots remains Dorothea Lange's "Migrant Mother." The subject of the photograph, Florence Owens Thompson, was embarrassed by the famous photo for most of her life. The most highly acclaimed of the FSA books is James Agee and Walker Evans's *Let Us Now Praise Famous Men* (1941). Lawrence Levine points out that Evans refused a request by one of the families in the study to include a photo of themselves posing in their Sunday best, clean-shaven and smiling. Lawrence Levine, "The Historian and Icon," in *Documenting America, 1935–1943*, ed. Lawrence Levine, Carl Fleischhauer, and Beverly Brannan (Berkeley: University of California Press, 1989), 21.

54. *Look*, June 12, 1944.

55. Stegner, "Who Persecutes Boston?" 52. Stegner moved closer to "unity in diversity" in *One Nation*, however.

56. Stegner, *One Nation*, 143.

57. Jackson, *Gunnar Myrdal and America's Conscience*, 231.

58. Because he used some FSA photographs and because it is a documentary book, I originally linked *One Nation* to other FSA books such as Richard Wright, *12 Million Black Voices* (New York: Basic Books, 1941/2002); Erskine Caldwell and

Margaret Bourke-White, *You Have Seen Their Faces* (Arno Press, 1937/1975); Dorothea Lange and Paul Taylor, *An American Exodus: A Record of Human Erosion* (New York: Reynal and Hitchcock, 1939); Archibald MacLeish, *Land of the Free* (New York: Harcourt, Brace, 1938); and Agee and Evans, *Let Us Now Praise Famous Men* (1941/2001). Upon further study, I realized that the optimism and journalistic tone of *One Nation* really prevent it from categorization in that genre. Though the last of the classics of the genre was published in 1941, the four years that separated Stegner's book from the others were very significant. Most obviously, *One Nation* betrays a confidence about possibilities for change that the other books can only summon as a distant hope. For analysis of the prominent FSA books, see Nicholas Natanson, *The Black Image in the New Deal: The Politics of FSA Photography* (Knoxville: University of Tennessee Press, 1992); Michael E. Staub, *Voices of Persuasion: Politics of Representation in 1930s America* (New York: Cambridge University Press, 1994); Jeff Allred, *American Modernism and Depression Documentary* (New York: Oxford University Press, 2010); Carl Fleischhauer and Beverly W. Brannan, eds., *Documenting America, 1935-1943* (Berkeley: University of California Press, 1988). None of these books refer to *One Nation*, reinforcing the point.

59. Stegner, *One Nation*, 253.

60. Ibid., 330. For criticism of Myrdal's liberalism and the "we" Stegner constructed in the article, see Ralph Ellison, *Shadow and Act* (New York: Vintage, 1995), 303-16. Ellison's review was written just after Myrdal's book but left unpublished until the 1960s. Both Myrdal and Ellison are discussed in Nikhil Pal Singh, *Black Is a Country: Race and the Unfinished Struggle for Democracy* (Cambridge: Harvard University Press, 2004).

61. Starr, *Golden Dreams*, 278. For "high modernist" see James C. Scott, *Seeing Like a State: How Certain Schemes to Improve the Human Condition Have Failed* (New Haven: Yale University Press, 1998).

62. Donald Worster, *A River Running West: The Life of John Wesley Powell* (New York: Oxford, 2000). This is not to imply that Stegner's book was poorly researched. It included extensive research in primary sources and the most significant secondary historical literature of the era, totaling over fifty pages of notes.

63. Limerick, "A Man for All Seasons: The Prescience of John Wesley Powell and the Meaning of His Legacy Today," *Los Angeles Times*, July 22, 2001.

64. On a "usable past," see Warren Susman, *Culture as History: The Transformation of American Society in the Twentieth Century* (Washington, DC: Smithsonian Institution Press, 2003).

65. Wallace Stegner, *Beyond the Hundredth Meridian: John Wesley Powell and the Second Opening of the West* (Boston: Houghton Mifflin Company, 1954), 304. For nuanced discussion of the promise and pitfalls of this choice to frame his historical figures as heroes and villains, see Gary Topping, "Wallace Stegner the Historian," in Rankin, *Wallace Stegner: Man and Writer*, 145-61.

66. Stegner, *Beyond the Hundredth*: on Gilpin, 343, 3; on Adams, 362; on King, 366. It should also be noted that Adams was the source of one of the sentences Stegner quoted as often as any other: "In plain words, Chaos was the law of nature, Order was the dream of man" (ibid., 363-64). Stegner also wrote that Adams's final lonely years were "more productive of humanly valuable observation and thinking and

writing than the whole lifetimes of any but the best" even if conducted "in the teeth of his insistent pessimism" (ibid., 345).

67. Ibid., 229.

68. Kevin Starr, *Coast of Dreams: California on the Edge, 1990–2003* (New York: Alfred A. Knopf, 2004), 533: "Going green characterized Republicans and Democrats alike and was making particular headway among the intelligentsia. No figure better epitomized this sensibility—educated, affluent, liberal, upper middle class—than did Stanford man of letters Wallace Stegner ... the undisputed spokesperson for environmentalism in his generation."

69. Stegner wrote other California stories, however. Stegner's first California novel, *Shooting Star* (1961), is about a wealthy family from Hillsborough, California, with New England roots. Prior to *Shooting Star*, he also wrote a novella and several short stories set in California. None of these early California stories, however, were written with a first-person narrator, and they lacked the ruminative complexity of Stegner's later attempts to reckon with the California suburbs. The novella is *The Potter's House*, a tragic novella set in Laguna Beach, California. His two short stories, "Pop Goes the Alley Cat" and "He Who Spits at the Sky," were drawn from his experiences in Los Angeles writing about the Chicano populations there for *One Nation*. Benson, *Wallace Stegner: His Life and Work*, 84. The two short stories are included in Stegner, *Collected Stories of Wallace Stegner* (New York: Random House, 1990).

70. Benson, *Wallace Stegner: His Life and Work*, 207, 243. "Field Guide" was written in 1952 and finished in 1953, but not published until 1956.

71. This was also the case with *The Big Rock Candy Mountain* (1943) and *Recapitulation* (1979), which are part of the same fictional universe and also include variations of previously published short stories. His other novels stand alone.

72. Wallace Stegner, *On Teaching and Writing Fiction* (New York: Penguin, 2002), 7.

73. Stegner, *Collected Stories*, 312.

74. Ibid., 311.

75. Ibid., 313–14. Thoreau: "Eastward I go only by force; but westward I go free." Henry David Thoreau, "Walking," *The Atlantic*, June 1862. San Francisco is to the west of Los Gatos, but the Bayshore Freeway connecting San Francisco to San Jose is to the east of Los Gatos.

76. Fishman, *Bourgeois Utopias*, 39.

77. For the contrast with the suburbanites of Orange County, see Lisa McGirr, *Suburban Warriors*.

78. Stegner, *Collected Stories*, 321.

79. Ibid.

80. Wendy Kaplan, ed. *California Design, 1930–1965* (Los Angeles: Los Angeles County Museum of Art and MIT Press, 2011), 27–33.

81. Stegner lived in Los Altos Hills. "Field Guide" is set in Los Gatos, around twenty miles southeast from Los Altos Hills. The rest of the stories take place on the Peninsula with no more specific designation given, but the descriptions from the books suggest Stegner had Los Altos Hills in mind as a setting.

82. The film was released in 1967. It was based on a novel by Charles Webb, which was published in 1963.

83. Stegner, *Collected Stories*, 319.

84. Ibid., 328.
85. Ibid., 327.
86. Murthi also appears in *All the Little Live Things*, 103.
87. Stegner, *Collected Stories*, 334.
88. Ibid., 337–38.
89. Ibid., 339.
90. Ibid., 340.
91. Ibid., 343.
92. Ibid., 358.
93. Ibid., 359.
94. See, for example, Wolfe's *Radical Chic and Mau-Mauing the Flak-Catchers* (New York: Picador, 2009).
95. For context for Salinger and his influence, see Hale, *A Nation of Outsiders*.
96. See Robert C. Solomon, "In Defense of Sentimentality," *Philosophy and Literature* 14, no. 2 (October 1990): 304–23.
97. See Mark McGurl's *The Program Era*, 190–94, for a discussion of closed and open systems. For criticism of the romantic artist ideal, see Wendell Berry, *Standing by Words: Essays* (Berkeley: Counterpoint, 1983), 7: "One of the oldest doctrines of the specialist-poets is that of the primacy of language and the primacy of poetry. They have virtually made a religion of their art, a religion based not on what they have in common with other people, but on what they do that sets them apart. For poets who believe in this way, a poem is not a point of clarification or a connection between themselves and the world on the one hand and between themselves and their readers on the other, nor is it an adventure into any reality or mystery outside themselves. It is a seeking of the self in words, the making of a word-world in which the word-self may be at home."
98. Edward Abbey, *The Journey Home: Some Words in Defense of the American West* (New York: Penguin, 1977), 183.
99. The two aims of the publication were to: "Speak for and about the new West, its vastly increased population, its new industrial importance, its nearness to Asia and the Pacific area; [and] to speak authoritatively and knowledgeably about Asia, and in doing so to make clear that America's view of her neighbors to the westward is not one of unimaginative colonialism, that enlightened Americans are respectful of the sovereignty of Asian peoples, curious about their cultural traditions, anxious to understand the systems of religious observance that make their daily lives so different from our own." *Pacifica*, September 1959.
100. In the novel *Live Things*, Stegner turns Weld into a multigeneration Californian. In this instance, where Weld is from Texas, Stegner includes a jibe about Weld's attempt to live on his land in California with means more suited to land in Texas, which is reminiscent of Marian's criticism of Joe and his garden (discussed in chapter 3).
101. Stegner, "Indoor-Outdoor Living," *Pacifica* (September 1959): 16–23, 22.

CHAPTER 2

1. Foote, in Rodman Paul, ed., *A Victorian Gentlewoman in the Far West: The Reminiscences of Mary Hallock Foote* (San Marino: Huntington Library Press, 2000), 400.

Foote's reminiscences were not published until 1972, but they were finished in the mid-1920s, based on intratextual evidence.

2. Ivan Doig, *This House of Sky: Landscapes of a Western Mind* (New York: Harcourt Brace, 1992), 239.

3. Richard White, *Remembering Ahanagran: A History of Stories* (Seattle: University of Washington Press, 1998), 303.

4. Wallace Stegner, *Second Growth* (Lincoln: University of Nebraska Press, 1985), title page. Stegner had read Frederick Jackson Turner in the 1930s, and his use of Turner's frontier thesis is explained in more detail below.

5. Benson, *Wallace Stegner: His Life and Work*, 128–29. The Stegners had to ski into town for anything they needed, given the amount of snow and unplowed roads.

6. Stegner, *Second Growth*, 191.

7. Ibid., 197.

8. Ibid., 123.

9. Ibid., 198.

10. Stegner's first novelette, *Remembering Laughter*, was criticized by Mary Stegner's family. *Joe Hill* and *Angle of Repose* also roused public controversy. I recount the controversy over *Angle of Repose* in chapter 4. For a brief summary of these controversies, see Fradkin, *Wallace Stegner and the American West*, 226–28.

11. Wallace Stegner to Phil Gray, July 24, 1947, box 15, folder 15, Stegner Papers.

12. Stegner, *Second Growth*, 208.

13. Phil Gray to Wallace Stegner, November 3, 1947, box 15, folder 15, Stegner Papers. Stegner maintained a correspondence with Louis and Esther Kesselman through the early 1980s. Stegner included copies of a 1944 note signed by over one hundred Greensboro residents wishing the Kesselmans well in the wake of Louis's illness. Note to Kesselmans, 1944, box 17, folder 22, Stegner Papers.

14. Stegner articulated his concerns about the potential extinction of the humanities in several essays and in a May 1959 letter to David Packard of Hewlett Packard. The letter criticized Packard for a speech to the Stanford American Association of University Professors (AAUP) that promoted shifting university resources towards applied science. Stegner argued that such a focus, if it took the place of the true "core" of the university—"the school of the humanities and sciences"—would "produce half-men, limited men, men with imperfect vision and low horizons." Page Stegner, *Selected Letters*, 302–3.

15. Etulain, *Stegner: Conversations*, 62.

16. Page Stegner, introduction to *Wolf Willow*, by Wallace Stegner (New York: Penguin Books, 2000), xi.

17. Here and throughout the chapter, I am indebted to Tara Penry for her analysis of *Wolf Willow* at the Idaho Humanities Council's 2017 Summer Teacher Institute.

18. Etulain, *Stegner: Conversations*, 73.

19. Benson, *Wallace Stegner*, 65–66. The dissertation was published by the University of Utah Press as *Clarence Edward Dutton: An Appraisal* in 1936 and reprinted by the press in 2006.

20. The closest Stegner came to traditional formal scholarship was in his two biographies: *Beyond the Hundredth Meridian* (1954) and *The Uneasy Chair: A Biography of Bernard DeVoto* (1974). Both were based on original research and included extensive bibliographies.

21. See Stegner's criticism of Gary Snyder and meditation in Page Stegner, *Selected Letters*, 207, 258–59.
22. See Forrest G. Robinson, "Clio Bereft of Calliope: Literature and the New Western History," included in Robinson, *The New Western History*. Robinson argues persuasively that Stegner's fiction anticipated the best insights of the New Western History, but that these insights were overlooked because they were often traced most intricately in his fiction.
23. In his acknowledgments, Stegner wrote: "Remembering is by no means a lonesome occupation. Remembering for this book, I have had the pleasure of help from a good many old Saskatchewan friends. . . . They are entitled to blame me if in spite of their help I have remembered wrong, or if I have occasionally warped fact a little in order to reach for the fictional or poetic truth that I would rank a little above history." Stegner, *Wolf Willow*, 307. This license to "warp" that Stegner granted himself was not uncontroversial. It was also at the root of the controversy I explore at the end of my discussion of *Angle of Repose*. It is also at the heart of "Fair Use," Sands Hall's play about *Angle of Repose* and Mary Hallock Foote.
24. Aaron Sachs, "Letters to a Tenured Historian: Imagining History as Creative Nonfiction—or Maybe Even Poetry," *Rethinking History: The Journal of Theory and Practice* 14, no. 1 (2010): 23–24.
25. Paul Fejos to Wallace Stegner, December 18, 1953, box 173, folder 52, Stegner Papers. Fejos is a fascinating figure in the history of international social science; unfortunately, his letters to Stegner were brief and never contained much more than pleasantries and brisk requests or updates. At the time of Stegner's study, Wenner-Gren was concurrently in the process of arranging and funding the June 1955 symposium that led to *Man's Role in Changing the Face of the Earth*, ed. William Thomas (Chicago: University of Chicago Press, 1956), a landmark text in geography and environmental history. See Susan Lindee and Joanna Radin, "Patrons of the Human Experience: A History of the Wenner-Gren Foundation for Anthropological Research, 1941–2016," *Current Anthropology* 56, no. 14 (October 2016): S252–56. See also Robert M. Wilson, "Retrospective Review: Man's Role in Changing the Face of the Earth," *Environmental History* 10, no. 3 (July 2005): 564–65.
26. Wallace Stegner to Paul Fejos, December 26, 1953, box 173, folder 52, Stegner Papers.
27. Stegner to Fejos, November 12, 1954, box 173, folder 52, Stegner Papers. For Kaare Svalastoga, see Peter Gundelach, "Kaare Svalastoga: The Unceasing Positivist," *Acta Sociologica* 43, no. 4 (2000): 365–73. Gundelach confirms Stegner's assessment, as Svalastoga started the first graduate program in sociology in Denmark. Svalastoga studied occupational prestige and mobility in Denmark in 1953–1954, interviewing 2,522 people. Svalastoga theorized that occupational prestige was the "central form of stratification" in Denmark and the study was published in 1959 as *Prestige, Class, and Mobility* in Danish. Gundelach, "Kaare Svalastoga," 367.
28. Stegner to Fejos, November 12, 1954, box 173, folder 52, Stegner Papers.
29. Memo by Wallace Stegner, December 10, 1954, box 173, folder 52, Stegner Papers.
30. For an exemplary model of the New England town study that became prominent in the 1970s, see Robert A. Gross, *The Minutemen and Their World* (New York: Hill and Wang, 1976). See also Michael Zuckerman, *Peaceable Kingdoms: New England Towns in the Eighteenth Century* (New York: Norton, 1970/1978). In his year at the Stanford CASBS, Stegner worked closely with Merle Curti, who was at work

on what would become *The Making of an American Community: A Case Study of Democracy in Frontier Country* (Stanford: Stanford University Press, 1959). Stegner is thanked in the acknowledgments. This book, written three times over for each place, is a variation of what Stegner seems to have envisioned writing when he started his project. Notably, *Wolf Willow* was reprinted in 2000 under the Penguin Classics imprint. Curti's book made it to paperback in 1969 but has not been reprinted since then.

31. Stegner spelled it Taasinge; currently it is spelled Tåsinge.
32. Wallace Stegner, Report on Research Conducted Under a Grant from the Wenner-Gren Foundation, 1953 and 1954, box 173, folder 52, Stegner Papers.
33. Ibid.
34. Stegner to Harold S. Jones, December 26, 1953, box 5, folder 9, Stegner Papers.
35. Stegner's former student Wendell Berry would later criticize the Green Revolution in *The Unsettling of America* (Berkeley: Counterpoint Press, 2015).
36. Stegner, Report on Research.
37. Ibid.
38. Stegner Cover Letter for Report to Fejos, December 14, 1954, box 173, folder 52, Stegner Papers. The report was dated December 10, 1954.
39. Stegner Cover Letter for Report to Fejos, January 17, 1956, box 173, folder 52, Stegner Papers. The final letter from Fejos closing the project was dated January 24, 1957.
40. Page Stegner, *Selected Letters*, 249–50.
41. Stegner's most thorough reaction to these issues in published form was "One Way to Spell Man," written in 1958 and included in his essay collection of the same name, *One Way to Spell Man: Essays with a Western Bias* (New York: Doubleday, 1982), 9–16. It was a poorly named essay, as it should be read, "here is one way to spell man," rather than "this is the one (and only) way to spell man." It made a case for art as a means of synthetic and relational thinking: "Art is all variables, all particulars—and yet at the moment of meeting, both work and reader must operate as wholes and must collaborate toward meaning. . . . It is a collaboration, a meeting of minds and spirits, a thing that lights up like love. It gets much of its virtue, as its detractors assert, from a controlled ambiguity. It does not state. It imitates or reflects, and is witnessed." Again, Stegner thought that art opened up relationships that were, in some cases, more intimate than in everyday life, even if across centuries: "The recognition of fellow humanity which art gives us more plainly than life generally does. . . . And if we are ever tempted to write or read by the rules of the quantitative method, if we ever approach literature as if it were 'subject matter,' we would do well to remind ourselves that the love and appreciation of literature come by exposure, by a meeting, not through paraphrase or explication."
42. Stegner, *Wolf Willow*, 5.
43. I will use Whitemud for Eastend when referring to *Wolf Willow* in order to be consistent with Stegner's usage. I use Eastend otherwise. The best study of *Wolf Willow* and the place and history in which it is set in relation to current historiography is in Beth LaDow, *The Medicine Line: Life and Death on a North American Borderland* (New York: Routledge, 2001).
44. Stegner, *Wolf Willow*, 6, 277.
45. Ibid., 281.

46. Ibid., 122.
47. Ibid., 8.
48. White, *Remembering Ahanagran*, 13. Stegner and White are closer in their methods than they might appear. Stegner would have agreed with White's warnings about the damage done by "cruel and idiot simplicities about memory, identity, and history," except that they would have disagreed on how many and which of these persisted. White writes, "Memory and identity are too powerful to go unquestioned and too important to be discarded as simply inventions and fabrications. They are the stuff out of which we fashion our lives and our stories. History can interrogate these stories; it can complicate them, but it cannot kill them. And I have no desire to do so." White, *Remembering Ahanagran*, 12.
49. Stegner, *Wolf Willow*, 53.
50. Ibid., 85.
51. Wallace Stegner, *The Uneasy Chair: A Biography of Bernard DeVoto* (Garden City: Doubleday, 1974), 240.
52. Stegner, *Wolf Willow*, 35–36.
53. Jeanette Maino to Wallace Stegner, August 5, 1963, Modesto, CA, box 54, folder 17, Stegner Papers.
54. Stegner, *Wolf Willow*, 36.
55. Ray Allen Billington, ed., *Frontier and Section: The Selected Essays of Frederick Jackson Turner* (Englewood Cliffs, NJ: Prentice Hall, 1961). Billington also edited a collection of essays debating the frontier thesis from the 1940s–1960s, which I have sampled for indications of the contemporaneous scholarship on the frontier thesis from the period when Stegner was writing *Wolf Willow*. Billington, ed., *The Frontier Thesis: Valid Interpretation of History?* (New York: Holt, Rinehart, and Winston, 1966). Limerick's *The Legacy of Conquest: The Unbroken Past of the American West* (New York: W. W. Norton, 1987) challenged Turner and sparked the renewal of the history of the American West from a different foundation. See also Richard W. Etulain, ed., *Writing Western History: Essays on Major Western Historians* (Albuquerque: University of New Mexico Press, 1991).
56. Etulain, *Stegner: Conversations*, 13, 159. To Richard Etulain, Stegner said that it was not until he began to write *Wolf Willow* that he began "to be serious about history" before saying instead that it started with *Mormon Country* (1942), but that his research for that book "didn't take me very far in." He had done substantial historical work for *Beyond the Hundredth Meridian* (1954), but he had also been working on *Wolf Willow* by that point as well, so the research undoubtedly fit together in his mind.
57. Note that Stegner was at the Stanford CASBS with Merle Curti, who he also had overlapping friendships with based on their residence in Wisconsin. Curti is listed in the acknowledgments, and Stegner's correspondence reveals that they kept up with each other. Stegner asked Curti to read *Wolf Willow* and Curti agreed, but unfortunately there is no record of his reading. In a letter dated February 18, 1988, Curti wrote to Stegner after finishing *Crossing to Safety* to tell him of the lingering effects of the Grays in Madison (Curti moved there in 1943) and mentions that he remembered "well and with gratitude your many kindnesses the year we were at the Center for Behavioral Sciences." Curti to Stegner, February 18, 1988, box 13, folder 38, Stegner Papers.

58. Billington, *Frontier and Section*, 61.
59. Ibid., 56, 61. Stegner still held to a variation of the frontier thesis into the early 1980s. He summarized it most clearly in this paragraph: "The continent has been tamed, but the average American's mind has not. Even yet there is a delusive spaciousness in our image of the continent, especially its western half, where the names on the map are sparse. Free land—arable and habitable land—was pretty well gone by 1890, but the free land of the mind, the notions and assumptions bred into us by centuries of spaciousness and waste, will last a long time and will more often be papered over than corrected. As it becomes harder to look forward to indefinite promise, we either project our expectations onto the new frontier of space, artificial and sterile and nonrenewable and incomprehensively expensive, or we convert the gilded future into the gilded past, warp expansive expectations into nostalgia for a golden age, sentimentalize the frontier and the frontier virtues into the grotesqueries of a Great Western Savings ad, and perpetuate our delusions with our myths. For complex reasons, the western half of the country inherits the memory and assumes the dream. It is younger and less altered, its vast open spaces create the illusion of a continuing opportunity that its prevailing aridity prohibits." Stegner, "Westword: The Call of the Wild," *New West* (August 1981): 142.
60. Stegner, *Wolf Willow*, 74.
61. Ibid., 75. Stegner was even harsher on the frontier in "A. B. Guthrie," a review of Guthrie's *The Big Sky*. Of Guthrie's main character, Stegner wrote: "Boone Caudill's savagery, admirable and even enviable though it is, can lead nowhere. The moral of his lapse from civilization is that such an absolute lapse is doomed and sterile, and in the end the savagery which has been his strength is revealed as his fatal weakness. . . . He is a killing machine, as dangerous to what he loves as to what he hates. . . . For this part we share too, and we grant, if we are honest, that the dream of primitive innocence is likewise, and simultaneously, a dream of violence and unrestraint. However inappropriate to the civilization with which we have infected Boone Caudill's mountains, it is a dream that dies hard." Stegner, *One Way to Spell Man*, 119–23.
62. Cook-Lynn, *Why I Can't Read Wallace Stegner*, 29–40. Finis Dunaway criticizes this tendency in relation to the environmentalist movement and the "Crying Indian" commercial of 1971 in *Seeing Green: The Use and Abuse of American Environmental Images* (Chicago: University of Chicago Press, 2015), 79–95. For a nuanced discussion of Stegner and the complications of a view of wilderness that erases the presence of Indian peoples, see also Elliott West, "Wallace Stegner's West, Wilderness, and History," in Meine, *Wallace Stegner and the Continental Vision*. More broadly, see Richard White's "'Are You an Environmentalist or Do You Work for a Living?'" in William Cronon, ed., *Uncommon Ground: Rethinking the Human Place in Nature* (New York: W. W. Norton, 1996), 171–85.
63. Stegner, *Wolf Willow*, 122.
64. LaDow, *Medicine Line*, 3.
65. Stegner, *Wolf Willow*, 125.
66. Ibid., 134.
67. Ibid., 133.
68. Ibid., 129.

69. Ibid., 136.
70. Peter Novick argues that "as it essentially was" is a better interpretation than "as it actually was" of Leopold von Ranke's famous statement of the historian's task, "*wie es eigentlich gewesen.*" This suggests idealist rather than empiricist foundations, contrary to the interpretation of the American historians that adopted him as the founder of modern historical method. *That Noble Dream: The 'Objectivity Question' and the American Historical Profession* (Cambridge: Cambridge University Press, 1988), 26–28. I am indebted to Eric Miller for highlighting this distinction.
71. See Richard Slatta, *Cowboys of the Americas* (New Haven: Yale University Press, 1990), 188–90, for a brief description of the winter of 1906–1907 in the Canadian plains.
72. Stegner, *Wolf Willow*, 138–42.
73. Ibid., 143.
74. Ibid., 148–49.
75. Ibid., 152.
76. Ibid., 150–51.
77. Ibid., 161.
78. Ibid., 193.
79. Ibid., 214–15.
80. Janet F. Moe to Stegner, December 12, 1962, box 54, folder 31, Stegner Papers. Moe wrote from Barneveld, New York.
81. Stegner, *Wolf Willow*, 218–19.
82. Ibid., 217.
83. Ibid., 219.
84. Ibid., 221.
85. Ibid., 223.
86. Ibid., 226.
87. Ibid., 224.
88. Ibid., 227.
89. Ibid., 238.
90. Ibid., 247–48.
91. Ibid., 248–49.
92. Ibid., 251.
93. Ibid., 255.
94. Ibid., 257–58.
95. Ibid., 262.
96. Ibid., 280.
97. Ibid., 268.
98. Ibid., 296.
99. Ibid., 297.
100. Ibid., 300; Stegner's criticism is reminiscent of Dwight Macdonald on masscult. *Masscult and Midcult: Essays Against the American Grain* (New York: New York Review Books Classics, 2011), 3–71.
101. Stegner, *Wolf Willow*, 301.
102. Ibid., 303.
103. Ibid., 306.

104. "Stegner's Book Triggers Epidemic of Reminiscing," *Salt Lake Tribune*, December 3, 1962, collected in box 71, folder 18, Stegner Papers. No author listed.

105. See Elliot West's essay in Rankin, *Wallace Stegner: Man and Writer*, 64–65. Patricia Limerick also examines the trend of whites making themselves at home in a multigenerational West in *Something in the Soil: Legacies and Reckonings in the New West* (New York: W. W. Norton, 2001). Three western memoirs that explore similar themes suggest the genre's continuing appeal: Ivan Doig, *This House of Sky* (New York: Harcourt Brace, 1978); Terry Tempest Williams, *Refuge* (New York: Pantheon Books, 1991); and Tara Westover, *Educated* (New York: Random House, 2018).

106. Limerick, *Something in the Soil*, 286.

107. Richard L. Knight also explores the impact of migration to the West due to technological innovation that has allowed "cappuccino cowboys" to work remotely and experience the West without sacrificing lucrative employment. "Field Report from the New American West," in Meine, *Wallace Stegner and the Continental Vision*, 182–88.

108. Comelia K. Francis to Wallace Stegner, April 21, 1963, box 52, folder 27, Stegner Papers. Francis was an English teacher at the Flathead Reservation in Arlee, Montana. She was fifty-four at the time she wrote the letter.

109. Nell W. Parsons to Stegner, June 12, 1963, box 55, folder 1, Stegner Papers. Parsons wrote from Seattle, Washington.

110. Ann Bonin to Stegner, September 8, 1967, box 51, folder 18, Stegner Papers. Bonin wrote from Dallas, Texas. She was forty-one at the time she wrote the letter.

111. Jean Gillette to Stegner, January 7, 1968, box 52, folder 29, Stegner Papers. Gillette wrote from Sunnyvale, California.

112. Stuart Kolbinson to Stegner, August 11, 1975, box 53, folder 41, Stegner Papers. Kolbinson wrote from Victoria, British Columbia. He was a farmer and owner of a hotel who had retired to write.

113. L. T. Hammond Jr. to Stegner, 1964, box 53, folder 1, Stegner Papers. Hammond wrote from Asheboro, North Carolina.

114. Desmond Arthur to Stegner, February 10, 1981, box 51, folder 5, Stegner Papers. Arthur wrote from San Francisco, California, at the age of fifty-five.

CHAPTER 3

1. I cite the article instead of the book, as the article was published only three years after Stegner's *Live Things*. Daniel Bell, "The Cultural Contradictions of Capitalism," *The Public Interest*, no. 21 (Fall 1970): 22.

2. Harrington, "We Few, We Happy Few, We Happy Bohemians: A Memoir of the Culture before the Counterculture," *Esquire* (August 1, 1972): 99.

3. Wallace Stegner, *All the Little Live Things* (New York: Viking Press, 1967), 139.

4. Wallace Stegner, *All the Little Live Things* (New York: Viking Press, 1967). Nancy Colberg includes the publication date for *Live Things* in *Wallace Stegner: A Descriptive Bibliography*, 93. The funeral notice for "Hippie, devoted son of Mass Media" was scheduled for October 6, 1967, and attended by a couple hundred people. See Danny Goldberg, *In Search of the Lost Chord: 1967 and the Hippie Idea* (Brooklyn: Akaschic Books, 2017). The fiftieth anniversary of the Summer of Love in 2017 sparked new scholarship on the counterculture. Hunter S. Thompson's report from May 14, 1967,

already reflects a jaded weariness about the posers flocking to what he called Hash-bury: "The thrust is no longer for 'change' or 'progress' or 'revolution,' but merely to escape, to live on the far perimeter of a world that might have been—perhaps should have been—and strike a bargain for survival on purely personal terms." Thompson, "The Hashbury Is the Capital of the Hippies," *New York Times*, May 14, 1967. See also Thomas Frank, *The Conquest of Cool* (Chicago: University of Chicago Press, 1997).

5. Todd Gitlin, *The Sixties: Years of Hope, Days of Rage* (New York: Bantam Press, 1987), 208–14. See also Anthony Chaney, *Runaway: Gregory Bateson, the Double Bind, and the Rise of Ecological Consciousness* (Chapel Hill: University of North Carolina Press, 2017), 185–211.

6. Terry Anderson, *The Movement and the Sixties: Protest in America from Greensboro to Wounded Knee* (Oxford: Oxford University Press, 1995), 170–76.

7. In a rare move, Stegner submitted the novel to his creative writing students for workshop because he was stuck and hadn't yet finished it in 1966; I have not been able to determine yet when he submitted the final draft for publication. Fradkin, *Wallace Stegner and the American West*, 157.

8. Stegner describes his preference for the literary tradition of Anton Chekhov that privileges revelation over resolution—"nuances, illuminations, epiphanies"—in *Where the Bluebird Sings*, 216.

9. Stegner does not name the area in his novel, but it is loosely based on Los Altos Hills. It is known to Californians as the Midpeninsula and is now solidly a suburb of Palo Alto.

10. Fradkin, *Wallace Stegner and the American West*, 160.

11. I am aware of literary theories that dissect the slipperiness of authorial intention. Briefly, Rita Felski's *The Limits of Critique* (Chicago: University of Chicago Press, 2015) has shaped my approach most significantly. Further, to the extent that Stegner's intentions can be discussed, I think it is a worthwhile effort given his prominence in the intellectual life of the American West.

12. Etulain, *Stegner: Conversations*, 74–75.

13. Benson, *Wallace Stegner: His Life and Work*, 309–10.

14. Etulain, *Stegner: Conversations*, 78.

15. David Dillon, "Time's Prisoners: An Interview with Wallace Stegner," *Southwest Review* 61, no. 3 (Summer 1976): 261–62.

16. I allude to Stegner's definition of place in "The Sense of Place": "At least to human perception, a place is not a place until people have been born in it, have grown up in it, lived in it, known it, died in it—have both experienced it and shaped it, as individuals, families, neighborhoods, and communities, over more than one generation. . . . [Space becomes] place only by slow accrual, like a coral reef." *Where the Bluebird Sings*, 201.

17. "All the Little Live Things—Notes," box 78, folder 1, undated, Stegner Papers.

18. Though discussing poetry, Wendell Berry's understanding of convocation describes the way Stegner incorporates these works. Berry argues: "Any poem worth the name is the product of a convocation. It exists, literally, by recalling past voices into presence." Benson, *What Are People For?*, 88–90. See also Phillip J. Donnelly, "Biblical Convocation in Wendell Berry's Remembering," *Christianity and Literature* 56, no. 2 (Winter 2007): 275–96, and Bilbro, *Wendell Berry's Sustainable Forms*.

19. Stegner, *Live Things*, 5–6.
20. It is important to note that though Stegner's neighborhood is now one of the wealthiest in the United States, they settled there before the exponential growth in land values connected to the rise of Silicon Valley. In 2017, Los Altos was ranked the third most expensive zip code in America. See Samantha Scharf, "Full List: America's Most Expensive ZIP Codes: 2017," *Forbes*, November 28, 2017. Joe is aware that they have "[bought] some quiet." Stegner, *Live Things*, 52.
21. I use "nature" with due caution; see Cronon, *Uncommon Ground*, for criticism of ahistorical conceptions of nature. On stereotypes of the suburbs, see Becky Nicolaides, "How Hell Moved from the City to the Suburbs: Urban Scholars and Changing Perceptions of Authentic Community," in Kruse and Sugrue, *The New Suburban History*. On the suburbs and the rise of environmentalism, see Heppler, "Suburban by Nature," and Adam Rome, *The Bulldozer in the Countryside: Suburban Sprawl and the Rise of American Environmentalism* (Cambridge: Cambridge University Press, 2001).
22. I have not been able to determine whether Stegner had read Leo Marx's work, which places *The Tempest* at the origin of the American pastoral tradition, before working on *Live Things*. See Marx, *The Machine in the Garden: Technology and the Pastoral Ideal in America* (Oxford: Oxford University Press, 1964). Stegner had definitely read Henry Nash Smith's *Virgin Land: The American West as Symbol and Myth* (1950; repr., Cambridge: Harvard University Press, 1970) by that point, as he cited it in *Beyond the Hundredth Meridian* (1954) and had corresponded with Smith. Stegner cited *Machine in the Garden* in *American Places* (1980), and Marx was Smith's student and an undergraduate at Harvard when Stegner was there as a Briggs-Copeland Fellow during the World War II years. For more on Stegner and pastoral imagery, see Russell Burrows, "Wallace Stegner's Version of Pastoral," *Western American Literature* 25, no. 1 (Spring 1990): 15–25.
23. Stegner, *Live Things*, 5.
24. See Miranda's famous exclamation: "O wonder! / How many goodly creatures are there here! / How beauteous mankind is! O brave new world / That has such people in't!" Shakespeare, *The Tempest* (New York: Signet Classics, 1998), 81.
25. Stegner, *Live Things*, 15.
26. Ibid.
27. For historical context on this dynamic, see Hale, *A Nation of Outsiders*. See also Walter J. Ong's contemporary assessment of the Beats in a discussion that is reminiscent of Allston's conflict with Peck: "The beatnik cannot avoid knowing that his outsideness guarantees that he is really in. But this makes him less an outsider, and hence less interesting. At this point his real motives become garbled to the point of total unmanageability. Does he really want to be out only in order to be in? Or does the fact that, being out, he is really in only annoy him and make him push harder to be out? No one knows. . . . Such a man is derivative in his very assertion of independence, and his program is an elaborate self-delusion at heart." Ong, *The Barbarian Within and Other Fugitive Essays and Studies* (New York: Macmillan, 1962), 283.
28. Shakespeare, *The Tempest*, 20–21. By concurring with Prospero and Miranda in their evaluation of Caliban as vicious and at best pitiable, Stegner was holding to an interpretation of *The Tempest* that was fraught and, in the American context,

increasingly suggestive of racism. Aime Cesaire's postcolonial interpretation of *The Tempest*, *Une Tempête* (1969), which reinterpreted Caliban's viciousness and Prospero's virtue, was just a few years away from being published. Stegner summarizes his interpretation of *The Tempest* briefly in a 1981 essay: "The woods, like Dante's *selva oscura*, were full of terror; we should not forget that the words wilderness and bewilder are related. Shakespeare, setting his last play on a West Indian island, made its sole inhabitant a misshapen monster whose name is an anagram for cannibal. Prospero's wilderness island is made habitable only by Prospero's magic, the arts of civilization." Stegner, *One Way to Spell Man*, 171.

29. This theme is discussed in chapter 1.

30. Stegner, *Live Things*, 22.

31. Ibid., 23.

32. See Anderson, *The Movement and the Sixties*, 241–91.

33. Two books that stress deeper continuities between the two generations are George Marsden, *The Twilight of the American Enlightenment* (New York: Basic Books, 2014), and Christopher Shannon, *A World Made Safe for Differences: Cold War Intellectuals and the Politics of Identity* (Lanham: Rowman and Littlefield, 2001).

34. On the generation gap, see David Steigerwald, *The Sixties and the End of Modern America* (New York: St. Martin's Press, 1995), 249. Discussing Kenneth Keniston's study *Young Radicals* (1967), Steigerwald argues, "For the most part, the activists were not children rebelling against authoritarian homes. Their upbringings were mostly normal. Their parents were mildly political and usually liberal; they had taken a keen interest in their children's educations and interests. By and large, Keniston's radicals enjoyed warm family relationships."

35. McGurl, *The Program Era*, 205–7.

36. Stegner asked for his harshest criticism of Kesey (in the original in-person conversations) to be deleted from the interviews with Richard Etulain in the early 1980s (the first edition of the conversations was published in 1983). This was the only major deletion, according to Etulain (in conversation with the author). In the deleted section, Stegner said he thought Kesey wanted to be a "guru" more than a writer, and that he did not take time to learn the intricacies of the English language. More relevant regarding the Nurse Ratched connection (and Stegner's antagonism to romantic primitivism), he also thought the primary characters were too simplistic in that "all of the sick are the right ones, and all of the people taking care of the sick are the wrong ones. The whole message of it is 'They won't let us inmates take care of the institution,' which is, I think, imbecile. I don't much take the message of One Flew Over the Cuckoo's Nest, though I grant you some scenes are pretty powerful" [underlining original]. See box 115, folder 19, Stegner Papers.

37. Fradkin, *Wallace Stegner and the American West*, 134–35.

38. Rick Dodgson highlights a particular nurse Kesey encountered in his work at the Menlo Park VA Hospital as being the more direct model for Nurse Ratched in *It's All a Kind of Magic: The Young Ken Kesey* (Madison: University of Wisconsin Press, 2013), 137.

39. Fradkin describes the well-known residents of Perry Lane during Stegner's era, which had been the bohemian quarter of Palo Alto since Thorstein Veblen lived there in the early 1900s. Fradkin, *Wallace Stegner and the American West*, 138–40.

For more on Perry Lane, see also Dodgson, *It's All a Kind of Magic*. Tom Wolfe's *The Electric Kool-Aid Acid Test* (New York: Farrar, Straus, and Giroux, 1969), offers a more colorful take.

40. Jim Wolpman, "Alive in the 60s: The Midpeninsula Free University," http:// midpeninsulafreeu.com. Wolpman's website includes a brief institutional history and links to pamphlets, brochures, catalogs, and other materials produced by the MFU.

41. Sam Whiting, "Antiwar Activist Ira Sandperl dies," *SF Gate*, April 19, 2013, www .sfgate.com/bayarea/article/Antiwar-activist-Ira-Sandperl-dies-4446447.php.

42. Stegner, Draft Notes for *Live Things*, box 78, folder 1, Stegner Papers.

43. Ibid.

44. Jim Fields to Stegner, November 1, 1983, box 52, folder 17. Fields wrote from Menlo Park, California.

45. The note is included in Fradkin, *Wallace Stegner and the American West*, 160–61. See also Gessner, *All the Wild that Remains*, 132–33. Gessner relates the following from McChesney: "'When I got home, Wally was sweeping off his patio. That was my regular job, part of my rent. He wouldn't look at me. But I did hear him mutter one phrase: 'Ruined a great university.'" Stegner's comments recall Irving Howe's reflections on that moment in *A Margin of Hope: An Intellectual Autobiography* (Orlando, FL: Harcourt Brace Jovanovich, 1982), 314–15. Howe wrote, "There was something peculiarly wounding in the New Left attacks on older liberals and radicals. I felt that some of its spokesmen wanted not just to refute my opinions—that would have been entirely proper—but also to erase, to eliminate, to 'smash' people like me. They wanted to deny our past, annul our history, wipe out our integrity, and not as people mistaken or even pusillanimous but as people who were 'finished,' 'used up.' . . . When New Left students painted the slogan 'Up against the wall, motherfuckers!' on campus buildings, they had in mind not just the corporate state or the Pentagon or the CIA; they had in mind the only 'enemy' they knew at first hand, their liberal and socialist teachers; they had in mind parents of the New Deal generation who had raised them on the deplorable doctrine of 'repressive tolerance.'"

46. Over time, Page was reconciled to his parents—more Wallace than Mary, however—and he and Wallace cowrote and published *American Places* (New York: E. P. Dutton, 1981). Fradkin, *Wallace Stegner and the American West*, 125–26. After a careful analysis of *Live Things* in addition to other works from Stegner, Forrest G. Robinson surmises that it is possible, given the tight parallels between life and art, that the book was an attempt by Stegner to expiate his own failures as a parent. In sum, it "acknowledges the failure of love, offers an etiology of that failure, and admits that hardness of heart has enduring guilt as its price." Robinson, "Fathers and Sons in Stegner's Ordered Dream of Man," *Arizona Quarterly: A Journal of American Literature, Culture, and Theory* 59, no. 3 (Autumn 2003): 108.

47. Fradkin also describes Stegner's dispute with poet Gary Snyder, *Wallace Stegner and the American West*, 153–57. See also Richard Etulain, *Stegner: Conversations*, 140–41, where Stegner says that he has been thinking a great deal about Snyder's claim about meditation. As with McChesney, Stegner seems to have tried very hard to understand his position, but without success. Richard Lyman's *Stanford in Turmoil: Campus Unrest, 1966–1972* (Stanford: Stanford University Press, 2009) describes the

protests at Stanford from the point of view of Lyman, a faculty member in history who rose through the administration and eventually served as Stanford's president from 1970–1980. George Packer's *The Blood of the Liberals* (New York: Farrar, Strauss, and Giroux, 2000) offers a particularly nuanced portrait of Palo Alto in the 1960s, as Packer was the child of a Stanford administrator (Herbert Packer) and a Stanford faculty member in the creative writing department (Nancy Packer, a close friend of Stegner's) during the era. For more context on the protests of the era, see Peniel Joseph, *Waiting 'Til the Midnight Hour: A Narrative History of Black Power in America* (New York: Henry H. Holt, 2006).

48. Stegner writing to Richard Scowcroft: "I doubt that truth is ever arrived at by the process of saying something preposterous, getting an angry and quite as preposterous reply, and ultimately forcing even the most level-headed people into saying things they don't mean." Page Stegner, *Selected Letters*, 310.

49. Stegner wrote one of his most direct attempts to discuss the students of the 1960s for *The Nation*. Interestingly, it was a one-decade-later reflection, as *The Nation* had also asked Stegner and others to reflect on the students of the 1950s. In the 1967 article, Stegner stressed continuity between the generations: "Moreover, in a permissive school and home atmosphere, these children were taught togetherness as an ideal. The Haight-Ashbury young, making love not war, are only doing what we taught them. And in questioning everything, including its elders, this generation is likewise proving the efficacy of its nurture, for it was taught to take nothing on faith, to question, to doubt. . . . Many would like to be told, more than they are, what is socially right, even if they have to find out later that it is wrong. Many crave a direction and an authority that we have taught them to distrust. . . . All of which is only to say that we have taught them to search and to experiment, and they are searching and experimenting. And few generations—forget the mistakes they are bound to make, and are making—have been more alert and alive. Idealism is highly visible among the college students I know in 1967, and that goes for some of the alarming ones as well as for those, less rebellious or more hopeful of the old order, who put their devotion into the Peace Corps or Head Start or something traditionally liberal and humanitarian." Stegner, "Class of '67: The Gentle Desperadoes," *The Nation*, June 19, 1967, 775–81.

50. Stegner, *Where the Bluebird Sings*, 222.

51. Stegner, *Live Things*, 41.

52. Ibid., 41.

53. Ibid., 44.

54. Ibid., 46.

55. Ibid., 47.

56. Ibid., 48.

57. Ibid., 48–49.

58. Ibid., 62.

59. See Stegner's "This I Believe" in *One Way to Spell Man* (1982). One of Joe's internal descriptions of Peck is also relevant: "He *is* dangerous, too, and all the more so because, as I now recognize, he has no more malice than he has sense, and has besides a considerable dedication to beliefs that he unquestionably considers virtuous. Dangerousness is not necessarily a function of malicious intent. If I were

painting a portrait of the father of evil, I wonder if I wouldn't give him the face of a high-minded fool" [italics original]. Stegner, *Live Things*, 74. Suggesting no special animus for the hippies, Stegner's novel *Joe Hill* (1950) explored similar "guru" dynamics.

60. Edward Abbey, *The Journey Home: Some Words in Defense of the American West* (New York: Penguin, 1977), 183.

61. This would extend Robinson's critique of Stegner's perceived failures as a parent in "Fathers and Sons in Stegner's Ordered Dream of Man" to his sense of guilt for participating in development that spun beyond Stegner's sense of proper ecological limits.

62. Stegner, *Live Things*, 66.

63. A phrase included in Stegner's notes on the novel, underlining original. Stegner, Notes on *Live Things*, box 78, folder 1, Stegner Papers. This phrase and the themes below, in addition to Stegner's uncanny resemblance to Spencer Tracy in the late 1960s, are particularly interesting in conversation with *Guess Who's Coming to Dinner* (1967). It came out in the same year as *Live Things* and was also set amid suburban liberals living in villas surrounded by beautiful gardens on the San Francisco Peninsula. Obviously, however, race is the central dynamic of the movie while it is conspicuously absent from *Live Things*. In the climax of the movie, Sidney Poitier says to his father: "You listen to me. You say you don't want to tell me how to live my life. So what do you think you've been doing? You tell me what rights I've got or haven't got, and what I owe to you for what you've done for me. Let me tell you something. I owe you nothing! If you carried that bag a million miles, you did what you're supposed to do! Because you brought me into this world. And from that day you owed me everything you could ever do for me like I will owe my son if I ever have another. But you don't own me!"

64. Stegner, *Live Things*, 127.

65. Ibid., 128.

66. Stegner's most succinct version came from 1952 and is not too distant from Joe's expressions in the argument: "However far I have missed achieving it, I know that moderation is one of the virtues I most believe in.... Everything potent, from human love to atomic energy, is dangerous; it produces ill about as readily as good; it becomes good only through the control, the discipline, and the wisdom with which we use it. Much of this control is social, a thing which laws and institutions and uniforms enforce, but much of it must be personal, and I do not see how we can evade the obligation to take full responsibility for what we individually do. Our reward for self-control and the acceptance of private responsibility is not usually money or power. Self-respect and the respect of others are quite enough." Stegner, *One Way to Spell Man*, 4. The interview was taken by Edward Murrow for his "This I Believe" series in 1952.

67. Stegner, *Live Things*, 129.

68. In Stegner's notes, Curt is born in 1925 and dies in 1962. Stegner, Notes on *Live Things*, box 78, folder 1, Stegner Papers.

69. Stegner, *Live Things*, 131.

70. Ibid., 133.

71. Ibid., 134.

72. Ibid., 136.

73. Ibid., 139.

74. George Cotkin's history of the New Sensibility offers a more sympathetic picture. See *Feast of Excess: A Cultural History of the New Sensibility* (Oxford: Oxford University Press, 2015). Hale's *Nation of Outsiders* allows for a more critical reading of the social effects of this cultural trend, even if not for the same reasons that Stegner raises via Joe Allston.

75. Stegner, *Live Things*, 140.

76. Ibid. Stegner made this critique most often without really considering more desperate migrations and/or forced migrations. It is interesting to compare Stegner's critique of hypermobility in the West with the experience of African Americans during the Great Migration(s) of 1915–1970. See Isabel Wilkerson's Pulitzer Prize–winning *The Warmth of Other Suns: The Epic Story of America's Great Migration* (New York: Vintage Press, 2010) for a history of these migrations written to capture the experiences on a personal level.

77. Stegner, *Live Things*, 141.

78. Marion Benasutti to Wallace Stegner, 1967, box 51, folder 17, Stegner Papers.

79. MA Arnold to Wallace Stegner, March 14, 1968, box 51, folder 5, Stegner Papers.

80. Paul Sanford to Wallace Stegner, August 23, 1971, box 55, folder 32, Stegner Papers.

81. Betty Hanson to Wallace Stegner, December 1, 1967, box 53, folder 1, Stegner Papers.

82. Stegner, *Live Things*, 178–79. Perhaps this passage was in the back of Kesey's mind when he made his remark at the time of Stegner's death about their difference being a matter of LSD and Jack Daniels.

83. Stegner, *Live Things*, 183.

84. Ibid., 192.

85. Kurt Vonnegut Jr., "Topics: Good Missiles, Good Manners, Good Night," *New York Times*, September 13, 1969.

86. Stegner, *Live Things*, 199–201.

87. Ibid., 215.

88. Ibid., 226.

89. Page Stegner witnessed an event like this. See Etulain, *Stegner: Conversations*, 75. Stegner also received a note from Janet Ewing, who said that her family owned the horse that broke its legs in the cattleguard. She read the book in 1976 and told Stegner that she "was a child of the 1960s" and she and her friends felt they had a "special claim on that land because we knew it so well, watched the changes so closely, and loved it with almost mystic passion. . . . I feel that those are my roots, my standard of beauty and also an Eden that no longer exists." Janet Ewing to Wallace Stegner, November 1, 1976, box 52, folder 13, Stegner Papers.

90. Joan Miller to Wallace Stegner, December 2, 1975, box 54, folder 28, Stegner Papers. Miller wrote from Sacramento, California.

91. Stegner, *Live Things*, 247–48. Stegner's description of Marian's death and Joe's reaction to it is reminiscent of Henry Adams's description of his sister's death in *The Education of Henry Adams* (Boston: Mariner Books, 2000), a book that Stegner quoted from throughout *Beyond the Hundredth Meridian* (1954). Of his sister's death, Adams wrote, "He found his sister, a woman of forty, as gay and brilliant in the terrors of lockjaw as she had been in the careless fun of 1859, lying in bed

in consequence of a miserable cab-accident that had bruised her foot. Hour by hour the muscles grew rigid, while the mind remained bright, until after ten days of fiendish torture she died in convulsions. . . . Death took features altogether new to him, in these rich and sensuous surroundings. Nature enjoyed it, played with it, the horror added to her charm, she liked the torture, and smothered her victim with caresses." Adams, *The Education of Henry Adams*, 287–88.

92. Stegner, *Live Things*, 247.

93. Ibid., 248.

94. Stegner was surprised when an interviewer told him that he thought Stegner's books "in relation to many modern novels" seemed "relatively optimistic in tone." Stegner replied: "I guess I'm not a very complete cynic, but I wouldn't have dared call myself an optimist. . . . I don't understand, quite, people who write books out of hatred or despair. I don't believe their despair, for one thing, because, if it's true despair, you don't write the book. I write about ordinarily decent people, and it seems to me that these very decent people have as much business in a book as Candys or Portnoys. . . . It's my faith that fiction is dramatized belief, and my beliefs include a notion that if you dislike life, there's an easy way out." Roger Hofheins and Dan Tooker, "Interview with Wallace Stegner," *The Southern Review* 11, no. 4 (October 1975): 795–96.

95. Kirk Bundy to Wallace Stegner, June 12, 1969, box 51, folder 34, Stegner Papers.

96. Rebecca Olsen to Wallace Stegner, February 3, 1987, box 54, folder 48, Stegner Papers.

97. Nina Miller to Wallace Stegner, June 25, 1988, box 54, folder 28. Miller wrote from Ithaca, New York.

98. "Curiously, I get a lot of very heartfelt, intimate letters even yet on that book, from people who have come up against the problem of someone close to them dying of cancer." Etulain, *Stegner: Conversations*, 74.

99. This phrase, a pun on Hegel, comes from Franco Moretti's "The Slaughterhouse of Literature," *Modern Language Quarterly* 61, no. 1 (March 2000): 207–27. It emphasizes the vast amount of published literature that is noncanonical or sifted out and lost to history.

100. Of the letters from readers marked with a definite location and sorted by Stegner into the category Fan Mail, about a third (566/1667) were from California. This is significantly higher than the total for any other state, as the next highest total from another state (New York) was less than 10 percent of the total (148/1667). This total represents a limited amount of Stegner's correspondence as a whole.

101. Of fiction, Stegner wrote: "Literature is a function of temperament, and thank God there are many kinds of temperament and therefore many kinds of literature. I can speak only for my own, and after considerable acquaintance I have determined that my temperament is quiet, recessive, skeptical, and watchful. . . . The shouters in thunder roar from their podiums and pulpits; I squeak from my corner. They speak to the deaf, but it takes good ears to hear me, for I want to be part of the common sound, a not-too-dominating element of the ambient noise." *Where the Bluebird Sings*, 221–22.

102. Todd Gitlin offers one attempt to understand the "fierce sense of difference" that divided the generations, even if he also argues that many descriptions of the

generation gap seem "overblown," as at least the student radicals of the New Left often "shared many more sentiments and values with their parents than with the rest of American society." Gitlin, *The Sixties*, 19.

103. Stegner, *The Sound of Mountain Water*, 38.

CHAPTER 4

1. The character Roald Duke, in Hunter S. Thompson, *Fear and Loathing in Las Vegas* (New York: Vintage Press, 1998), 66–68.

2. The character Lyman Ward, in Stegner, *Angle of Repose*, 6.

3. Stegner modeled his narrator's house on the North Star House in Grass Valley, which was designed by Julia Morgan in 1905. Fradkin, *Wallace Stegner and the American West*, 316.

4. Recent scholarship following the Long Civil Rights Movement framework has resisted this declension narrative of the 1960s. For example, see Annelise Orleck, *Storming Caesars Palace: How Black Mothers Fought Their Own War on Poverty* (New York: Beacon Press, 2005), and Joseph, *Waiting 'Til the Midnight Hour*.

5. This publication history is related in Colberg, *Wallace Stegner: A Descriptive Bibliography*, 223.

6. Wallace Stegner, *The Sound of Mountain Water* (New York: Penguin, 1997), 193.

7. Ibid., 199–201. See Newberry, "Wallace Stegner's 'Wolf Willow.'" Alan Jacobs uses the term "temporal bandwidth," to describe a similar idea. Jacobs has elaborated on the idea as it is expressed by a character in Thomas Pynchon's *Gravity's Rainbow* (1973), who describes temporal bandwidth as "the width of your present, your now.... The more you dwell in the past and future, the thicker your bandwidth, the more solid your persona. But the narrower your sense of Now, the more tenuous you are." Jacobs, "To survive our high-speed society, cultivate 'temporal bandwidth,'" *The Guardian*, June 16, 2018, online at https://www.theguardian.com/commentisfree/2018/jun/16/temporal-bandwith-social-media-alan-jacobs.

8. Stegner, *Angle of Repose*, 579.

9. Harold Swanton, a screenwriter for *Alfred Hitchcock Presents*, writing from Northridge, California, in a letter dated August 4, 1992. He refers specifically to Joe Allston in *Spectator Bird*: "Curiously, your virtuoso grumblings about the woes of ageing have had a therapeutic effect, and I grumble less about mine." Swanton to Stegner, August 4, 1992, box 56, folder 2, Stegner Papers.

10. Stegner, *Angle of Repose*, 291. According to Stegner's contemporary Paul Fussell, in his satirical guide to American social classes, this confirms Lyman's middle-class sensibility: "The middle class is the place where table manners assume an awful importance and where net curtains flourish to conceal activities like 'hiding the salami' (a phrase no middle-class person would indulge in, surely: the fatuous *making love* is the middle-class equivalent)." Fussell, *Class: A Guide Through the American Status System* (New York: Summit Books, 1983), 39.

11. On this dynamic, see Jane Tompkins, *West of Everything: The Inner Life of Westerns* (New York: Oxford University Press, 1993).

12. Stegner, in his last essay collection: "A lot of people have mistakenly recognized me in Lyman Ward's wheelchair." Stegner, *Where the Bluebird Sings*, 224.

13. Stegner, *Angle of Repose*, 4.

14. Ibid., 453, for Lyman's title.
15. Audrey C. Peterson, "Narrative Voice in Wallace Stegner's *Angle of Repose*," *Western American Literature* 10, no. 2 (Summer 1975): 125–33.
16. James Hepworth highlights the postmodern features of *Angle of Repose* in "Wallace Stegner's *Angle of Repose*: One Reader's Response" (PhD diss., University of Arizona, 1989).
17. According to his Amazon page sales rankings, *Angle of Repose* (1971) and *Crossing to Safety* (1987) alternate between first and second among Stegner's books. Nancy Colberg's *Wallace Stegner: A Descriptive Bibliography* provides totals for printings as of 1990.
18. Mary Ellen Williams Walsh was first to raise these concerns when she delivered a conference paper, "Succubi and Other Monsters: The Women in *Angle of Repose*," at the Western Literature Association's 1979 meeting. It was not received well at the time, but the essay was later revised and published as "*Angle of Repose* and the Writings of Mary Hallock Foote: A Source Study," in Anthony Arthur, ed., *Critical Essays on Wallace Stegner* (Boston: G. K. Hall, 1982), 184–209. On the conference paper, see Fradkin, *Wallace Stegner and the American West*, 257. David Lavender was another early critic—and one of the most prominent male critics—in his "The Tyranny of Facts," collected in Judy Nolte Lensink, ed., *Old Southwest/New Southwest: Essays on a Region and Its Literature* (Tucson: Tucson Public Library, 1987), 62–73. Jackson Benson defends Stegner fairly strenuously in *Wallace Stegner: His Life and Work*. Philip Fradkin gives a more balanced view in his biography. Historian John Demos addresses it in "Real Lives and Other Fictions: Reconsidering Wallace Stegner's *Angle of Repose*," in Mark C. Carnes, *Novel History: Historians and Novelists Confront America's Past (and Each Other)* (New York: Simon and Schuster, 2001). Susan Salter Reynolds wrote about it in a cover story for the *Los Angeles Times Magazine*, "Tangle of Repose," March 23, 2003. Sands Hall's 2001 play, "Fair Use," dramatizes the situation and raises some of the more existential questions about the issue in a compelling way. It was performed in Grass Valley at the North Star House as recently as May 27, 2018, and in Boise, Idaho, on June 4, 2016.
19. On Foote, see Paul, *A Victorian Gentlewoman in the Far West*; Christine Hill Smith, *Social Class in the Writings of Mary Hallock Foote* (Reno: University of Nevada Press, 2009); Darlis A. Miller, *Mary Hallock Foote: Author-Illustrator of the American West* (Norman: University of Oklahoma Press, 2002).
20. Sands Hall's play is still being performed, for example.
21. John Demos's article in Carnes's *Novel History* highlights some of these ironies as well, 132–45.
22. Lyman Ward and *All in the Family*'s Archie Bunker, one of the most (in)famous fictional American curmudgeons, entered the world in the same year, 1971. Jefferson Cowie highlights the ways that Carroll O'Connor, the actor who played Archie Bunker, and the character were intertwined, similarly to what I do here with Stegner. See *Stayin' Alive: The 1970s and the Last Days of the Working Class* (New York: The New Press, 2010), 194–96. Curmudgeons can be simply reactionary, but a slightly more positive assessment that explains their resilience in American culture—other than simply American conservatism—is that the curmudgeon is resisting the planned obsolescence of the elderly and insisting that age might imply wisdom rather than

simply obsolescence. See Hans Jonas on this interpretation of wisdom and obsolescence: "If . . . a man in his advancing years has to turn to his children, or grandchildren, to have them tell him what the present is about; if his own acquired knowledge and understanding no longer avail him; if at the end of his days he finds himself to be obsolete rather than wise—then we may term the rate and scope of change that thus overtook him, 'revolutionary.'" Jonas, *Philosophical Essays: From Ancient Creed to Technological Man* (Englewood Cliffs, NJ: Prentice Hall, 1974), 46.

23. Stegner, *Angle of Repose*, 3.

24. Ibid., 6.

25. Ibid., 14.

26. Stegner, *Where the Bluebird Sings*, 220.

27. Stegner, *Angle of Repose*, 5.

28. Stegner: "If any object is important enough to be mentioned, it should be put to some use. As Chekhov says, if you hang a gun on the wall at the beginning, it has to go off before the end." Stegner, *On Teaching and Writing Fiction*, 93.

29. Stegner, *Angle of Repose*, 9. On the "library" Stegner "builds . . . around Susan Ward," see Melody Graulich, "Book Learning: *Angle of Repose* as Literary History," in Rankin, *Wallace Stegner: Man and Writer*, 233.

30. Stegner, *Angle of Repose*, 5.

31. Stegner's notes suggest he envisioned a more prominent role for this character and potentially another male graduate student hired as a caretaker, but fortunately he resisted, as it would have likely made the novel seem too close to a rehashing of *Live Things*. Stegner, Notes on Angle of Repose, box 95, folder 1, Stegner Papers.

32. Stegner, *Angle of Repose*, 37.

33. See Bruce Seymour, *Lola Montez: A Life* (New Haven: Yale University Press, 1996).

34. On Royce in terms similar to the themes I explore here, see Robert V. Hine, *Josiah Royce: From Grass Valley to Harvard* (Norman: University of Oklahoma Press, 1992).

35. Stegner, *Angle of Repose*, 12. Compare with Susan's reactions to the mining camp in New Almaden: "The people here were not people. Except for Oliver, she was alone and in exile, and her heart was back where the sun rose." *Angle of Repose*, 107.

36. Stegner was sensitive to the fact that this settler-colonialism was in fact a form of conquest that displaced the Indian peoples of the American West. He condemned it but also made distinctions between forms of settlement that were more destructive or less, primarily in environmental terms. While not a major theme, he alludes to it in one internal monologue Lyman has regarding Oliver's decision to move to Deadwood which likewise makes him uneasy, as the land had been "lately stolen from the Sioux." Reporting that Oliver is working for George Hearst, Lyman writes that he "does not fear for his scalp. I fear for his soul." But Lyman also recognizes degrees of guilt: "There is no reason that Oliver should not have been [like George Hearst and other 'raiders'] except character. Pioneer or not, resource-raider or not, afflicted or not with the frontier faith that exploitation is development, and development is good, he was simply an honest man. His gift was not for money-making and the main chance. He was a builder, not a raider." Oliver had, according to his grandson, "an uncomplicated ambition to leave the world a little better for his passage through it, and his notion of how to better it was to develop it for human use." Stegner, *Angle of Repose*, 206.

37. See Richard Slotkin's nearly contemporaneous history, *Regeneration through Violence: The Mythology of the American Frontier, 1600–1860* (Middletown: Wesleyan University Press, 1973).

38. Stegner, *Angle of Repose*, 401–2.

39. Ibid., 201.

40. "Susan Ward came West not to join a new society, but to endure it, not to build anything but to enjoy a temporary experience and make it yield whatever instruction it contained." Ibid., 77.

41. Ibid., 107. See also Smith, *Social Class*, 3–12. Considering Smith's analysis of Foote, Stegner's depiction of Foote's sense of class superiority was not exaggerated much, if at all.

42. Lyman's particularly vivid description of Susan's process of becoming "a western woman": "Time hung unchanging, or with no more visible change than a slow reddening of poison oak leaves, an imperceptible darkening of the golden hills. It dripped like a slow percolation through limestone, so slow that she forgot it between drops. Nevertheless every drop, indistinguishable from every other, left a little deposit of sensation, experience, feeling. In thirty or forty years the accumulated deposits would turn my cultivated, lady-like, talkative, talented, innocently snobbish grandmother into a western woman in spite of herself." Stegner, *Angle of Repose*, 104.

43. Ibid., 118.

44. Ibid., 127.

45. Ibid., 183.

46. See Tara Westover, *Educated: A Memoir*, xiv, 274, 310, 319, 320, and Westover's descriptions of Buck's Peak for a modern variation on this theme.

47. This is a theme that is carried throughout the novel: "'Each move leaves me less myself.'" Stegner, *Angle of Repose*, 507. Stegner is sympathetic to Susan's desire to establish herself in a place and be a part of a community, but challenges the terms that she has set for this endeavor. Susan will not submit to the community on its terms, and for some understandable reasons.

48. Of his students at the time, Stegner said, "They didn't give a damn what happened up to two minutes ago and would have been totally unable to understand a Victorian lady. I could conceive students of mine confronting Mary Hallock Foote and thinking, 'My God, fantastic, inhuman,' because they themselves were so imprisoned by the present that they had no notion of how various humanity and human customs can be." Etulain, *Stegner: Conversations*, 88.

49. Ram Dass, *Be Here Now* (Taos: Lama Foundation, 1971).

50. Stegner, *Angle of Repose*, 172.

51. Ibid., 290.

52. The allusion works in several ways. Paolo and Francesca's fate in Dante's *Inferno* is interesting in light of Stegner's themes: they are stuck in an eternal whirlwind and therefore placeless.

53. Stegner, *Angle of Repose*, 294.

54. Ibid., 295.

55. Ibid., 296.

56. Ibid., 298.

57. Bennett, *Workshops of Empire*, 118–19. Bennett's summary of Stegner in the 1970s is also fairly biting: "His view of American reality, which seemed so perspicacious in his prime years, was revealed by the counterculture to possess no metaphysical or immutably authoritative cultural grounding. He knew it and loathed the fact, and made great art from his loathing in *Angle of Repose*" (118).

58. Page Stegner, *Selected Letters*, 270. Stegner was writing to Merrill Joan Gerber, a former Stegner Fellow, in 1974.

59. William Bevis, in Rankin, *Wallace Stegner: Man and Writer*, 255–67.

60. Stegner, *Angle of Repose*, 301.

61. Ibid., 302.

62. Stegner also includes a brief vignette of Susan's sister, who feels less nostalgic for Milton because she is still living there with a husband who "says he's smothering here" and envies Susan and Oliver's western freedom. Ibid., 307.

63. Lyman's reflections on Susan leaving New Almaden: "Gone, and as painful now as the thought of a stillborn child. Sentimental? Of course. Riddled with the Anglo-American mawkishness about home, quicksandy with assumptions about monogamy and Woman's Highest Role, buttery with echoes of the household poets. All that. But I find that I don't mind her emotions and her sentiments. Home is a notion that only the nations of the homeless fully appreciate and only the uprooted comprehend. What else would one plant in a wilderness or on a frontier? What loss would hurt more? So I don't snicker backward ninety years at poor Grandmother pacing her porch and biting her knuckle and hating the loss of what she had never quite got over thinking her exile. I find her moving." Ibid., 166. For analysis of this theme and its complexities in the era of Mary Hallock Foote, see Richard White, *The Republic for Which It Stands: The United States during Reconstruction and the Gilded Age, 1865–1896* (New York: Oxford University Press, 2017), 136–71. Following the Civil War, White writes, "The production of homes was the ultimate rationale for the economy, for the nation itself, and for the public policies and the activist government embraced by the Republicans" (p. 137).

64. Stegner, *Angle of Repose*, 303. Suggesting the resonance of the metaphor, the recent Christopher Nolan film *Interstellar* (2014) includes a paean to pioneers and ends with a space colony.

65. On the distinction, see Henry S. Richardson, "Moral Reasoning," The Stanford Encyclopedia of Philosophy (Fall 2018 Edition), ed. Edward N. Zalta, online at https://plato.stanford.edu/archives/fall2018/entries/reasoning-moral/.

66. Nancy B. Harris to Wallace Stegner, April 1, 1972, box 53, folder 1, Stegner Papers. Harris was a mental health counselor at Free Clinic in Laguna. She wrote from Niguel, California.

67. The comment was about *Live Things* specifically, but in the context of it echoing themes in *Angle of Repose*. Beverly Boekel to Wallace Stegner, May 12, 1971, box 51, folder 27, Stegner Papers.

68. Mary Jayne Willis to Wallace Stegner, July 11, 1971, box 56, folder 38, Stegner Papers. Willis wrote from Columbus, Ohio.

69. Joan S. Van Ness to Wallace Stegner, May 9, 1971, box 56, folder 24, Stegner Papers. Van Ness wrote from New York City.

70. Janet F. Moe to Wallace Stegner, June 24, 1971, and July 17, 1964, box 54, folder 31, Stegner Papers. Moe wrote from Barneveld, New York.

71. Ann Cochran to Wallace Stegner, July 30, 1975, box 51, folder 49, Stegner Papers. Cochran wrote from Palo Alto, California. She worked at the Office of Facilities at Stanford.

72. Kacie Conner to Wallace Stegner, July 11, 1971, box 51, folder 49, Stegner Papers. Conner wrote from Des Moines, Iowa.

73. Shelbee Matis to Wallace Stegner, August 1971, box 54, folder 22, Stegner Papers. Matis wrote from Evanston, Illinois. She was in her forties at the time and worked as an artist and sculptor.

74. Matis wrote Stegner another letter about *Spectator Bird* in 1978, and then another about *Live Things* in 1992, all of them appreciative but still challenging. As of 2017, Matis was still hosting art exhibitions. See Gayle Worland, "Shelbee Matis: At 89, a Life of Crafting Art," *Wisconsin State Journal*, November 18, 2017. https://madison .com/wsj/entertainment/arts-and-theatre/shelbee-matis-at-a-life-of-crafting-art /article_589493f0-b941-5051-a32d-b31296dfcced.html.

75. Stegner, *Angle of Repose*, 402, 406.

76. Ibid., 407. Stegner resists using the term "big rock candy mountain," but his father and the story of him and his mother that he told most vividly in the book with that title is clearly on his mind.

77. Susan, in a letter to Augusta: "Like everything here, it is large and raw. It is for the future, it sacrifices the present for what is to come." Ibid., 526.

78. Ibid., 411.

79. Ibid., 416–17.

80. Ibid., 418.

81. Ibid., 427.

82. Ibid., 432.

83. Ibid.

84. Ibid.

85. Ibid., 424.

86. Ibid., 476.

87. Ibid., 486.

88. Ibid., 552–67.

89. Ibid., 571.

90. Ibid., 573.

91. Ibid., 574–75.

92. Ibid., 576–77.

93. Ibid.

94. Ibid., 581.

95. Ibid., 582–600.

96. On the theme of "webs" in *Angle of Repose*, see Graulich, "Book Learning," 232. She builds on Clifford Geertz's metaphor in *The Interpretation of Cultures: Selected Essays* (New York: Basic Books, 1973), 5.

97. Stegner, *Angle of Repose*, 569.

98. See Susan Salter Reynolds, "Tangle of Repose," especially. The historian John Lukacs defines "the purpose of history" as "less a definite establishment of truths than"

an attempt at the "reduction of untruths." Stegner would not have agreed. Lukacs, *The Future of History* (New Haven: Yale University Press, 2011), 151.

99. Stegner, *Angle of Repose*, 622.

100. On "positive negative space," see Stephen Kern, *The Culture of Time and Space* (Cambridge: Harvard University Press, 2003), 152–80.

101. See also Rob Williams, "'Huts of Time': Wallace Stegner's Historical Legacy," for a good reflection on Stegner's fiction versus western myth that illuminates parallel concerns. Williams's essay is included in Rankin, ed., *Wallace Stegner: Man and Writer*, 119–43.

102. On the Footes' marriage, see Rodman Paul's introduction to *A Victorian Gentlewoman*, 25–44.

103. Of her time in Grass Valley, Foote concludes, "All that has happened here since [the death of Agnes Foote in 1904] would be too difficult to tell for one so deeply implicated through her relations to the chief actors, yet so powerless, as myself." Paul, *A Victorian Gentlewoman*, 399.

104. Stegner, *Angle of Repose*, 625.

105. Ibid., 631. It should be noted that the reflection on "angle of repose" as metaphor started with Foote's actual writings.

106. Ibid. According to *Merriam-Webster*, the false arch or corbel arch is "a structure which spans an opening like an arch by having successive courses of masonry project farther inward as they rise on each side of the gap." False arches are not as efficient or stable—or as beautiful, it should be added—as true arches with a keystone.

107. See Hepworth, "*Angle of Repose*: One Reader's Response."

108. Rodman Paul's research into Foote and his decision to edit her autobiography was not directly related to Stegner's work, however.

109. See especially Melody Graulich, "Book Learning," 246–50, for a defense of this reading.

110. Berry, *What Are People For?*, 54–55.

111. Etulain, *Stegner: Conversations*, 86–87.

112. Ibid., 162–63.

113. J. Stephen Sheppard to Wallace Stegner, November 20, 1971, box 55, folder 41, Stegner Papers. Writing from New York City, Sheppard was a literary agent for Paul R. Reynolds.

114. Stegner, *Angle of Repose*, 600.

115. Berry quoted in Bilbro, *Wendell Berry's Sustainable Forms*, 10.

CHAPTER 5

1. Stegner, *The Sound of Mountain Water*, 284–85.

2. Though he returned to the characters of *Live Things*, he did not consider himself bound to them or the timeline of the book. Joe has aged only four years. In *Live Things*, Curtis has just died in the 1960s. This being the case, the changes are only worth noting as Stegner's imagined developments and should be taken as such.

3. On the 1970s more broadly, see Philip Jenkins, *Decade of Nightmares: The End of the Sixties and the Making of Eighties America* (New York: Oxford University Press, 2006); Daniel Rodgers, *Age of Fracture* (Cambridge: Belknap Press, 2011);

Thomas Borstelmann, *The 1970s: A New Global History from Civil Rights to Economic Inequality* (Princeton: Princeton University Press, 2012).

4. Benson, *Wallace Stegner: His Life and Work*, 288.
5. Etulain, *Stegner: Conversations*, 44.
6. Wallace Stegner, Notes on Spectator Bird, box 107, folder 3, Stegner Papers.
7. Ibid.
8. On Faulkner, see Etulain, *Stegner: Conversations*, 78–79. On O'Connor, see Stegner, *Where the Bluebird Sings*, 220–21. Stegner thought O'Connor's justification for her use of the grotesque—that "when speaking to the hard-of-hearing one must shout"—was a poor justification, and not adequate to the achievement of her stories themselves.
9. Stegner, *Spectator Bird* (New York: Penguin, 2010): Tennyson, 101; Goethe, 192; Pascal, 198; the Venerable Bede, 203.
10. For more on "The Seafarer," see Jack Baker, "Re-Membering the Past Rightly: The *Ubi Sunt* Tradition in Wendell Berry's Fiction," in *Telling the Stories Right*, ed. Jack Baker and Jeffrey Bilbro (Eugene: Wipf and Stock Publishers, 2018).
11. Wallace Stegner, *The Spectator Bird*, 48.
12. Ibid., 58.
13. Ibid., 48.
14. Ibid., 49. See Stegner's "Sense of Place" essay: "[We] are nostalgic before history has taken its second step.... We have made a tradition out of mourning the passing of things we never had time really to know, just as we have made a culture out of the open road, out of movement without place." Stegner, *Where the Bluebird Sings*, 203–4.
15. Stegner, *Spectator Bird*, 53.
16. Ibid. It is interesting to note the inclusion of the category hippie, and Joe's agreement with a sentiment that would not be able to condemn Jim Peck or Tom Weld.
17. Ibid., 60.
18. Ibid., 62. Note the similarity to this feeling and the way Joe feels when he is challenged by Peck.
19. Wallace Stegner, "The Artist as Environmental Advocate," an oral history conducted in 1982 by Ann Lage (Sierra Club History Series, Regional Oral History Office, The Bancroft Library, University of California, Berkeley, 1983), 9. The interview took place in Stegner's study in Los Altos Hills.
20. See Heppler, "Machines in the Valley," 146–216.
21. "Not In My Backyard."
22. Stegner in Phyllis Filiberti Butler, ed., *20-20 Vision: In Celebration of the Peninsula Hills* (Palo Alto: Western Tanager Press, 1982), 12–14.
23. Stegner, *Spectator Bird*, 5.
24. See Cowie, *Stayin' Alive*, 313–69.
25. Stegner, *Spectator Bird*, 12.
26. Ibid., 13.
27. For more context, see Matthew Frye Jacobson, *Roots Too: White Ethnic Revival in Post-Civil Rights America* (Cambridge: Harvard University Press, 2006). Stegner's *Spectator Bird* won the National Book Award in the same year as Irving Howe's *The World of Our Fathers: The Journey of the East European Jews to America and the*

Life They Found and Made, another reflection on American migration intertwined with a search for a personal and possessed past.

28. Stegner, *Spectator Bird*, 28–29.
29. Ibid., 32–33.
30. Ibid., 34.
31. This situation, as well as the meeting with Karen Blixen, was drawn from a real experience of Stegner's. See Benson, *Wallace Stegner: His Life and Work*, 371.
32. Stegner, *Spectator Bird*, 94.
33. Ibid.
34. Ibid., 95–97.
35. Ibid., 101.
36. Ibid.
37. Ibid., 102.
38. Ibid., 97. This book was published just before Wendell Berry's *The Unsettling of America* (1977), a critique of industrial farming practices built on essays written over the course of the 1970s. Stegner would have likely read these essays, as Wendell Berry was his former student and close friend. In his notes, Stegner refers to his fellow Californian Luther Burbank as an inspiration and he shows up briefly in the novel. Stegner, Notes on Spectator Bird, box 107, folder 3, Stegner Papers.
39. Stegner, *Spectator Bird*, 144.
40. Ibid., 169.
41. On Ferdinand Tönnies' terms Gemeinschaft and Gesellschaft in the study of American history, see Thomas Bender, *Community and Social Change in America* (New Brunswick: Rutgers University Press, 1978), 16–24.
42. Zygmunt Bauman, *Modernity and the Holocaust* (Ithaca: Cornell University Press, 2000), 13.
43. Stegner, *Spectator Bird*, 198.
44. Translation by Henry Wadsworth Longfellow.
45. Ibid., 197.
46. Stegner refers to a character from James Joyce's *Dubliners* (1914). Wallace Stegner, Notes on Spectator Bird, box 107, folder 3, Stegner Papers.
47. Stegner, *Spectator Bird*, 199.
48. Ibid., 203.
49. Ibid.
50. For more connections on Stegner's use of birds in his fiction, see Melody Graulich, "Ruminations on Stegner's Protective Impulse and the Art of Storytelling," in Meine, *Wallace Stegner and the Continental Vision*, 59.
51. Abby Cohen to Wallace Stegner, October 28, 1989, box 51, folder 49. Cohen wrote from Berkeley, California.
52. Sudie Duncan Sides to Wallace Stegner, April 19, 1979, box 55, folder 44. Sides wrote from San Francisco, California. He told Stegner that he had read many of his books and was a professor of history at San Francisco State University.
53. Dorothy Fabian to Wallace Stegner, June 18, 1976, box 52, folder 17, Stegner Papers.
54. Philip S. Bernstein to Wallace Stegner, April 20, 1977, box 51, folder 14, Stegner Papers. Bernstein identified himself as Rabbi at Temple B'rith Kodesh in Rochester, New York.

55. Terri Sweat to Wallace Stegner, October 7, 1988, box 56, folder 1, Stegner Papers.
56. Jeannette Maino to Wallace Stegner, June 14, 1977, box 54, folder 17, Stegner Papers. Maino wrote from Modesto, California.
57. Mrs. Frank Hrisomalos to Wallace Stegner, March 8, 1978, box 53, folder 23, Stegner Papers. Hrisomalos wrote from Bloomington, Indiana.
58. Sterling R. Johnson to Wallace Stegner, May 22, 1978, box 53, folder 29, Stegner Papers. Johnson wrote from Palm Springs, California.
59. Vance Morgan to Wallace Stegner, September 19, 1979, box 54, folder 32, Stegner Papers. Morgan wrote from Chesapeake, Virginia.
60. Raymond Hensel, February 14, 1981, box 53, folder 12, Stegner Papers. Hensel wrote from San Mateo, California.

CONCLUSION

1. The "Wilderness Letter" is reprinted in Stegner's *The Sound of Mountain Water*, 145–53, among other collections. I find James Morton Turner's more appreciative assessment of the political defense of wilderness areas more convincing than the criticism of the concept of wilderness found in William Cronon's influential essay "The Trouble with Wilderness; or, Getting Back to the Wrong Nature." See Turner's *The Promise of Wilderness: American Environmental Politics since 1964* (Seattle: University of Washington Press, 2103); and Cronon, *Uncommon Ground*, 69–91.
2. Stegner, "Born a Square: The Westerner's Dilemma," *The Atlantic* 213 (January 1964): 46–50.
3. The context for the letter is described in Stegner, *Marking the Sparrow's Fall*. The report was being composed for the Outdoor Recreation Resources Review Commission.
4. See the first of several books to borrow the phrase in its title: Joseph Wood Krutch and Eliot Porter, *Baja California and the Geography of Hope* (New York: Ballantine Books, 1967).
5. Stegner, *Marking the Sparrow's Fall*, 114.
6. Ibid., 112. In this, Stegner's arguments were consistent with Arthur Schlesinger's *The Vital Center: The Politics of Freedom* (Cambridge: The Riverside Press, 1962), 241–47.
7. See Fradkin, *Wallace Stegner and the American West*, 205–13.
8. Stegner, *Marking the Sparrow's Fall*, 113. He did share concerns about the state of American culture that gave him pause: "our novelists are the declared enemies of their society" and the producers of a literature that is "sick, embittered, losing its mind, losing its faith."
9. Mark W. T. Harvey describes Stegner's earlier conservation activism during the Echo Park Dam controversy in the 1950s and highlights the connections between the Wilderness Letter and the 1964 Wilderness Act in *A Symbol of Wilderness: Echo Park and the American Conservation Movement* (Seattle: University of Washington Press, 2000), 258–59. Harvey's *Wilderness Forever: Howard Zahniser and the Path to the Wilderness Act* (Seattle: University of Washington Press, 2005) provides more context on the development of the Wilderness Act itself, but only mentions Stegner briefly.
10. Stegner, *Sound of Mountain Water*, 38.

11. For example, in *Beyond the Hundredth Meridian* (1954), Stegner highlights the way that John Wesley Powell's cooperative vision was rejected. But he also highlighted cultures that were cooperative with resources, citing the irrigation projects of the Latter-day Saints in Utah and the *ejidos* in New Mexico as examples. These "wests" were perhaps what he had in mind. For a historical study of this issue in terms similar to Stegner's, see Robert Hine, *Community on the American Frontier: Separate but Not Alone* (Norman: University of Oklahoma Press, 1981).

12. Stegner, *Where the Bluebird Sings*, 84.

13. See Patricia Nelson Limerick, Charles E. Rankin, and Clyde A. Milner, eds., *Trails: Toward a New Western History* (Lawrence: University Press of Kansas, 2017). This conference brought together most of the historians that would bring "new western history" into public discussion outside of the academy.

14. Gary Holthaus et al., eds., *A Society to Match the Scenery: Personal Visions of the Future of the American West* (Boulder: University Press of Colorado, 1991), 229.

15. In *This Is Dinosaur*, a book Stegner edited for the Sierra Club, he expressed this ideal: "It is legitimate to hope that there may be left in Dinosaur the special kind of human mark, the special record of human passage, that distinguishes man from all other species. It is rare enough among men, impossible to any other form of life. It is simply the deliberate and chosen refusal to make any marks at all. Sometimes we have withheld our power to destroy, and have left a threatened species like the buffalo, a threatened beauty spot like Yosemite or Yellowstone or Dinosaur, scrupulously alone. We are the most dangerous species of life on the planet, and every other species, even the earth itself, has cause to fear our power to exterminate. But we are also the only species which, when it chooses to do so, will go to great effort to save what it might destroy." *This Is Dinosaur: Echo Park Country and Its Magic Rivers* (New York: Alfred A. Knopf, 1955), 17.

16. Stegner to Limerick, August 26, 1988, envelope 1, FF1–FF4, Patricia Nelson Limerick Literary Papers, WH 542, Denver Public Library.

17. Fradkin, *Wallace Stegner and the American West*, 197–98, 345n3. Stegner's son, Page, also used the phrase "geography of despair" when discussing his father's later life in the documentary *Wallace Stegner*, dir. John Howe, 2009, PBS-KUED.

18. Stegner wrote a critical essay about Reagan's probable policies for public lands in the West in the *Washington Post*'s inauguration issue. While he raised rhetorical questions about Reagan's policies more than he stated outright his opinions, the concluding paragraphs were not sanguine: "The more James Watt's policies succeed, the less open space the West will provide for natives or tourists, the less unhassled life will be discoverable by those seeking it, the dirtier the air will be, the scarcer the water, the lower and more impure the groundwater tables, the less irrigated farming, the less ranching, the less grass, the less of the West itself as we have known it. . . . Whether he [Reagan] is a real gun hand or only a figurehead, whether he acts out of ignorance, indifference or political expediency, it looks to a lot of westerners as if he has decided to throw the West to the raiders and the Sagebrush rebels of the right wing." Stegner, "Will Reagan Ride with the Raiders?" *Washington Post*, January 20, 1981.

19. Qoheleth is "the assembler" or "the Preacher" who narrates the biblical book of Ecclesiastes. See especially Ecclesiastes 1:11: "There is no remembrance of former

things, / nor will there be any remembrance / of later things yet to be / among those who come after." Holy Bible (ESV).

20. Holthaus et al., *Society to Match the Scenery*, 229.
21. Comer, *Landscapes of the New West*, 44–45.
22. Donald Worster to Wallace Stegner, April 14, 1988, box 22, folder 44, Stegner Papers.
23. It is noted as "adapted" from the "Geography of Hope" lecture and included as the introduction to *Where the Bluebird Sings*, xix.
24. Ibid., xxvi–xxvii.
25. Ibid., xxvii–xxviii.
26. Assuming his hindsight is accurate. Susan Bartlett Weber, ed., *The History of Greensboro: The First Two Hundred Years* (Greensboro, VT: Greensboro Historical Society, 1990), xiii–xv.
27. Ibid.
28. Ibid.
29. Ibid.
30. Ibid.
31. Benson, *Wallace Stegner: His Life and Work*, 422.
32. Stegner, *Angle of Repose*, 69–70. This recalls the similarly cranky reflections on place and suburbanization in James Howard Kunstler's *The Geography of Nowhere: The Rise and Decline of America's Man-Made Landscape* (New York: Simon and Schuster, 1993).
33. Stegner, *Wolf Willow*, 23.
34. Ibid., 12.

BIBLIOGRAPHY

ARCHIVAL SOURCES

Creative Writing Program: Correspondence and Manuscripts, 1949–1992. Stanford University, Palo Alto, California.

Patricia Nelson Limerick Literary Papers. Denver Public Library, Denver, Colorado.

Philip Fradkin Papers. University of Utah, Salt Lake City, Utah.

Research Material about Wallace Stegner (compiled by Jackson J. Benson). Stanford University, Palo Alto, California.

Wallace Earle Stegner Papers. University of Utah, Salt Lake City.

Wallace Stegner Collection. Stanford University, Palo Alto, California.

PUBLISHED SOURCES

Abbey, Edward. *Desert Solitaire: A Season in the Wilderness*. New York: Touchstone, 1990.

———. *The Journey Home: Some Words in Defense of the American West*. New York: Penguin, 1977.

Abbott, Carl. *The Metropolitan Frontier: Cities in the Modern American West*. Tucson: University of Arizona Press, 1993.

Adams, Henry. *The Education of Henry Adams*. Boston: Mariner Books, 2000.

Agee, James, and Walker Evans. *Let Us Now Praise Famous Men*. Boston: Houghton Mifflin, 1960.

Allitt, Patrick. *Climate of Crisis: America in an Age of Environmentalism*. New York: Penguin Press, 2014.

Allred, Jeff. *American Modernism and Depression Documentary*. New York: Oxford University Press, 2010.

Anderson, Carol. *Eyes off the Prize: The United Nations and the African American Struggle for Human Rights, 1944–1955*. New York: Cambridge University Press, 2003.

Anderson, Terry. *The Movement and the Sixties: Protest in America from Greensboro to Wounded Knee*. Oxford: Oxford University Press, 1995.

Aron, Stephen. "Convergence, California, and the Newest Western History." *California History* 86, no. 4 (January 1, 2009): 4–13, 79–81.

Arras, Paul. *The Lonely Nineties: Visions of Community in Contemporary U.S. Television*. Cham, Switzerland: Palgrave, Macmillan, 2018.

Arthur, Anthony, ed. *Critical Essays on Wallace Stegner*. Boston: G. K. Hall, 1982.

Ashbolt, Anthony. "'Go Ask Alice': Remembering the Summer of Love Forty Years On." *Australasian Journal of American Studies* 26, no. 2 (2007): 35–47.

Baker, Jack, and Jeffrey Bilbro, eds. *Telling the Stories Right*. Eugene: Wipf and Stock Publishers, 2018.

Barnhisel, Greg. *Cold War Modernists: Art, Literature, and American Cultural Diplomacy.* New York: Columbia University Press, 2015.

Bauman, Zygmunt. *Modernity and the Holocaust.* Ithaca, NY: Cornell University Press, 2000.

Bederman, Gail. *Manliness and Civilization: A Cultural History of Gender and Race in the United States, 1880–1917.* Chicago: University of Chicago Press, 1995.

Bell, Daniel. "The Cultural Contradictions of Capitalism." *The Public Interest,* no. 21 (Fall 1970).

Bender, Thomas. *Community and Social Change in America.* New Brunswick: Rutgers University Press, 1978.

Bennett, Eric. *Workshops of Empire: Stegner, Engle, and American Creative Writing in the Cold War.* Iowa City: University of Iowa Press, 2015.

Benson, Jackson J. *Down by the Lemonade Springs: Essays on Wallace Stegner.* Reno: University of Nevada Press, 2001.

———. *Wallace Stegner: His Life and Work.* New York: Viking, 1996.

Berry, Wendell. *Imagination in Place.* Berkeley: Counterpoint Press, 2010.

———. *Standing by Words: Essays.* Berkeley: Counterpoint Press, 1983.

———. *The Unsettling of America.* Berkeley: Counterpoint Press, 2015.

———. *What Are People For?* New York: North Point Press, 1990.

Bevis, William. "Stegner: The Civic Style." In Rankin, *Wallace Stegner: Man and Writer,* 255–67.

Bilbro, Jeffrey. *Virtues of Renewal: Wendell Berry's Sustainable Forms.* Lexington: University of Kentucky Press, 2019.

Billington, Ray Allen, ed. *Frontier and Section: The Selected Essays of Frederick Jackson Turner.* Englewood Cliffs, NJ: Prentice, Hall, 1961.

———, ed. *The Frontier Thesis: Valid Interpretation of History?* New York: Holt, Rinehart, and Winston, 1966.

Borstelmann, Thomas. *The 1970s: A New Global History from Civil Rights to Economic Inequality.* Princeton: Princeton University Press, 2012.

Bradley, Dorothy. "Contemporary Western Politics of the Land." In Meine, *Wallace Stegner and the Continental Vision,* 201–7.

Brick, Howard. *Age of Contradiction: American Thought and Culture in the 1960s.* Ithaca, NY: Cornell University Press, 2000.

———. *Daniel Bell and the Decline of Intellectual Radicalism: Social Theory and Political Reconciliation in the 1940s.* Madison: University of Wisconsin Press, 1986.

Buell, Lawrence. *The Dream of the Great American Novel.* Cambridge: Belknap Press, 2014.

———. *Writing for an Endangered World: Literature, Culture, and Environment in the U.S. and Beyond.* Cambridge: Belknap Press, 2003.

Burns, Jennifer. *Goddess of the Market: Ayn Rand and the American Right.* Oxford: Oxford University Press, 2009.

Burrows, Russell. "Wallace Stegner's Version of Pastoral." *Western American Literature* 25, no. 1 (Spring 1990): 15–25.

Butler, Phyllis Filiberti, ed. *20-20 Vision: In Celebration of the Peninsula Hills.* Palo Alto: Western Tanager Press, 1982.

Caldwell, Erskine, and Margaret Bourke-White. *You Have Seen Their Faces.* 1937. Reprint, New York: Arno Press, 1975.

Camp, Jennie A. "Angling for Repose: Wallace Stegner and the De-Mythologizing of the American West." Ph.D. diss., University of Denver, 2004.

Carnes, Mark C. *Novel History: Historians and Novelists Confront America's Past (and Each Other)*. New York: Simon and Schuster, 2001.

Chafe, William. *Civilities and Civil Rights*. Oxford: Oxford University Press, 1980.

Chaney, Anthony. *Runaway: Gregory Bateson, the Double Bind, and the Rise of Ecological Consciousness*. Chapel Hill: University of North Carolina Press, 2017.

Colberg, Nancy. *Wallace Stegner: A Descriptive Bibliography*. Lewiston, ID: Confluence Press, 1990.

Comer, Krista. *Landscapes of the New West: Gender and Geography in Contemporary Women's Writing*. Chapel Hill: University of North Carolina Press, 1999.

Cook-Lynn, Elizabeth. *Why I Can't Read Wallace Stegner and Other Essays: A Tribal Voice*. Madison: University of Wisconsin Press, 1996.

Cooney, Terry A. *The Rise of the New York Intellectuals: Partisan Review and Its Circle*. Madison: University of Wisconsin Press, 1986.

Cotkin, George. *Existential America*. Baltimore: Johns Hopkins University Press, 2003.

———. *Feast of Excess: A Cultural History of the New Sensibility*. Oxford: Oxford University Press, 2015.

———. *Morality's Muddy Waters: Ethical Quandaries in Modern America*. Philadelphia: University of Pennsylvania Press, 2013.

Cowie, Jefferson. *Stayin' Alive: The 1970s and the Last Days of the Working Class*. New York: The New Press, 2010.

Cronon, William, ed. *Uncommon Ground: Rethinking the Human Place in Nature*. New York: W. W. Norton, 1996.

Curti, Merle. *The Making of an American Community: A Case Study of Democracy in Frontier County*. Stanford: Stanford University Press, 1959.

Dass, Ram. *Be Here Now*. Taos, NM: Lama Foundation, 1971.

Demos, John. "Real Lives and Other Fictions: Reconsidering Wallace Stegner's *Angle of Repose*." In Carnes, *Novel History*, 132–45.

Denning, Michael. *The Cultural Front: The Laboring of American Culture in the Twentieth Century*. New York: Verso, 2014.

Deverell, William, ed. *A Companion to the American West*. Oxford: Blackwell Publishing, 2004.

———. "Western Vistas: Historiography, 1971 to Today." *The Western Historical Quarterly* 42, no. 3 (October 2011): 355–60.

Diggins, John Patrick. *The Promise of Pragmatism: Modernism and the Crisis of Knowledge and Authority*. Chicago: University of Chicago Press, 1994.

Dillon, David. "Time's Prisoners: An Interview with Wallace Stegner." *Southwest Review* 61, no. 3 (Summer 1976): 252–67.

Dodgson, Rick. *It's All a Kind of Magic: The Young Ken Kesey*. Madison: University of Wisconsin Press, 2013.

Doherty, Maggie. *The Equivalents: A Story of Art, Female Friendship, and Liberation in the 1960s*. New York: Alfred A. Knopf, 2020.

Doig, Ivan. *This House of Sky: Landscapes of a Western Mind*. New York: Harcourt Brace, 1992.

Donnelly, Phillip J. "Biblical Convocation in Wendell Berry's Remembering." *Christianity and Literature* 56, no. 2 (Winter 2007): 275–96.

Dorman, Robert. *Hell of a Vision: Regionalism and the Modern American West*. Tucson: University of Arizona Press, 2012.

———. *Revolt of the Provinces: The Regionalist Movement in America, 1920–1945*. Chapel Hill: University of North Carolina Press, 1993.

Dudziak, Mary. *Cold War Civil Rights: Race and the Image of American Democracy*. Princeton: Princeton University Press, 2000.

Dunaway, Finis. *Seeing Green: The Use and Abuse of American Environmental Images*. Chicago: University of Chicago Press, 2015.

Egan, Timothy. "Stegner's Complaint." *Opinionator*. Accessed October 15, 2015. http://opinionator.blogs.nytimes.com/2009/02/18/stegners-complaint/.

Ellison, Ralph. *Shadow and Act*. New York: Vintage, 1995.

Etulain, Richard. *Re-Imagining the Modern American West: A Century of Fiction, History, and Art*. Tucson: University of Arizona Press, 1996.

———. *Stegner: Conversations on History and Literature*. Reno: University of Nevada Press, 1996.

———. *Telling Western Stories: From Buffalo Bill to Larry McMurtry*. Albuquerque: University of New Mexico Press, 1999.

———, ed. *Writing Western History: Essays on Major Western Historians*. Albuquerque: University of New Mexico Press, 1991.

Fea, John, Jay Green, and Eric Miller, eds. *Confessing History: Explorations in Christian Faith and the Historian's Vocation*. South Bend, IN: University of Notre Dame Press, 2010.

Felski, Rita. *The Limits of Critique*. Chicago: University of Chicago Press, 2015.

Fernlund, Kevin J., ed. *The Cold War: American West, 1945–1989*. Albuquerque: University of New Mexico Press, 1998.

Fiege, Mark. "A Country without Illusions: Wallace Stegner in His Time and Ours." Lecture, Montana State University, October 2016. Accessed March 29, 2019. https://www.youtube.com/watch?v=DJTuuqQIsvA.

———. *The Republic of Nature: An Environmental History of the United States*. Seattle: University of Washington Press, 2012.

Findlay, John M. *Magic Lands: Western Cityscapes and American Culture after 1940*. Berkeley: University of California Press, 1992.

Fishman, Robert. *Bourgeois Utopias: The Rise and Fall of Suburbia*. New York: Basic Books, 1987.

Fleischhauer, Carl, and Beverly Brannan, eds. *Documenting America: 1935–1943*. Berkeley: University of California Press, 1989.

Foner, Eric, and Lisa McGirr. *American History Now*. Philadelphia: Temple University Press, 2011.

Fradkin, Philip L. *Wallace Stegner and the American West*. New York: Alfred A. Knopf, 2008.

Frank, Thomas. *The Conquest of Cool: Business Culture, Counterculture, and the Rise of Hip Consumerism*. Chicago: University of Chicago Press, 1997.

Fussell, Paul. *Class: A Guide Through the American Status System*. New York: Summit Books, 1983.

———. *The Great War and Modern Memory*. Oxford: Oxford University Press, 1975.

Geertz, Clifford. *The Interpretation of Cultures: Selected Essays*. New York: Basic Books, 1973.

Gessner, David. *All the Wild That Remains: Edward Abbey, Wallace Stegner, and the American West*. New York: W. W. Norton, 2015.

Gitlin, Todd. *The Sixties: Years of Hope, Days of Rage*. New York: Bantam Books, 1987.

Goldberg, Danny. *In Search of the Lost Chord: 1967 and the Hippie Idea*. Brooklyn: Akaschic Books, 2017.

Gonda, Jeffrey. *Unjust Deeds: The Restrictive Covenant Cases and the Making of the Civil Rights Movement*. Chapel Hill: University of North Carolina Press, 2015.

Graebner, William. *The Age of Doubt: American Thought and Culture in the 1940s*. Boston: Twayne Publishers, 1991.

Grana, Cesar, and Marigay Grana, eds. *On Bohemia: The Code of the Self-Exiled*. New Brunswick: Transaction Publishers, 1990.

Graulich, Melody. "Book Learning: *Angle of Repose* as Literary History." In Rankin, *Wallace Stegner: Man and Writer*, 231–54.

———. "Ruminations on Stegner's Protective Impulse and the Art of Storytelling." In Meine, *Wallace Stegner and the Continental Vision*, 43–59.

Greenberg, Clement. "Avant-Garde and Kitsch." *Partisan Review* (1939): 34–49.

Greif, Mark. *The Age of the Crisis of Man: Thought and Fiction in America, 1933–1973*. Princeton: Princeton University Press, 2015.

———. "What's Wrong with Public Intellectuals?" *The Chronicle of Higher Education*, February 13, 2015. http://chronicle.com/article/Whats-Wrong-With-Public/189921/.

Gross, Robert A. *The Minutemen and Their World*. New York: Hill and Wang, 1976.

Gundelach, Peter. "Kaare Svalastoga: The Unceasing Positivist." *Acta Sociologica* 43, no. 4 (2000): 365–73.

Hale, Grace Elizabeth. *A Nation of Outsiders: How the White Middle Class Fell in Love with Rebellion in Postwar America*. New York: Oxford University Press, 2014.

Hall, Jacquelyn Dowd. "The Long Civil Rights Movement and the Political Uses of the Past." *The Journal of American History* (March 2005): 1233–63.

Harrington, Michael. "We Few, We Happy Few, We Happy Bohemians: A Memoir of the Culture before the Counterculture." *Esquire* (August 1, 1972): 99–103, 162–64.

Hartman, Andrew. *A War for the Soul of America: A History of the Culture Wars*. Chicago: University of Chicago Press, 2014.

Harvey, Mark W. T. *A Symbol of Wilderness: Echo Park and the American Conservation Movement*. Seattle: University of Washington Press, 2000.

———. *Wilderness Forever: Howard Zahniser and the Path to the Wilderness Act*. Seattle: University of Washington Press, 2005.

Hazlett, John D. "Generational Theory and Collective Autobiography." *American Literary History* 4, no. 1 (April 1, 1992): 77–96.

Heilbut, Anthony. *Exiled in Paradise: German Refugee Artists and Intellectuals in America, from the 1930s to the Present*. New York: Viking Press, 1983.

Heppler, Jason. "Machines in the Valley: Community, Urban Change, and Environmental Politics in Silicon Valley, 1945–1990." PhD diss., University of Nebraska, 2016.

Hepworth, James R. *Stealing Glances: Three Interviews with Wallace Stegner*. Santa Fe: University of New Mexico Press, 1998.

———. "Wallace Stegner, The Art of Fiction No. 118." *Paris Review* (Summer 1990). http://www.theparisreview.org/interviews/2314/the-art-of-fiction-no-118-wallace -stegner.

———. "Wallace Stegner's *Angle of Repose*: One Reader's Response." PhD diss., University of Arizona, 1989.

Hine, Robert. *Community on the American Frontier: Separate but Not Alone.* Norman: University of Oklahoma Press, 1981.

———. *Josiah Royce: From Grass Valley to Harvard.* Norman: University of Oklahoma Press, 1992.

Hofheins, Roger, and Dan Tooker. "Interview with Wallace Stegner." *The Southern Review* 11, no. 4 (October 1975): 794–801.

Hollinger, David A. "How Wide the Circle of the 'We'? American Intellectuals and the Problem of the Ethnos since World War II." *The American Historical Review* 98, no. 2 (April 1, 1993): 317–37.

———, ed. *The Humanities and the Dynamics of Inclusion since World War II.* Baltimore: Johns Hopkins University Press, 2006.

———. *In the American Province: Studies in the History and Historiography of Ideas.* Bloomington: Indiana University Press, 1985.

Hollinger, David, and Charles Capper, eds. *The American Intellectual Tradition Volume II: 1865 to the Present.* New York: Oxford University Press, 2006.

Holthaus, Gary, et al., eds. *A Society to Match the Scenery: Personal Visions of the Future of the American West.* Boulder: University Press of Colorado, 1991.

Howe, Irving. *A Margin of Hope: An Intellectual Autobiography.* Orlando, FL: Harcourt Brace Jovanovich, 1982.

Hungerford, Amy. *Postmodern Belief: American Literature and Religion since 1960.* Princeton: Princeton University Press, 2010.

Iber, Patrick. *Neither Peace, nor Freedom: The Cultural Cold War in Latin America.* Cambridge: Harvard University Press, 2015.

Immerwahr, Daniel. *Thinking Small: The United States and the Lure of Community Development.* Cambridge: Harvard University Press, 2015.

Irvine, Colin Charles. "Reading into It: Wallace Stegner's Novelistic Sense of Time and Place." PhD diss., Marquette University, 2002.

Isserman, Maurice, and Michael Kazin. *America Divided: The Civil War of the 1960s.* New York: Oxford University Press, 2000.

Jackson, Walter A. *Gunnar Myrdal and America's Conscience: Social Engineering and Racial Liberalism, 1938–1987.* Chapel Hill: University of North Carolina Press, 1990.

Jacobson, Matthew Frey. *Roots Too: White Ethnic Revival in Post-Civil Rights America.* Cambridge: Harvard University Press, 2006.

Jenkins, Philip. *Decade of Nightmares: The End of the Sixties and the Making of Eighties America.* New York: Oxford University Press, 2006.

Johnson, Lee Ann. *Mary Hallock Foote.* Boston: Twayne Publishers, 1980.

Jonas, Hans. *Philosophical Essays: From Ancient Creed to Philosophical Man.* Englewood Cliffs, NJ: Prentice Hall, 1974.

Joseph, Peniel. *Waiting 'Til the Midnight Hour: A Narrative History of Black Power in America.* New York: Henry Holt, 2006.

Kabaservice, Geoffrey M. *Rule and Ruin: The Downfall of Moderation and the Destruction of the Republican Party, from Eisenhower to the Tea Party.* New York: Oxford University Press, 2012.

Kaplan, Wendy, ed. *California Design: 1930–1965.* Los Angeles: Los Angeles County Museum of Art and MIT Press, 2011.

Kennedy, David M. *Freedom from Fear: The American People in Depression and War 1929–1945*. New York: Oxford University Press, 1999.

Kern, Stephen. *The Culture of Time and Space*. Cambridge: Harvard University Press, 2003.

Klein, Kerwin. *Frontiers of Historical Imagination: Narrating the European Conquest of Native America, 1890–1990*. Berkeley: University of California Press, 1997.

Knight, Richard L. "Field Report from the New American West." In Meine, *Wallace Stegner and the Continental Vision*, 182–88.

Kolodny, Annette. *The Land Before Her: Fantasy and Experience of the American Frontiers, 1630–1860*. Chapel Hill: University of North Carolina Press, 1984.

Kramer, Michael J. "Hot Fun in the Summertime: Micro and Macrocosmic Views on the Summer of Love." *The Sixties* 10, no. 2 (2017): 221–41.

Kruse, Kevin M. *White Flight: Atlanta and the Making of the Modern Conservative Movement*. Princeton: Princeton University Press, 2005.

Kruse, Kevin M., and Thomas J. Sugrue, eds. *The New Suburban History*. Chicago: University of Chicago Press, 2006.

Krutch, Joseph Wood, and Eliot Porter. *Baja California and the Geography of Hope*. New York: Ballantine Books, 1967.

Krystal, Arthur, et al. *A Company of Readers: Uncollected Writings of W. H. Auden, Jacques Barzun, and Lionel Trilling from the Readers' Subscription and Mid-Century Book Clubs*. New York: Free Press, 2001.

Kunstler, James Howard. *The Geography of Nowhere: The Rise and Decline of America's Man-Made Landscape*. New York: Simon and Schuster, 1993.

LaDow, Beth. *The Medicine Line: Life and Death on a North American Borderland*. New York: Routledge, 2001.

Lange, Dorothea, and Paul Taylor. *An American Exodus: A Record of Human Erosion*. New York: Reynal and Hitchcock, 1939.

Lasch, Christopher. *The Culture of Narcissism*. New York: W. W. Norton, 1978.

———. *The True and Only Heaven: Progress and Its Critics*. New York: W. W. Norton, 1991.

Lasch-Quinn, Elisabeth. *Ars Vitae: The Fate of Inwardness and the Return of the Ancient Arts of Living*. South Bend, IN: University of Notre Dame Press, 2020.

———. *Race Experts: How Racial Etiquette, Sensitivity Training, and New Age Therapy Hijacked the Civil Rights Revolution*. New York: W. W. Norton, 2001.

Latour, Bruno. *Reassembling the Social: An Introduction to Actor-Network-Theory*. Oxford: Oxford University Press, 2005.

Lavender, David. *The Great West*. New York: Mariner Books, 2000.

———. "The Tyranny of Facts." In *Old Southwest/New Southwest: Essays on a Region and Its Literature*, edited by Judy Nolte Lensink, 62–73. Tucson: Tucson Public Library, 1987.

Levine, Lawrence. "The Historian and Icon." In Fleischhauer and Brannan, eds., *Documenting America*, 15–42.

Lewis, Merrill, and Lorene Lewis. *Wallace Stegner*. Boise: Boise State University Press, 1972.

Lewis, Nathaniel. *Unsettling the Literary West: Authenticity and Authorship*. Lincoln: University of Nebraska Press, 2003.

Limerick, Patricia Nelson. *Legacy of Conquest: The Unbroken Past of the American West*. New York: W. W. Norton, 1987.

———. "Precedents to Wisdom." In Rankin, *Wallace Stegner: Man and Writer*, 108–13.

———. *Something in the Soil: Legacies and Reckonings in the New West*. New York: W. W. Norton, 2001.

Limerick, Patricia Nelson, Clyde A. Milner, and Charles E. Rankin, eds. *Trails: Toward a New Western History*. Lawrence: University Press of Kansas, 1991.

Lindee, Susan, and Joanna Radin. "Patrons of the Human Experience: A History of the Wenner-Gren Foundation for Anthropological Research, 1941–2016." *Current Anthropology* 57, no. 14 (October 2016): S218–301.

Lippman, Walter. *A Preface to Morals*. New Brunswick: Transaction Publishers, 1982.

Lukács, Gyorgy. *The Meaning of Contemporary Realism*. Translated by John Mander and Necke Mander. Talgarth, Wales: The Merlin Press, 1979.

Lukacs, John. *The Future of History*. New Haven: Yale University Press, 2011.

Lyman, Richard. *Stanford in Turmoil: Campus Unrest, 1966–1972*. Stanford: Stanford University Press, 2009.

MacDonald, Dwight. *Masscult and Midcult: Essays Against the American Grain*. New York: New York Review Books Classics, 2011.

MacIntyre, Alasdair. *After Virtue: A Study in Moral Theory*. South Bend, IN: University of Notre Dame Press, 2007.

MacLeish, Archibald. *Land of the Free*. New York: Harcourt, Brace, 1938.

Mailer, Norman. *The White Negro*. San Francisco: City Lights Books, 1972.

Marsden, George. *The Twilight of the American Enlightenment: The 1950s and the Crisis of Liberal Belief*. New York: Basic Books, 2014.

Marx, Leo. *The Machine in the Garden: Technology and the Pastoral Ideal in America*. Oxford: Oxford University Press, 1964.

McClay, Wilfred. *The Masterless: Self and Society in Modern America*. Chapel Hill: University of North Carolina Press, 1994.

McGilchrist, M. M. R. "Across a Great Divide: Views of Landscape and Nature in the American West, before and after the Cultural Watershed of the 1960s and 1970s: Wallace Stegner and Cormac McCarthy." PhD diss., University of Derby (United Kingdom), 2008.

McGirr, Lisa. *Suburban Warriors: The Origins of the New American Right*. Princeton: Princeton University Press, 2015.

McGurl, Mark. *The Program Era: Postwar Fiction and the Rise of Creative Writing*. Cambridge: Harvard University Press, 2011.

McKibben, Bill. *The End of Nature*. New York: Random House, 1989.

McMurtry, Larry. "How the West Was Won or Lost." *The New Republic*, October 22, 1990.

———. *Sacagawea's Nickname: Essays on the American West*. New York: New York Review of Books, 2001.

McWilliams, Carey. *California: The Great Exception*. Berkeley: University of California Press, 1998.

Meine, Curt, ed. *Wallace Stegner and the Continental Vision: Essays on Literature, History, and Landscape*. Washington, DC: Island Press, 1997.

Miller, Darlis A. *Mary Hallock Foote: Author-Illustrator of the American West*. Norman: University of Oklahoma Press, 2002.

Miller, Eric. *Hope in a Scattering Time: A Life of Christopher Lasch*. Grand Rapids: Eerdmans, 2010.

Minter, David. *A Cultural History of the American Novel: 1890–1940, Henry James to William Faulkner*. Cambridge: Cambridge University Press, 1994.

Mitchell, Lee Clark. *Westerns: Making the Man in Fiction and Film*. Chicago: University of Chicago Press, 1996.

Moretti, Franco. "The Slaughterhouse of Literature." *Modern Language Quarterly* 61, no. 1 (March 2000): 207–27.

Murphy, Paul V. *The Rebuke of History: The Southern Agrarians and American Conservative Thought*. Chapel Hill: University of North Carolina Press, 2001.

Myers, D. G. *The Elephants Teach: Creative Writing since 1880*. Englewood Cliffs: Prentice Hall, 1996.

Natanson, Nicholas. *The Black Image in the New Deal: The Politics of FSA Photography*. Knoxville: University of Tennessee Press, 1992.

Nesson, Liam Conway. "Reactionary and Progressive Environmentalism: Edward Abbey, Wallace Stegner, and Stances in Defense of the American West." PhD diss., University of Arkansas, 2009.

Newberry, Ruth. "Wallace Stegner's *Wolf Willow* and 1960s Critical Essays: Renarrativizing Western American Literature for the West and for America." PhD diss., Duquesne University, 2011.

Nicolaides, Becky. "How Hell Moved from the City to the Suburbs: Urban Scholars and Changing Perceptions of Authentic Community." In Kruse and Sugrue, *The New Suburban History*, 80–98.

Nisbet, Robert. *The Quest for Community*. 1953. Reprint, Wilmington: ISI Books, 2014.

Novick, Peter. *That Noble Dream: The 'Objectivity Question' and the American Historical Profession*. Cambridge: Cambridge University Press, 1988.

Oakeshott, Michael. *The Voice of Liberal Learning*. New Haven: Yale University Press, 1989.

O'Mara, Margaret. *Cities of Knowledge: Cold War Science and the Search for the Next Silicon Valley*. Princeton: Princeton University Press, 2005.

Ong, Walter J. *The Barbarian Within and Other Fugitive Essays and Studies*. New York: Macmillan, 1962.

Orleck, Annelise. *Storming Caesars Palace: How Black Mothers Fought Their Own War on Poverty*. New York: Beacon Press, 2005.

Packer, George. *Blood of the Liberals*. New York: Farrar, Straus, and Giroux, 2000.

Packer, Nancy Huddleston. "Wallace Stegner: A Passionate and Committed Heart." *Sewanee Review* 117, no. 2 (Spring 2009): 208–22.

Patterson, James T. *Grand Expectations: The United States, 1945–1974*. Oxford: Oxford University Press, 1996.

Paul, Rodman, ed. *A Victorian Gentlewoman in the Far West: The Reminiscences of Mary Hallock Foote*. San Marino: Huntington Library Press, 2000.

Penry, Tara. "A Motorcar Runs through It: Imagining the Unwritten Western Book." *The Thomas Wolfe Review* 37 (2013): 110–18.

Perlstein, Rick. *Before the Storm: Barry Goldwater and the Unmaking of the American Consensus*. New York: Hill and Wang, 2001.

Peterson, Audrey C. "Narrative Voice in Wallace Stegner's *Angle of Repose*," *Western Literature* 10, no. 2 (Summer 1975): 125–33.

Rankin, Charles E., ed. *Wallace Stegner: Man and Writer*. Albuquerque: University of New Mexico Press, 1996.

Ratner-Rosenhagen, Jennifer. *The Ideas That Made America: A Brief History*. New York: Oxford University Press, 2019.

Ratner-Rosenhagen, Jennifer, et al., eds. *Worlds of American Intellectual History*. Oxford: Oxford University Press, 2017.

Rieff, Philip. *The Triumph of the Therapeutic: Uses of Faith after Freud*. Wilmington: ISI Books, 2007.

Richardson, Peter. *American Prophet: The Life and Work of Carey McWilliams*. Ann Arbor: University of Michigan Press, 2005.

Robinson, Forrest G. "Fathers and Sons in Stegner's Ordered Dream of Man." *Arizona Quarterly: A Journal of American Literature, Culture, and Theory* 59, no. 3 (Autumn 2003): 97–114.

———, ed. *The New Western History: The Territory Ahead*. Tucson: University of Arizona Press, 1998.

Robinson, Forrest G., and Margaret G. Robinson. *Wallace Stegner*. Boston: Twayne Publishers, 1977.

Rodgers, Daniel. *Age of Fracture*. Cambridge: Belknap Press, 2011.

Rome, Adam. *The Bulldozer in the Countryside: Suburban Sprawl and the Rise of American Environmentalism*. Cambridge: Cambridge University Press, 2001.

Rossinow, Douglas. *The Politics of Authenticity: Liberalism, Christianity, and the New Left in America*. New York: Columbia University Press, 1998.

Rothstein, Richard. "De Facto Segregation: A National Myth." In *Facing Segregation: Housing Policy Solutions for a Stronger Society*, edited by Molly W. Metzger and Henry S. Webber, 15–34. New York: Oxford University Press, 2019.

Rubin, Joan Shelley. *The Making of Middlebrow Culture*. Chapel Hill: University of North Carolina Press, 1992.

Ruffin, Herbert. *Uninvited Neighbors: African Americans in Silicon Valley, 1769–1990*. Norman: University of Oklahoma Press, 2014.

Sachs, Aaron. "Letters to a Tenured Historian: Imagining History as Creative Nonfiction—or Maybe Even Poetry." *Rethinking History: The Journal of Theory and Practice* 14, no. 1 (2010): 5–38.

Said, Edward. *Orientalism*. New York: Pantheon Books, 1978.

Sandeen, Eric J. *Picturing an Exhibition: The Family of Man and 1950s America*. Albuquerque: University of New Mexico Press, 1995.

Saunders, Frances Stonor. *The Cultural Cold War: The CIA and the World of Arts and Letters*. New York: W. W. Norton, 2000.

Saunders, George. "My Writing Education: A Time Line—The New Yorker." Accessed October 23, 2015. http://www.newyorker.com/books/page-turner/my-writing-education-a-timeline?src=longreads.

Schlesinger, Arthur. *The Vital Center: The Politics of Freedom*. Cambridge: The Riverside Press, 1962.

Scott, James C. *Seeing Like a State: How Certain Schemes to Improve the Human Condition Have Failed*. New Haven: Yale University Press, 1998.

Seymour, Bruce. *Lola Montez: A Life*. New Haven: Yale University Press, 1996.

Shakespeare, William. *The Tempest*. New York: Signet Classics, 1998.

Shannon, Christopher. *A World Made Safe for Differences: Cold War Intellectuals and the Politics of Identity*. Lanham: Rowman and Littlefield, 2001.

Singh, Nikhil Pal. *Black Is a Country: Race and the Unfinished Struggle for Democracy*. Cambridge: Harvard University Press, 2004.

Slatta, Richard. *Cowboys of the Americas*. New Haven: Yale University Press, 1990.

Slotkin, Richard. *Regeneration Through Violence: The Mythology of the American Frontier, 1600–1860*. Middletown: Wesleyan University Press, 1973.

Smith, Christine Hill. *Social Class in the Writings of Mary Hallock Foote*. Reno: University of Nevada Press, 2009.

Smith, Henry Nash. *Virgin Land: The American West as Symbol and Myth*. 1950. Reprint, Cambridge: Harvard University Press, 1970.

Smith, Richard Candida. *The Modern Moves West: California Artists and Democratic Culture in the Twentieth Century*. Philadelphia: University of Pennsylvania Press, 2009.

Solomon, Robert C. "In Defense of Sentimentality." *Philosophy and Literature* 14, no. 2 (October 1990): 304–23.

Sontag, Susan. "Notes on Camp." *Partisan Review* 31, no. 4 (Fall 1964): 515–30.

Starr, Kevin. *Coast of Dreams: California on the Edge, 1990–2003*. New York: Alfred A. Knopf, 2004.

———. *Golden Dreams: California in an Age of Abundance, 1950–1963*. Oxford: Oxford University Press, 2009.

Staub, Michael. *Voices of Persuasion: Politics of Representation in 1930s America*. New York: Cambridge University Press, 1994.

Steensma, Robert C. *Wallace Stegner's Salt Lake City*. Salt Lake City: University of Utah Press, 2007.

Stegner, Mary, and Page Stegner, eds. *The Geography of Hope: A Tribute to Wallace Stegner*. New York: Sierra Club Books, 1996.

Stegner, Page, ed. *The Selected Letters of Wallace Stegner*. Berkeley: Shoemaker and Hoard, 2007.

Stegner, Wallace. *20-20 Vision: In Celebration of the Peninsula Foothills*. Edited by Phyllis Filiberti. Palo Alto: Western Tanager Press, 1982.

———. *All the Little Live Things*. New York: The Viking Press, 1967.

———. *The American West as Living Space*. Ann Arbor: University of Michigan Press, 1987.

———. *Angle of Repose*. New York: Vintage, 2014.

———. "The Artist as Environmental Advocate." Sierra Club History Series, Regional Oral History Office, The Bancroft Library. Berkeley: University of California, 1983.

———. *Beyond the Hundredth Meridian: John Wesley Powell and the Second Opening of the West*. Boston: Houghton Mifflin, 1954.

———. *The Big Rock Candy Mountain*. New York: Duell, Sloan and Pierce, 1943.

———. "Born a Square: The Westerner's Dilemma." *The Atlantic* 213 (January 1964): 46–50.

———. *The City of the Living and Other Stories*. Boston: Houghton Mifflin Company, 1956.

———. *Collected Stories of Wallace Stegner*. New York: Random House, 1990.

———. "The Colleges in Wartime." *Delphian Quarterly* 25 (April 1942): 2–7.

———. *Crossing to Safety*. New York: Modern Library Classics, 2002.

———. "A Decade of Regional Publishing." *Publisher's Weekly*, March 11, 1939.

———. *Fire and Ice*. New York: Duell, Sloan and Pierce, 1941.

———. "Four Hundred Families Plan a House." *'47 Magazine* 1 (April 1947): 63–67.

———. *The Gathering of Zion: The Story of the Mormon Trail*. New York: McGraw-Hill, 1964.

———. "Indoor-Outdoor Living." *Pacifica* (September 1959).

———. "Introduction: Water Warnings, Water Futures." *Plateau* 53, no. 1 (1981).

———. "Is the Novel Done For?" *Harper's* (December 1942).

———. *Marking the Sparrow's Fall: The Making of the American West*. Edited by Page Stegner. New York: Henry Holt and Company, 1998.

———. *Mormon Country*. New York: Duell, Sloan and Pierce, 1942.

———. *One Nation*. Boston: Houghton Mifflin, 1945.

———. *One Way to Spell Man: Essays with a Western Bias*. New York: Doubleday, 1982.

———. *On a Darkling Plain*. New York: Harcourt, Brace and Company, 1940.

———. *On Teaching and Writing Fiction*, with Lynn Stegner. New York: Penguin Books, 2002.

———. *The Potter's House*. Muscatine: The Prairie Press, 1938.

———. *The Preacher and the Slave*. Boston: Houghton Mifflin Company, 1950.

———. "Publishing in the Provinces." *Delphian Quarterly* 22, no. 3 (Summer 1939).

———. *Recapitulation*. Garden City: Doubleday, 1979.

———. "Regionalism in Art." *Delphian Quarterly* 21, no. 1 (Winter 1939).

———. *Remembering Laughter*. Boston: Little, Brown and Company, 1937.

———. *Second Growth*. Boston: Houghton Mifflin and Company, 1947.

———. *The Sense of Place*. Madison: Silver Buckle Press, 1986.

———. *A Shooting Star*. New York: The Viking Press, 1961.

———. *The Sound of Mountain Water*. New York: Doubleday & Company, 1969.

———. *The Spectator Bird*. New York: Doubleday, 1976.

———. *This Is Dinosaur: Echo Park Country and Its Magic Rivers*. New York: Alfred A. Knopf, 1955.

———. "To a Young Writer." *Atlantic* 204 (November 1959).

———. "The Trail of the Hawkeye: Literature Where the Tall Corn Grows." *Saturday Review of Literature*, July 30, 1938.

———. *The Uneasy Chair: A Biography of Bernard DeVoto*. Garden City: Doubleday, 1974.

———. "Westword: The Call of the Wild." *New West* (August 1981).

———. *Where the Bluebird Sings to the Lemonade Springs*. New York: Random House, 1992.

———. "Who Persecutes Boston?" *Atlantic Monthly* 174 (July 1944): 45–52.

———. "Will Reagan Ride with the Raiders?" *Washington Post*, January 20, 1981.

———. *Wolf Willow: A History, a Story, and a Memory of the Last Plains Frontier*. New York: The Viking Press, 1962.

———. *The Women on the Wall*. Boston: Houghton Mifflin Company, 1950.

———. *The Writer in America*. Kanda: The Hokuseido Press, 1952.

Stegner, Wallace, and James Hepworth. *Stealing Glances: Three Interviews with Wallace Stegner*. 1st ed. Albuquerque: University of New Mexico Press, 1998.

Stegner, Wallace, and Page Stegner. *American Places*. New York: E. P. Dutton, 1981.

Steigerwald, David. *The Sixties and the End of Modern America*. New York: St. Martin's Press, 1995.

———. "Where Have You Gone, Holden Caulfield? Why We Aren't 'Alienated' Anymore." *Origins: Current Events in Historical Perspective* 4, no. 4 (January 2011). http://origins.osu.edu/article/where-have-you-gone-holden-caulfield-why-we-aren-t-alienated-anymore/page/0/1.

Steigerwald, David, and Michael Flamm, eds. *Debating the 1960s: Liberal, Conservative, and Radical Perspectives.* New York: Rowman and Littlefield, 2008.

Sugrue, Thomas. *The Origins of the Urban Crisis.* Princeton: Princeton University Press, 1996.

Susman, Warren. *Culture as History: The Transformation of American Society in the Twentieth Century.* Washington, DC: Smithsonian Institution Press, 2003.

Swingrover, Elizabeth Anne. "'The Way Things Are': The Later Novels of Wallace Stegner." PhD diss., University of Nevada, Reno, 1988.

Taylor, Bron Raymond. *Dark Green Religion: Nature Spirituality and the Planetary Future.* Berkeley: University of California Press, 2010.

Taylor, Charles. *A Secular Age.* Cambridge: Belknap Press of Harvard University Press, 2007.

———. *Sources of the Self: The Making of Modern Identity.* Cambridge: Harvard University Press, 1989.

Thomas, William, ed. *Man's Role in Changing the Face of the Earth.* Chicago: University of Chicago Press, 1956.

Thompson, Hunter S. *Fear and Loathing in Las Vegas.* New York: Vintage Press, 1998.

Tipton, Steven M. *Getting Saved from the Sixties: Moral Meaning in Conversion and Cultural Change.* Berkeley: University of California Press, 1984.

Tocqueville, Alexis de. *Democracy in America.* Edited by J. P. Mayer. Translated by George Lawrence. New York: HarperCollins Publishers, 2000.

Tompkins, Jane. *West of Everything: The Inner Life of Westerns.* New York: Oxford University Press, 1993.

Topping, Gary. "Wallace Stegner the Historian." In Rankin, *Wallace Stegner: Man and Writer,* 145–61.

Trilling, Lionel. "On the Teaching of Modern Literature." In *The American Intellectual Tradition Volume 2: 1865 to the Present,* ed. David A. Hollinger and Charles Capper, 377–89. New York: Oxford University Press, 2006.

Tuan, Yi-Fu. *Space and Place: The Perspective of Experience.* Minneapolis: University of Minnesota Press, 1977.

Turner, Frederick Jackson. *Frontier and Section: Selected Essays of Frederick Jackson Turner.* Englewood Cliffs: Prentice-Hall, 1961.

Turner, James Morton. *The Promise of Wilderness: American Environmental Politics since 1964.* Seattle: University of Washington Press, 2013.

Von Eschen, Penny M. *Satchmo Blows up the World: Jazz Ambassadors Play the Cold War.* Cambridge, MA: Harvard University Press, 2006.

Wagnleitner, Reinhold. *Coca-Colonization and the Cold War: The Cultural Mission of the United States in Austria after the Second World War.* Chapel Hill: University of North Carolina Press, 1994.

Wald, Alan M. *The New York Intellectuals: The Rise and Decline of the Anti-Stalinist Left from the 1930s to the 1980s.* Chapel Hill: University of North Carolina Press, 1987.

Walker, Richard A. *The Country in the City: The Greening of the San Francisco Bay Area.* Seattle: University of Washington Press, 2007.

Wall, Wendy. *Inventing the "American Way": The Politics of Consensus from the New Deal to the Civil Rights Movement*. Oxford: Oxford University Press, 2008.

Weber, Susan Bartlett, ed. *The History of Greensboro: The First Two Hundred Years*. Greensboro, VT: Greensboro Historical Society, 1990.

West, Elliott. "Wallace Stegner's West, Wilderness, and History." In Meine, *Wallace Stegner and the Continental Vision*, 85–96.

———, ed. *The Way to the West: Essays on the Central Plains*. Albuquerque: University of New Mexico Press, 1995.

Western Literature Association (U.S.), ed. *Updating the Literary West*. Fort Worth: Texas Christian University Press, 1997.

Westover, Tara. *Educated: A Memoir*. New York: Random House, 2018.

White, Richard. "Are You an Environmentalist or Do You Work for a Living?" In Cronon, *Uncommon Ground*, 171–85.

———. *"It's Your Misfortune and None of My Own": A New History of the American West*. Norman: University of Oklahoma Press, 1991.

———. *Remembering Ahanagran: A History of Stories*. Seattle: University of Washington Press, 1998.

———. *The Republic for Which It Stands: The United States during Reconstruction and the Gilded Age, 1865–1896*. New York: Oxford University Press, 2017.

Wickberg, Daniel. "Intellectual History vs. the Social History of Intellectuals." *Rethinking History* 5, no. 3 (November 2001): 383–95.

———. "What Is the History of Sensibilities? On Cultural Histories, Old and New." *The American Historical Review* 112, no. 3 (June 2007): 661–84.

Wiggershaus, Rolf, and Michael Robertson. *The Frankfurt School: Its History, Theories, and Political Significance*. Cambridge, MA: MIT Press, 1995.

Wilkerson, Isabel. *The Warmth of Other Suns: The Epic Story of America's Great Migration*. New York: Vintage Press, 2010.

Williams, Rob. "'Huts of Time': Wallace Stegner's Historical Legacy." In Rankin, *Wallace Stegner: Man and Writer*, 119–43.

Williams, Terry Tempest. *Refuge: An Unnatural History of Family and Place*. New York: Pantheon Books, 1991.

Wilson, Robert M. "Retrospective Review: Man's Role in Changing the Face of the Earth." *Environmental History* 10, no. 3 (July 2005): 564–66.

Wolfe, Tom. *The Electric Kool-Aid Acid Test*. New York: Farrar, Straus, and Giroux, 1969.

———. *Radical Chic and Mau-Mauing the Flak-Catchers*. New York: Picador, 2009.

Worster, Donald. *Dust Bowl: The Southern Plains in the 1930s*. Oxford: Oxford University Press, 2004.

———. *A River Running West: The Life of John Wesley Powell*. New York: Oxford University Press, 2000.

Wreszin, Michael. *A Rebel in Defense of Tradition: The Life and Politics of Dwight Macdonald*. New York: Basic Books, 1994.

Wright, Richard. *12 Million Black Voices*. 1941. Reprint, New York: Basic Books, 2002.

Wroebel, David, and Michael C. Steiner. *Many Wests: Place, Culture, and Regional Identity*. Lawrence: University Press of Kansas, 1997.

Zuckerman, Michael. *Peaceable Kingdoms: New England Towns in the Eighteenth Century*. New York: W. W. Norton, 1970.

INDEX

Barnes, Flo (character), 52
Barnhisel, Greg, 187n26
Bauman, Zygmunt, 163
Beat generation, 91, 97, 200n27
Beatnik, 91, 97, 200n27
Bell, Daniel, 81
belonging: experience of, 51; in "Genesis,"
    71; sense of, 22–24; in *Spectator Bird*,
    148, 166–69
Bennett, Eric, 127–28, 211n57
Benson, Jackson, 9–10, 182n38, 208n18
Berry, Wendell: convocation and, 199n18;
    Green Revolution and, 194n35;
    industrial farming and, 215n38;
    regionalism and, 144–45; romantic
    artist ideal and, 191n97; Stanford
    Writing Program and, 215n38
Bertelson, Mr. and Mrs. (characters),
    156–57
Bevis, William, 12, 127
Beyond the Hundredth Meridian: Adams
    and, 205–6n91; cooperation in,
    217n11; as Powell's biography, 35–37;
    scholarship of, 192n20
The Big Rock Candy Mountain: *Angle of
    Repose* and, 212n76; organization of,
    38, 190n71; protagonist of, 5, 66–67;
    readers' responses to, 13; success of,
    17
Bilbro, Jeffrey, 8, 181n28
Blake, William, 165
Blixen, Karen, 157–59, 162, 215n31
boomer paradigm: in *Angle of Repose*, 133;
    definition of, 8; legacy of, 173; mobil-
    ity of, 181n28; Oliver and, 133. *See
    also* sticker paradigm
Boston racism, 31
bourgeois utopia, 21–24
Bradley, Dorothy, 13
"brave new world," 87, 103, 140, 200n24
Bread Loaf Writer's Conference, 17
Brook Farm, 134, 136
Brower, David, 182n38
Buddha, 165
Bunker, Archie, 208–9n22
Burbank, Luther, 215n38

Caldwell, Idaho, 26–27
Caliban, 87–88, 200–201n28
California: after World War II, 17, 41;
    counterculture of, 81–93, 198–99n4;
    fiction about, 37–38, 190n69; signifi-
    cance of, 15; Stegner's assessment of,
    18; Stegner's move to, 16–19, 24
Candide (character), 86, 106–7
Candide (Voltaire), 86
"Carrion Spring," 73–74
Carroll O'Connor, 208–9n22
CASBS, 54, 61–62, 83–84
Casement, Bill and Sue (characters),
    41–42, 45
Catlin, John (character), 82, 94, 102,
    105–6
Catlin, Marian (character): in *All the
    Little Live Things*, 47, 82–83, 93–97,
    102–8; death of, 106–8, 205–6n91;
    The Tempest and, 87–88
Caxton Press, Idaho, 26–27
Chekhov, Anton, 119, 199n8, 209n28
Chopin, Frederick, 43
CIA, 187n26, 202n45
Clark, Walter Van Tilburg, 69
Comer, Krista, 173, 184–85n53
commune: in *Angle of Repose*, 132–38;
    suburbs and, 90
community: achievement of, 85; in *All the
    Little Live Things*, 83–84, 96, 106–7;
    in *Angle of Repose*, 127–28, 132–37,
    210n47; in Eastend, 59; fictional
    approach to, 84; Foote and, 116–17;
    in "Genesis," 72–73; in Greensboro,
    60, 174–75; planned, 19–20; respon-
    sibility of, 74–76; in *Second Growth*,
    51–52; in *Spectator Bird*, 148, 159,
    169; Susan and, 124, 210n47; in Taas-
    inge, 60–61; transience of, 146–47;
    in Whitemud, 74–76
Conrad, Joseph, 68–69
consenting adult, 165–66
conservationism, 154–55
"conviction of belonging," 8, 22, 68,
    181n25
convocation, 199n18